Non-Verbal Reasoning

The 11+ Practice Book

with Assessment Tests

For the CEM (Durham University) test

Ages

10-11

Practise • Prepare • Pass

Everything your child needs for 11+ success

How to use this Practice Book

This book is divided into three parts — Spotting Patterns, 3D Shapes and Assessment Tests. There are answers and detailed explanations in the pull-out section at the back of the book.

Spotting Patterns

- Each section contains practice questions focusing on one of the main concepts your child will need to understand for the Non-Verbal Reasoning part of the test.
- These pages can help your child build up the different skills they'll need for the real test.

3D Shapes

- This part concentrates on the skills your child will need to tackle the 3D shape questions in the test.

Assessment Tests

- The third section of the book contains eight assessment tests, each with a mix of question types.
- You can print off multiple-choice answer sheets from our website, www.cgplearning.co.uk/11+, so your child can practise taking the tests as if they're sitting the real thing.
- If you want to give your child timed practice, set a time limit of 20 minutes for each test.
- The tests get harder from 1 to 8, so don't be surprised if your child finds the later ones more tricky.
- Talk your child through the answers to the questions they got wrong. This will help them understand questions that work in a similar way when they come up against them in later tests.
- Your child should aim for a mark of around 85% (39 questions correct) in each test. If they score less than this, use their results to work out the areas they need more practice on.
- If they haven't managed to finish the test in time, they need to work on increasing their speed, whereas if they have made a lot of mistakes, they need to work more carefully.
- Keep track of your child's scores using the progress chart on the inside back cover of the book.

Published by CGP

Editors:
Chris Burton, Ceara Hayden, Sharon Keeley-Holden, Rachel Kordan, Kirstie McHale, Anthony Muller, Rebecca Tate and Ben Train.

With thanks to Judy Hornigold and Anthony Muller for the proofreading.

ISBN: 978 1 84762 566 3
www.cgpbooks.co.uk
Printed by Elanders Ltd, Newcastle upon Tyne
Clipart from Corel®

Based on the classic CGP style created by Richard Parsons.

Contents

Spotting Patterns

3D Shapes

Assessment Tests

Shapes

Most questions will be based around shapes, so you need to get to know them.

Warm Up

1. How many **sides** does each shape have?

a. 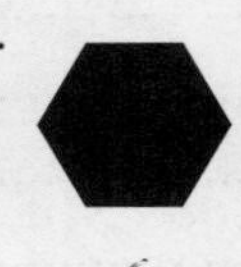 6

b. 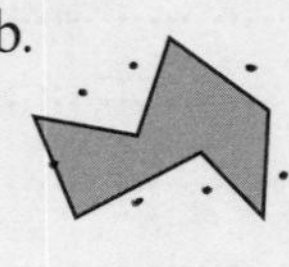 7

c.  8

d.  8

e. 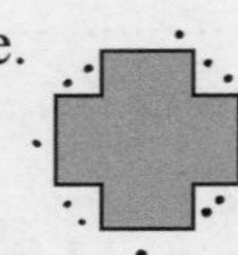 12

f. 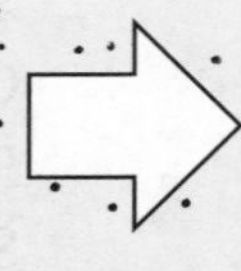 7

2. How many **lines of symmetry** does each shape have?

a.  1

b. 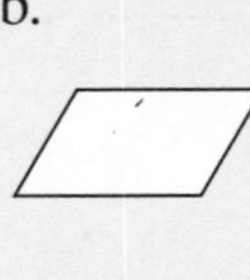 0

c.  1

d.  1

e. 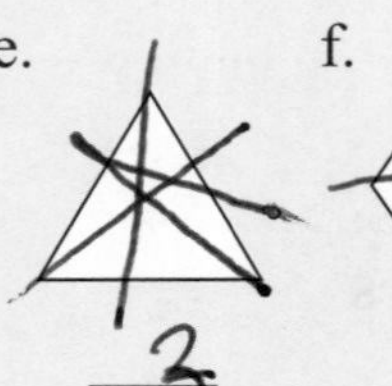 3

f. 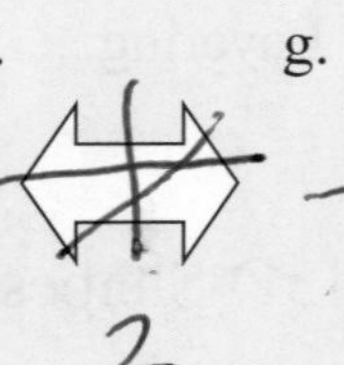 2

g. 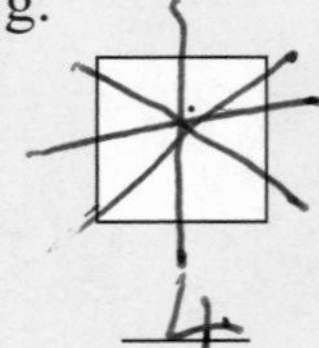 4

3. How many of these shapes have **five** sides?

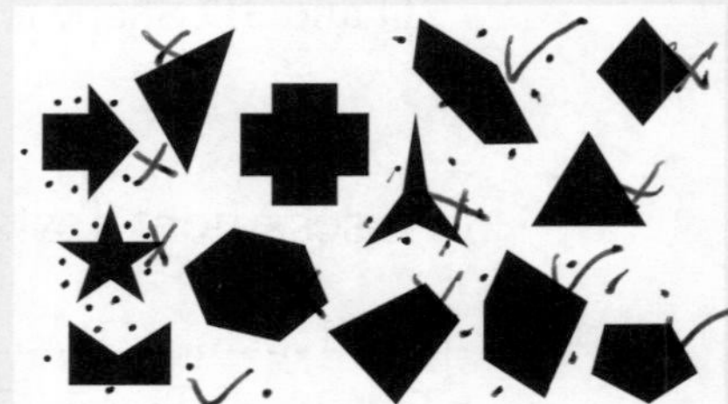

Number of **five-sided** shapes: 4

Complete the Series

Work out which of the options best fits in place of the missing square in the series.

Example:

 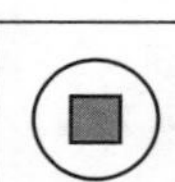 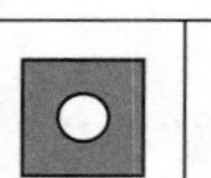 

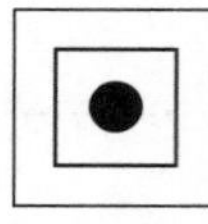 a 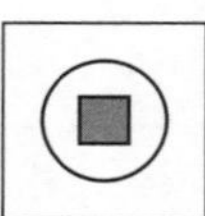 b 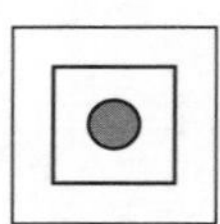 c 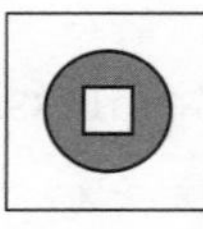 d

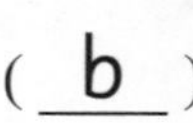

(b)

The series alternates between a white circle in a grey square and a grey square in a white circle.

4. 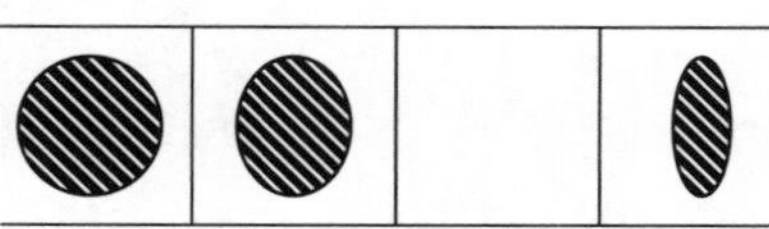

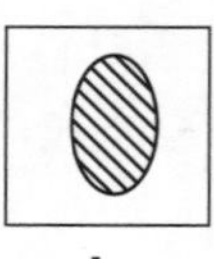 a  b c d (c)

5. 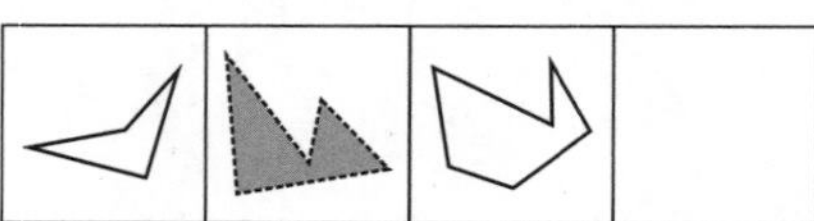

a b c d (a)

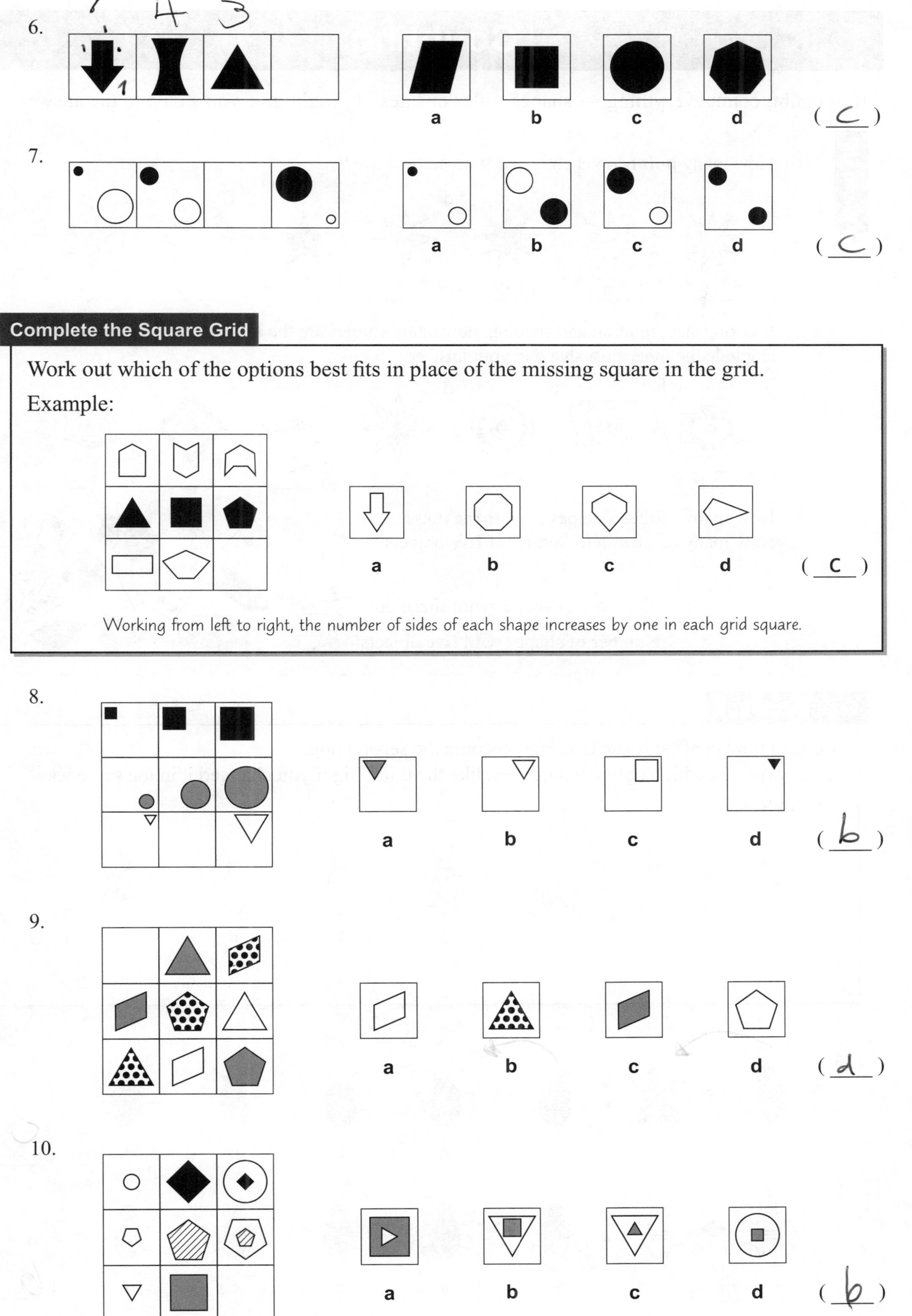

6.
a
b
c
d
(c)
7.
a
b
c
d
(c)
Complete the Square Grid
Work out which of the options best fits in place of the missing square in the grid.
Example:
a
b
c
d
(C)
Working from left to right, the number of sides of each shape increases by one in each grid square.
8.
a
b
c
d
(b)
9.
a
b
c
d
(d)
10.
a
b
c
d
(b)

Counting

If in doubt, count everything — shapes, sides or lines. It might give you a clue to the answer.

Warm Up

1. How many **points** do each of the stars below have?

a. b. c. d. e. f. g.

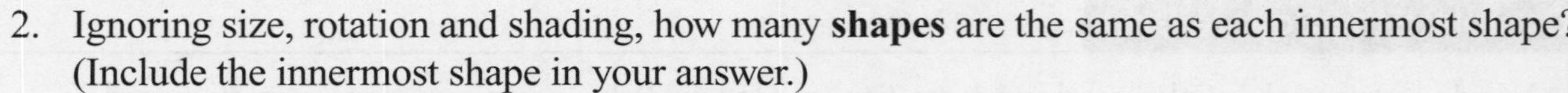

2. Ignoring size, rotation and shading, how many **shapes** are the same as each innermost shape? (Include the innermost shape in your answer.)

a. b. c. d. e. f. g.

 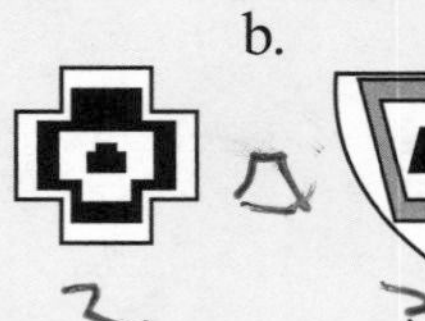  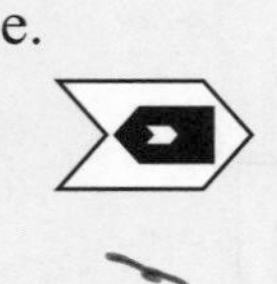  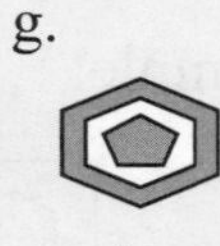

3. How many of these shapes have **three** dots?
How many of them have a total of **five** objects?

Number of shapes with **three** dots: ____

Number of shapes with **five** objects: ____

Changing Bugs

Look at how the first bug changes to become the second bug.
Then work out which option would look like the third bug if you changed it in the same way.

Example:

  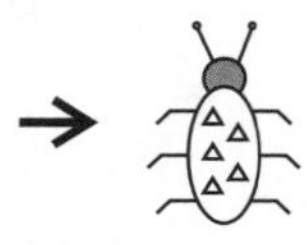 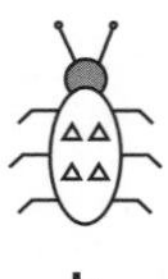 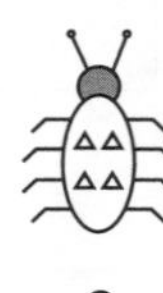 

a b c d (b)

The bug loses one shape from its back.

4.

 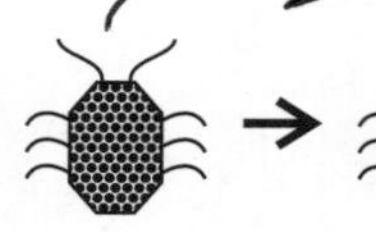   

a b c d

(____)

5.

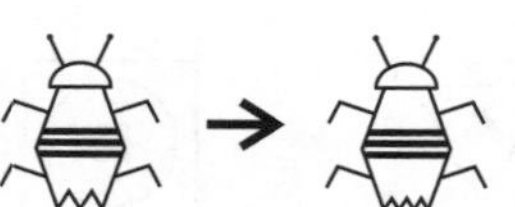 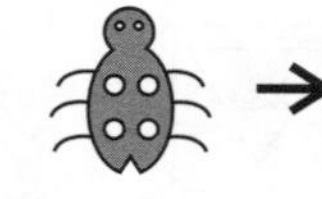 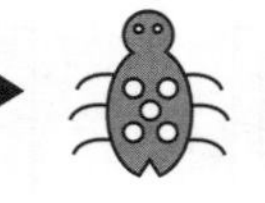 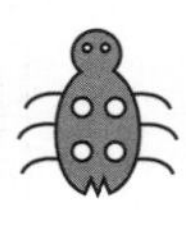 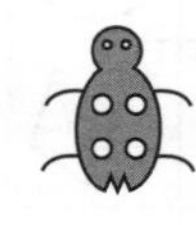 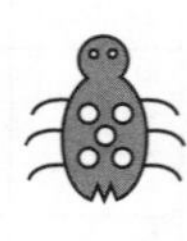

a b c d

(____)

6.

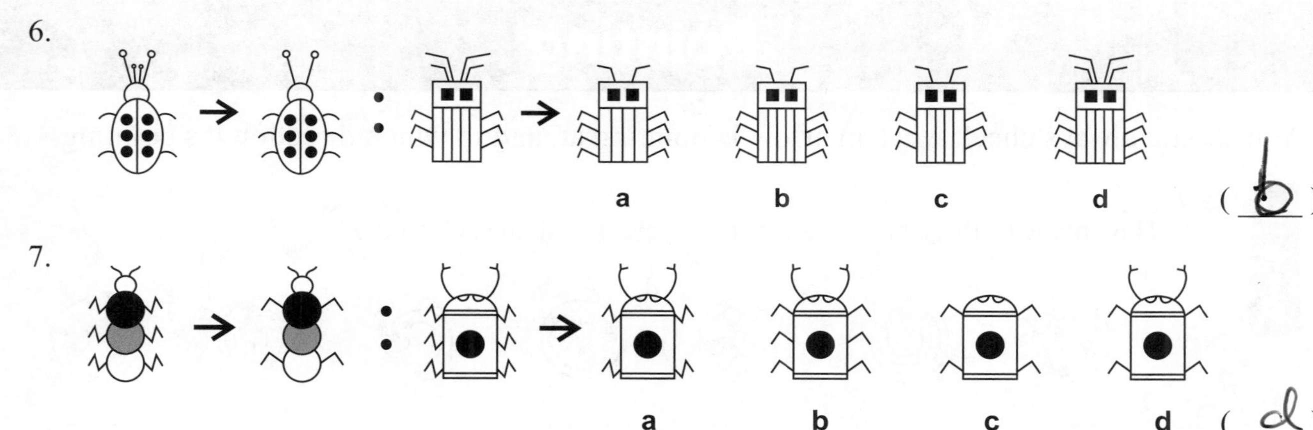

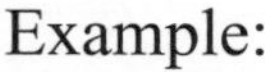

Work out which of the options best fits in place of the missing hexagon in the grid.

Example:

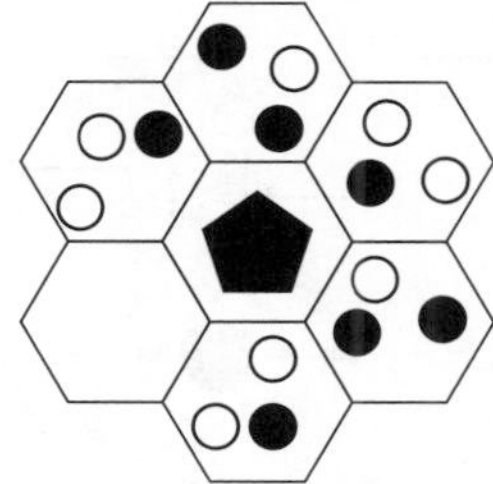

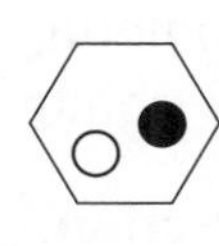

a

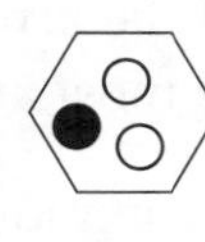

b

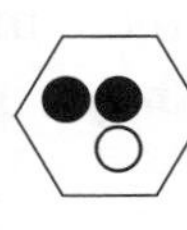

c

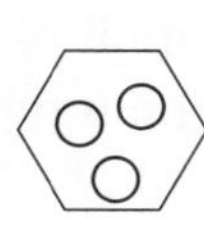

d

(C)

In each hexagon the number of black and white circles alternates between one and two.

8.

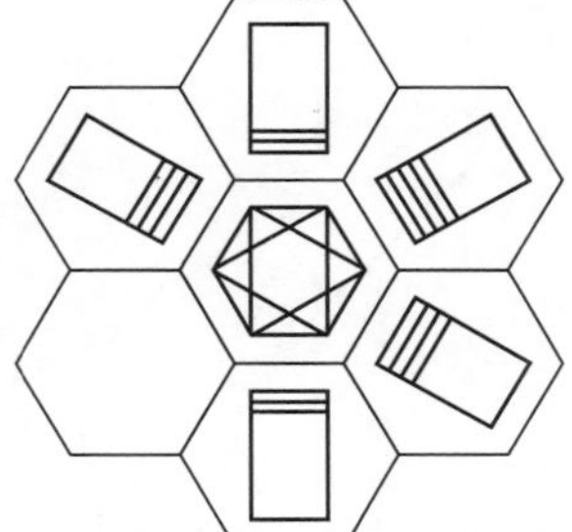

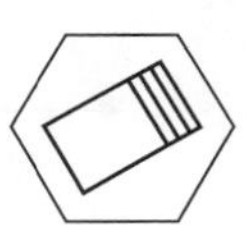

a

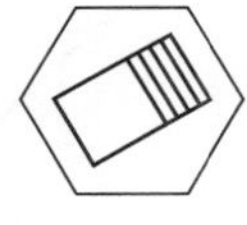

b

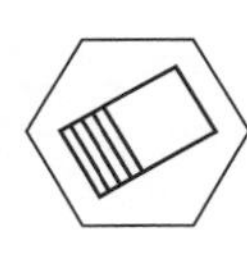

c

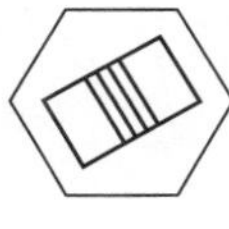

d

9.

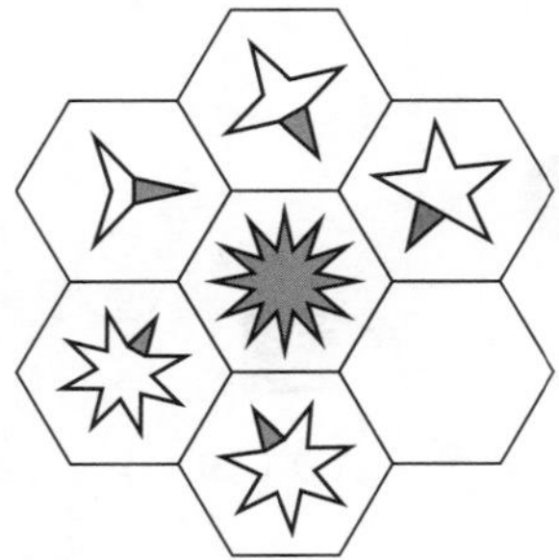

a

b

c

d

10.

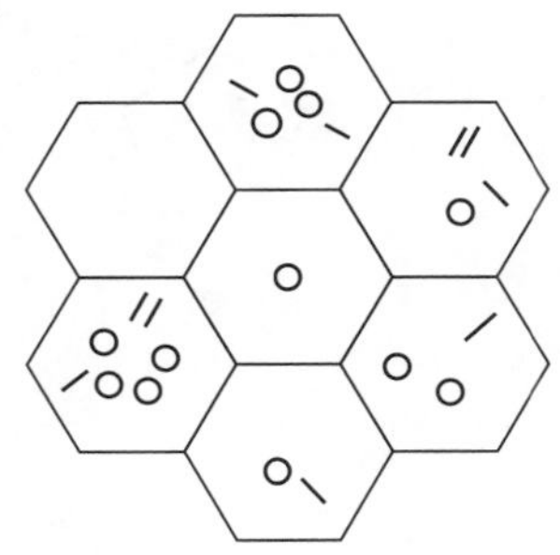

a

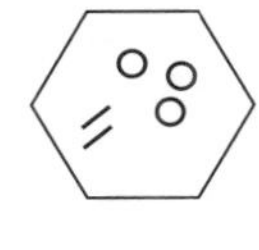

b

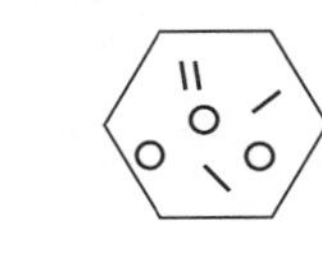

c

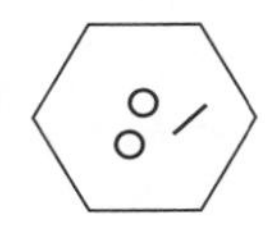

d

Pointing

You should always check what an arrow is pointing at, and in which direction it's pointing.

Warm Up

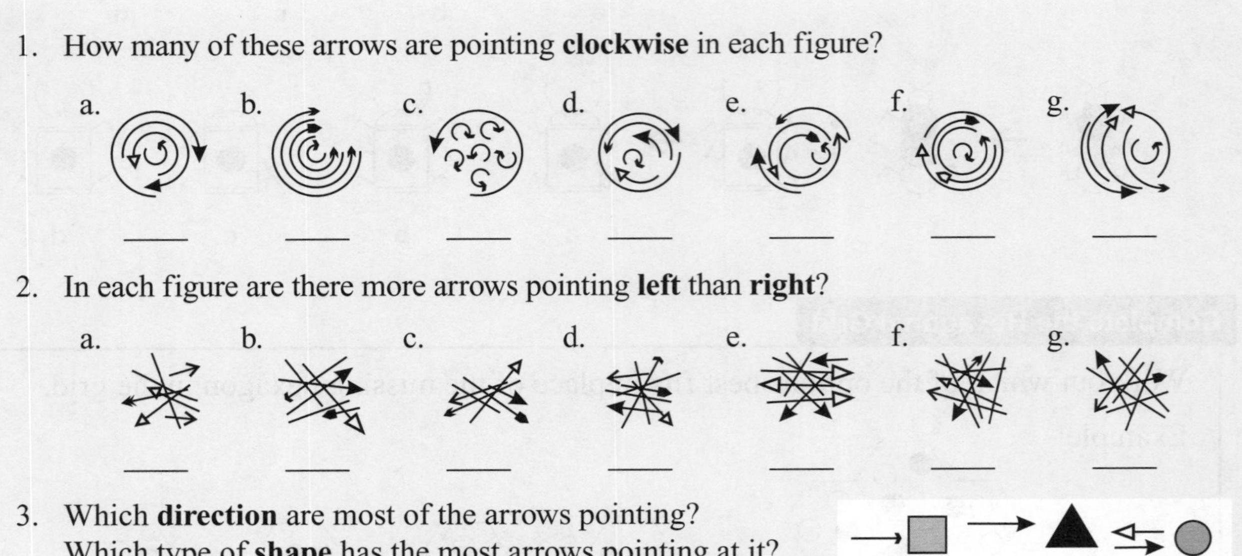

1. How many of these arrows are pointing **clockwise** in each figure?

a. ____ b. ____ c. ____ d. ____ e. ____ f. ____ g. ____

2. In each figure are there more arrows pointing **left** than **right**?

a. ____ b. ____ c. ____ d. ____ e. ____ f. ____ g. ____

3. Which **direction** are most of the arrows pointing?
Which type of **shape** has the most arrows pointing at it?

Most common **direction**: __________

Type of **shape**: __________

Odd One Out

Find the figure in each row that is most unlike the other figures.

Example:

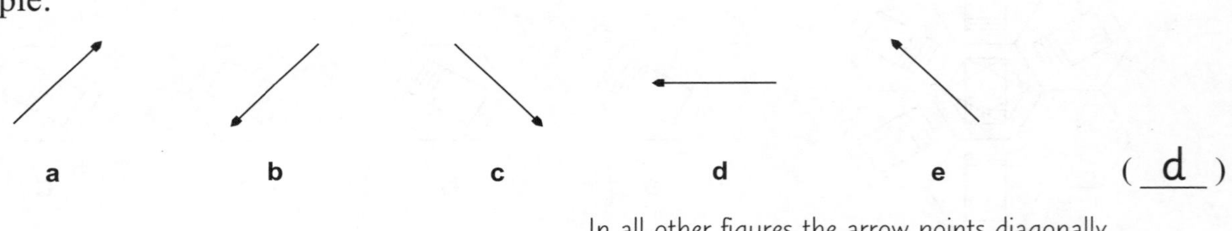

a b c d e (d)

In all other figures the arrow points diagonally.

4. a b c d e (____)

5. a b c d e (____)

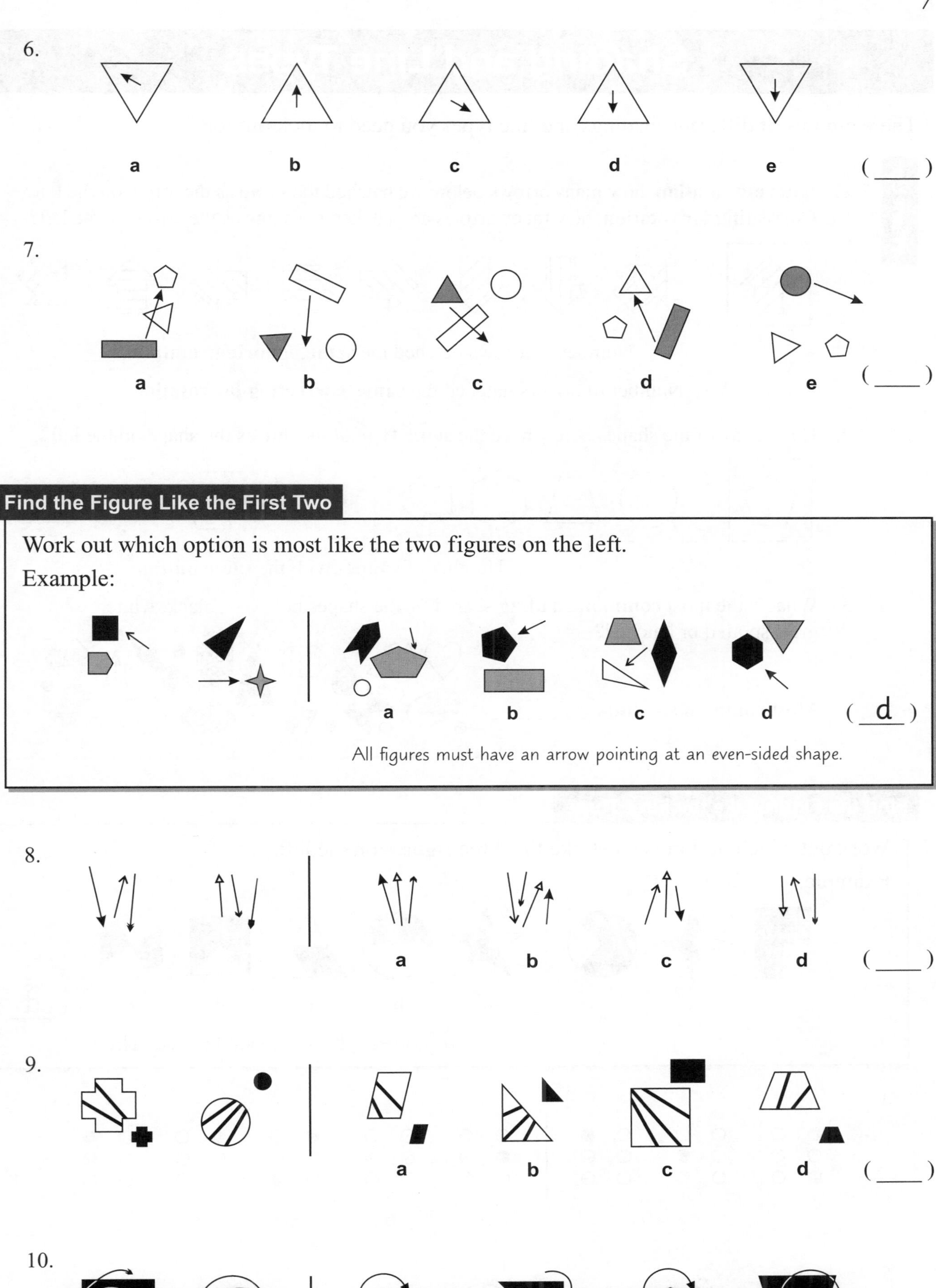

6.

a b c d e (____)

7.

a b c d e (____)

Find the Figure Like the First Two

Work out which option is most like the two figures on the left.

Example:

a b c d (d)

All figures must have an arrow pointing at an even-sided shape.

8.

a b c d (____)

9.

a b c d (____)

10.

a b c d (____)

Shading and Line Types

There are lots of different shadings and line types you need to look out for.

Warm Up

1. **Ignoring rotation**, how many arrows below are hatched the **same** as the arrow on the left?
Correcting for rotation, how many arrows are hatched the **same** as the arrow on the left?

    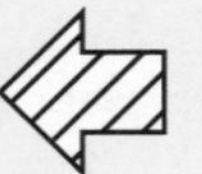    

Number of arrows hatched the **same**, **ignoring rotation**: ____

Number of arrows hatched the **same**, **correcting for rotation**: ____

2. How many of the shapes below have the **same type** of **outline** as the shape on the left?

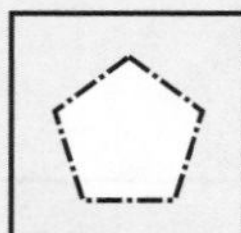   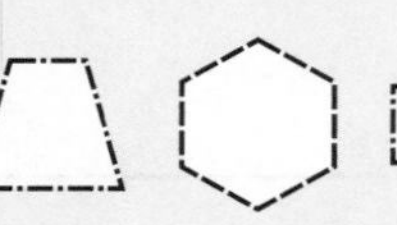 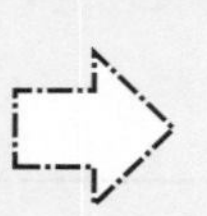    

Number of **shapes** with the **same outline**: ____

3. What is the most **common shading** shared by the shapes below — black, white, grey, spotted or hatched?

Most **common shading**: __________

Find the Figure Like the First Three

Work out which option is most like the three figures on the left.

Example:

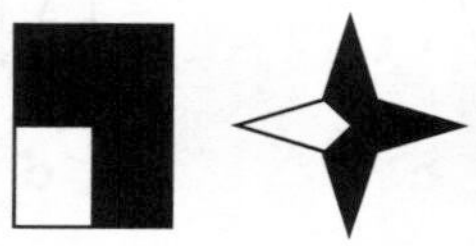   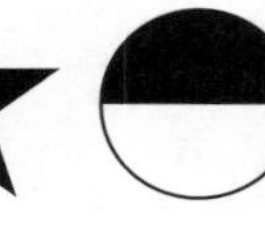 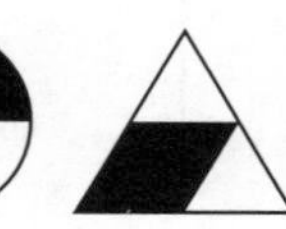 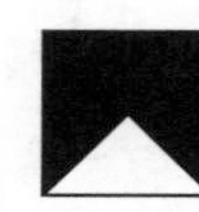 

a b c d e (d)

Three quarters of the shape must be shaded black.

4.

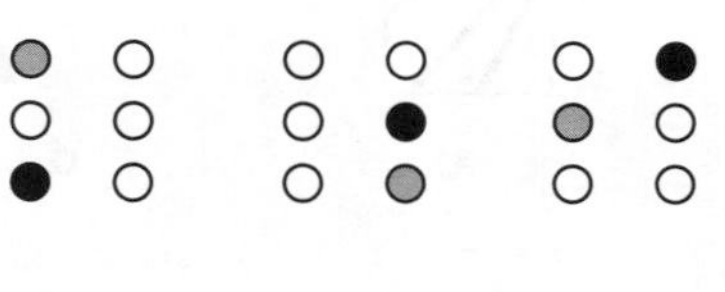  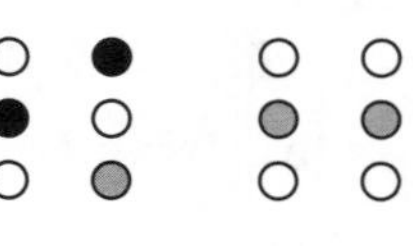 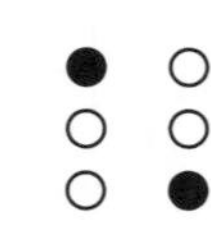 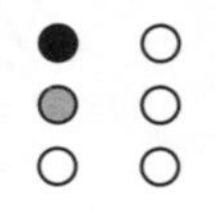 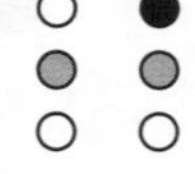

a b c d e (____)

5.

  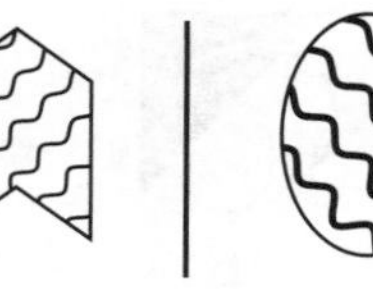 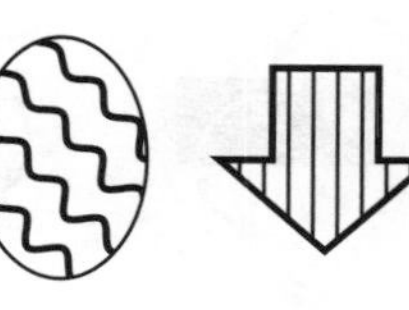 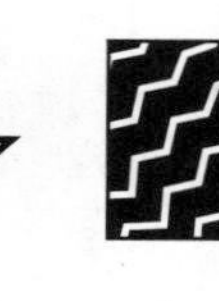 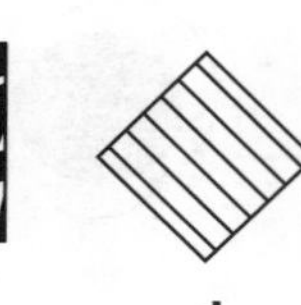 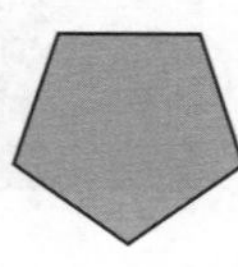

a b c d e (____)

6.

7.

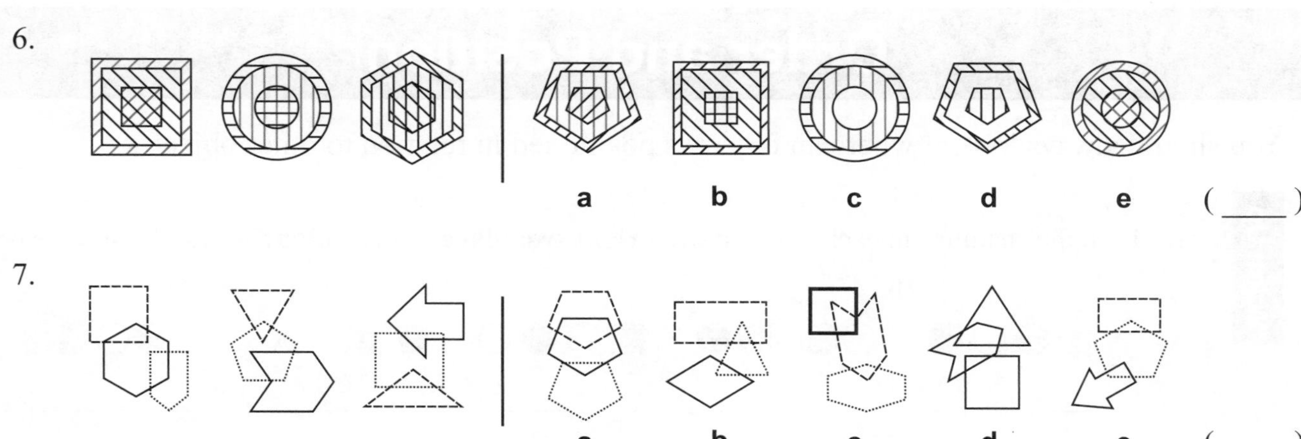

6. (____)

7. (____)

Complete the Hexagonal Grid

Work out which of the options best fits in place of the missing hexagon in the grid.

Example:

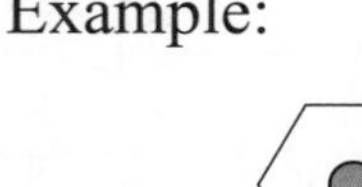

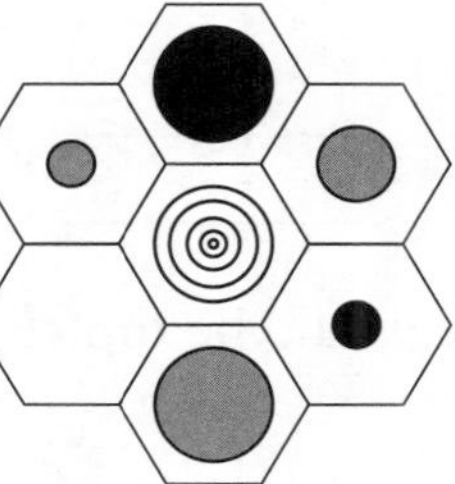

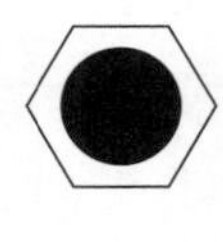

a

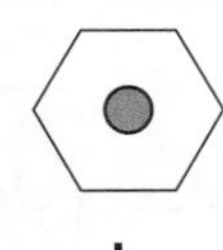

b

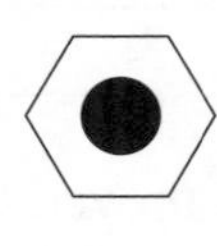

c

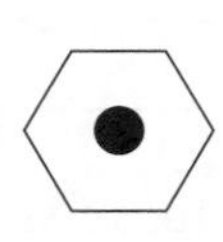

d

(C)

The circles alternate between black and grey. The size of the circle changes from big to medium to small and then starts from big again.

8.

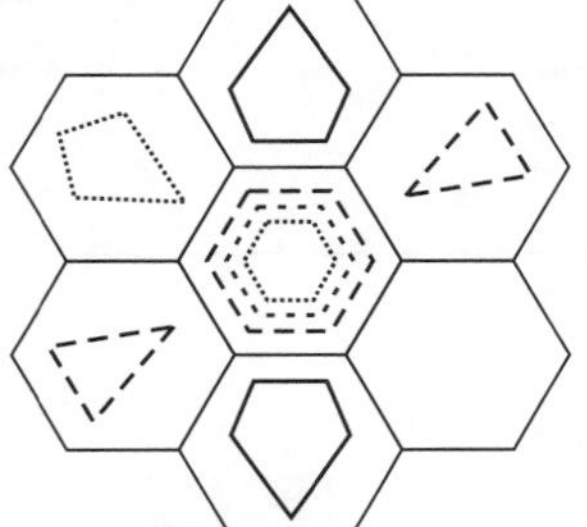

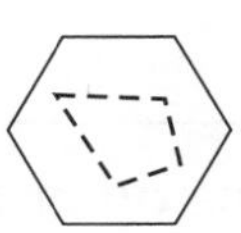

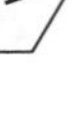

a

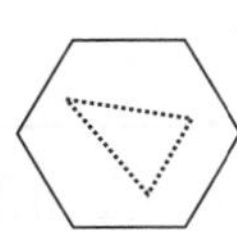

b

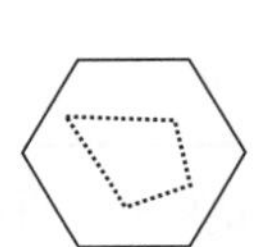

c

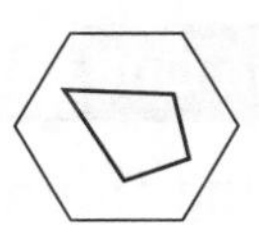

d

(____)

9.

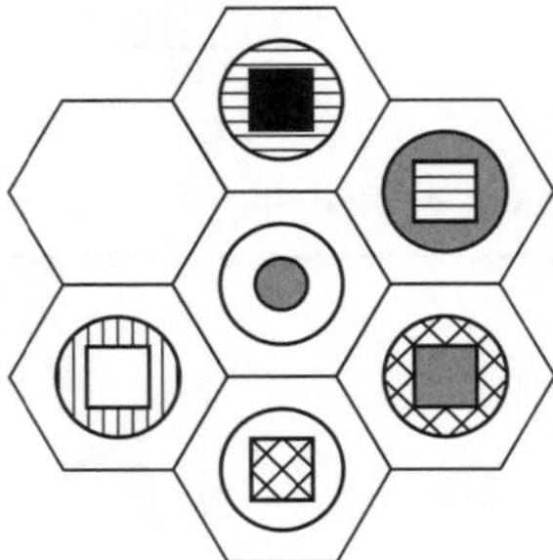

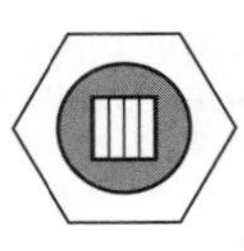

a

b

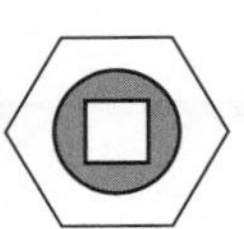

c

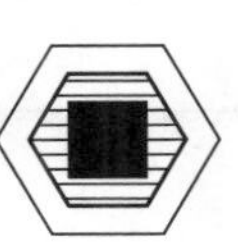

d

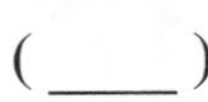

(____)

10.

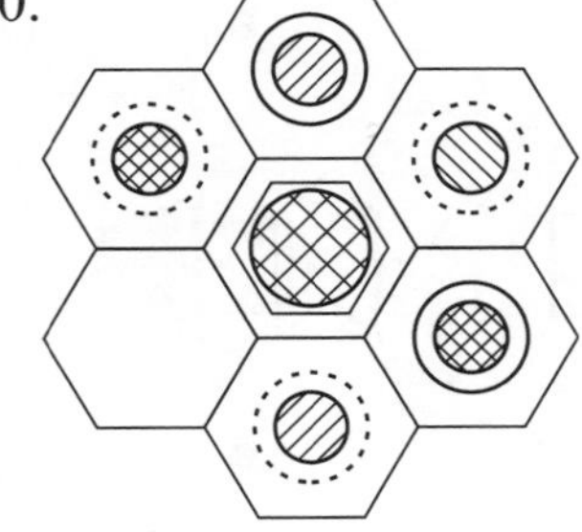

a

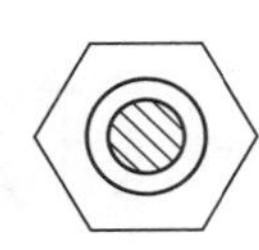

b

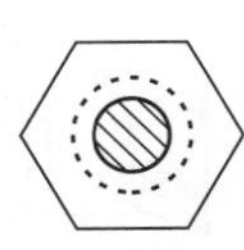

c

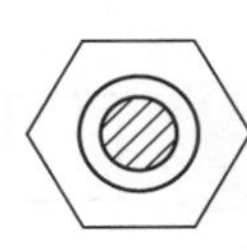

d

(____)

Order and Position

You should always look at where an object is positioned in relation to other objects.

Warm Up

1. If all the shadings in each figure moved **right two places**, what **colour** would the **square** be?

a. b. c. d. e.

2. i) What **shape** is **two places anticlockwise** from the X in each of the figures below?
ii) What **colour** is the shape **one place clockwise** from the X in each of the figures?

a. b. c. d. e. f.

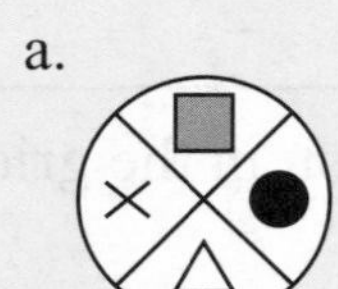
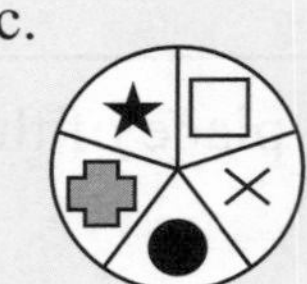
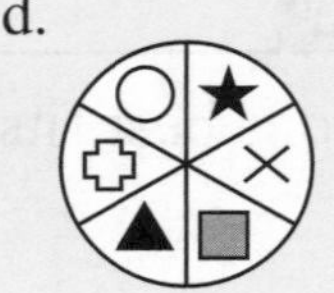
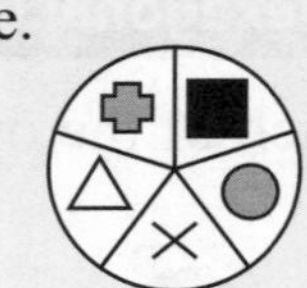

i) ______ ______ ______ ______ ______ ______
ii) ______ ______ ______ ______ ______ ______

3. If all these **shapes** moved **two places clockwise**, what **shape** would be **top right**?

a. b. c. d. e.

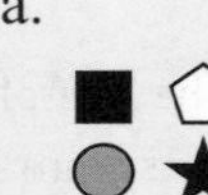

Odd One Out

Find the figure in each row that is most unlike the other figures.

Example:

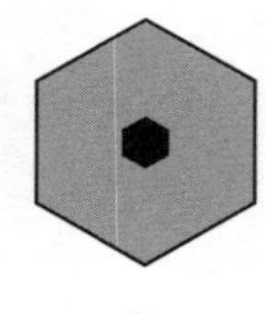
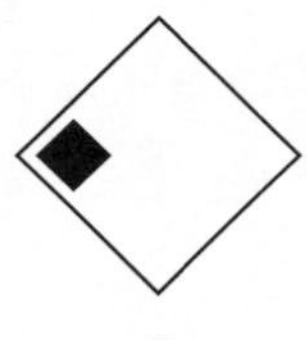
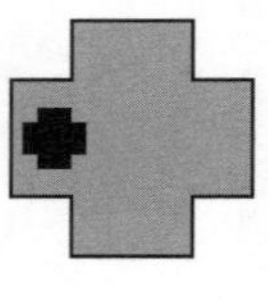

a b c d e (b)

All the other figures have the black inner shape on the left-hand side.

4.

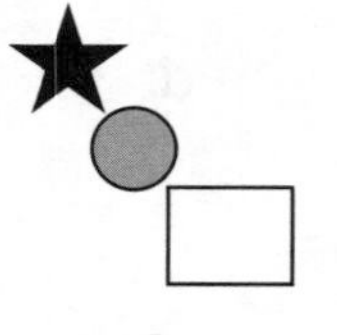
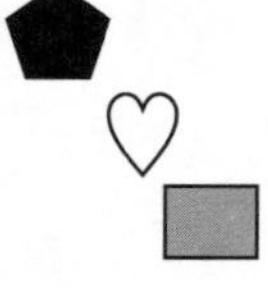
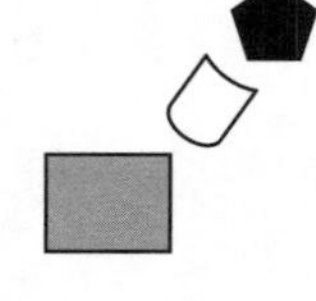

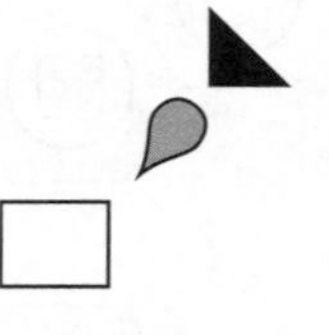

a b c d e (____)

5.

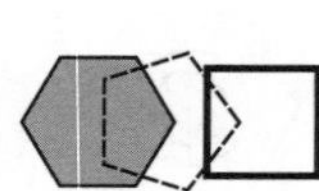
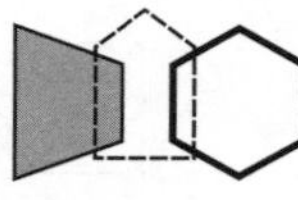
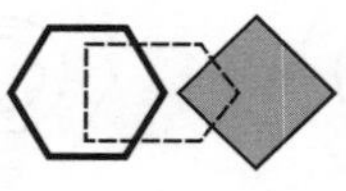
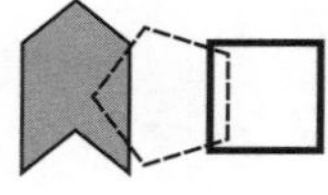
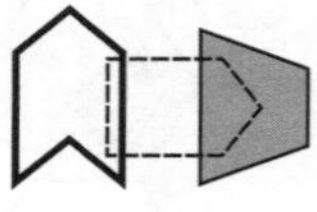

a b c d e (____)

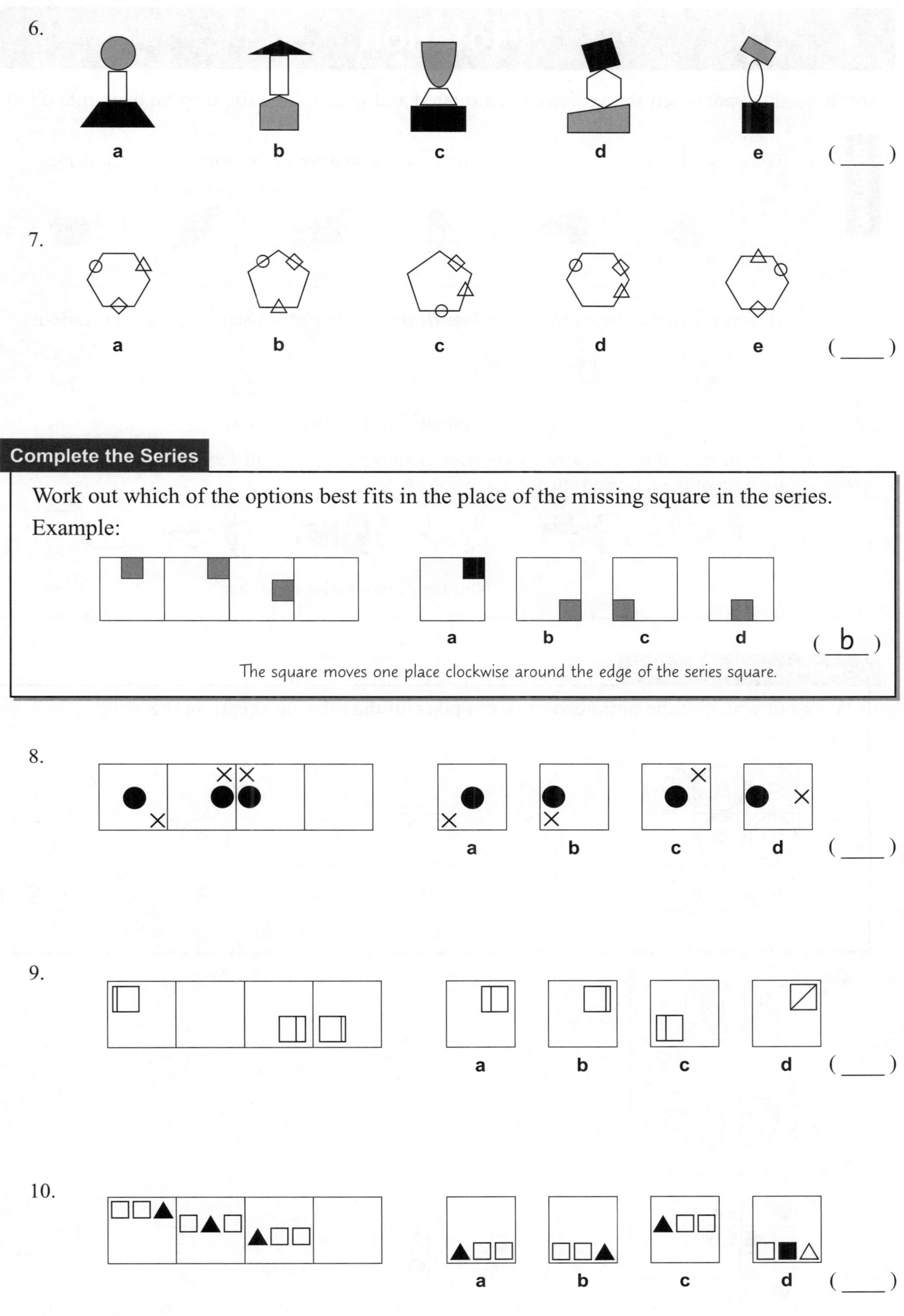

6. a b c d e (____)

7. a b c d e (____)

Complete the Series

Work out which of the options best fits in the place of the missing square in the series.

Example:

a b c d (b)

The square moves one place clockwise around the edge of the series square.

8. a b c d (____)

9. a b c d (____)

10. a b c d (____)

Rotation

You'll need to spot when shapes have been rotated and which direction they've been rotated in.

Warm Up

1. Work out whether these white shapes rotate **45** or **90 degrees** to become the black shapes.

a. b. c. d. e. f.

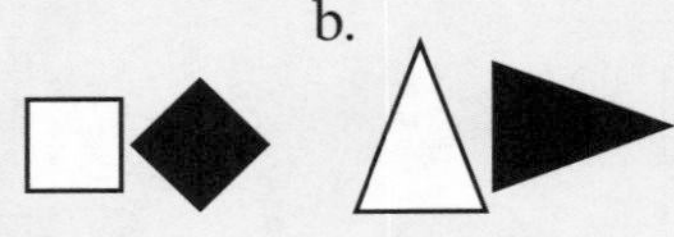

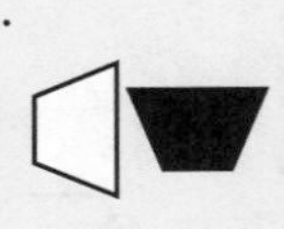

____ ____ ____ ____ ____ ____

2. How many of the shapes below are **identical** to the left hand shape apart from **rotation**?

Number of **identical shapes**: ____

3. Including shading, how many right hand shapes below are a 90 degree **clockwise** rotation of the left hand shape?

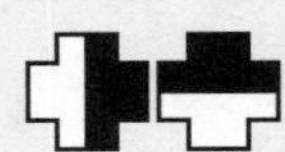

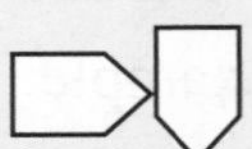

Number of **clockwise** rotations: ____

Complete the Square Grid

Work out which of the options best fits in place of the missing square in the grid.

Example:

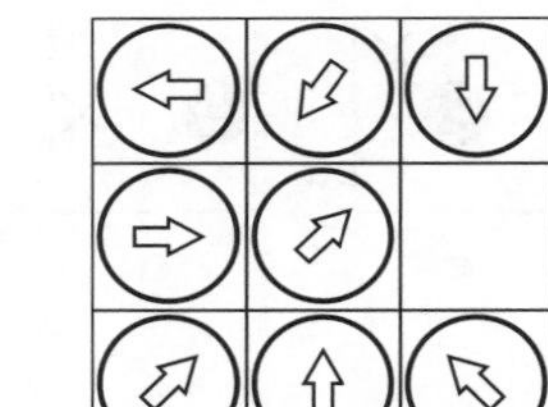

a b c d (C)

Moving from left to right, the arrow rotates 45 degrees anticlockwise.

4.

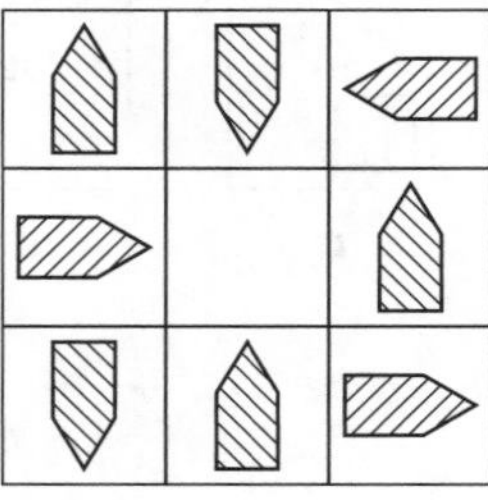

a b c d (____)

5.

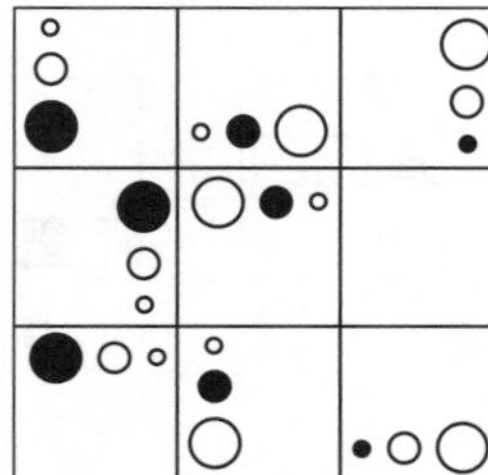

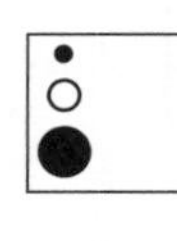
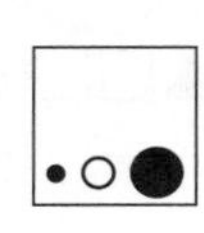
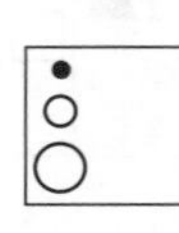

a b c d (____)

6.

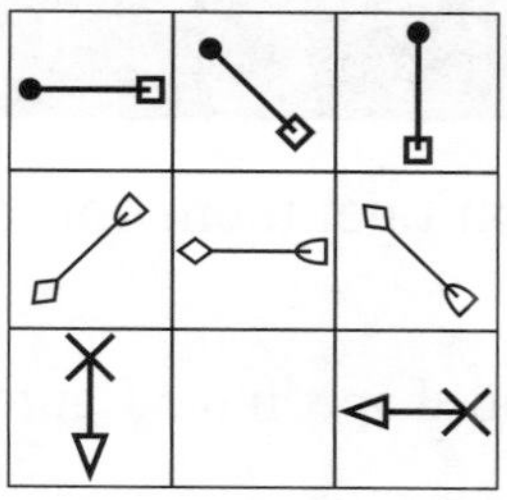

a b c d (____)

7.

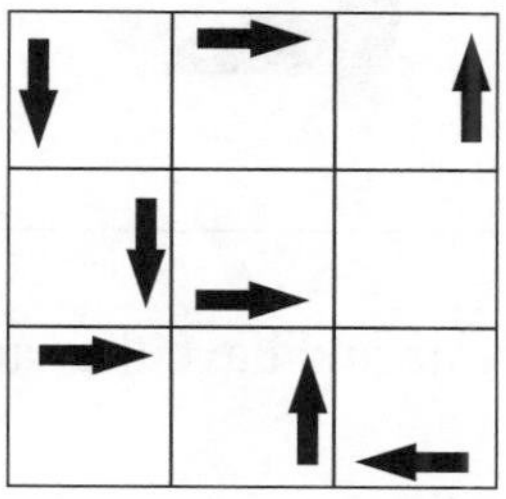

a b c d (____)

Rotate the Figure

Work out which option would look like the figure on the left if it was rotated.

Example:

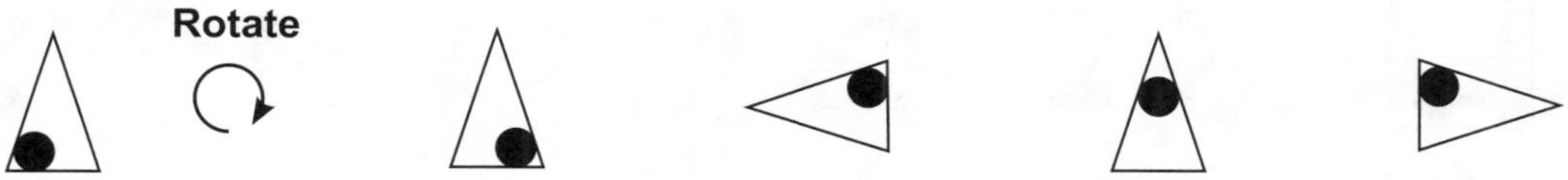

Rotate

a b c d (d)

The figure has been rotated 90 degrees clockwise.

8.

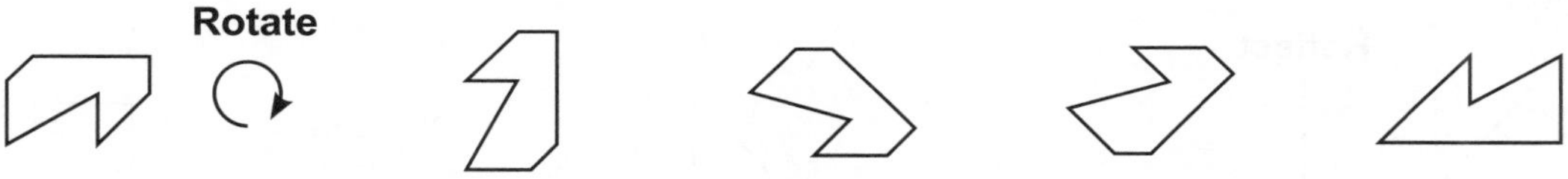

Rotate

a b c d (____)

9.

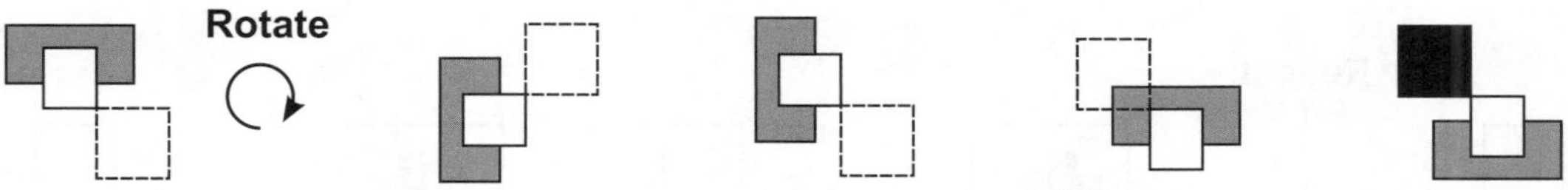

Rotate

a b c d (____)

10.

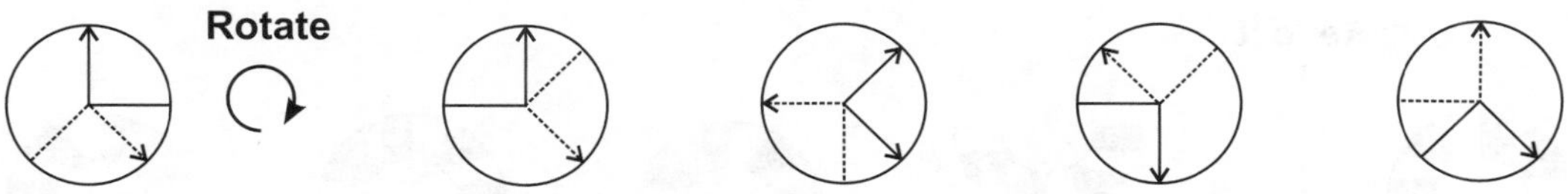

Rotate

a b c d (____)

Reflection

Reflection and rotation can look very similar so make sure you don't get them confused.

Warm Up

1. Is the right hand shape a **reflection** or **rotation** of the left hand shape in the figures below?

a.  ______

b.  ______

c. 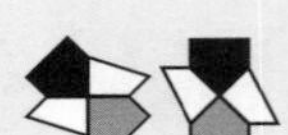 ______

d.  ______

e.  ______

f. 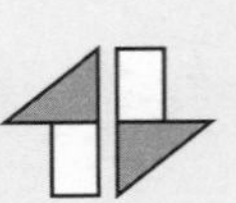 ______

2. If each figure is **reflected** across the line, will it still look the same and have the same rotation?

a.  ____

b. 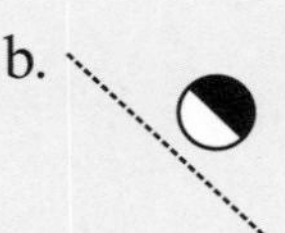 ____

c.  ____

d. 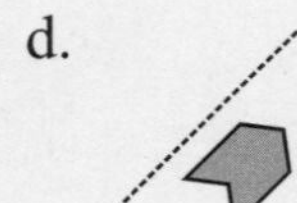 ____

e. 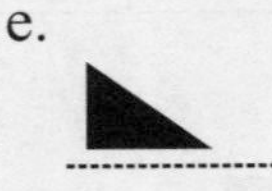 ____

f.  ____

3. How many of the right hand shapes below are **reflections** of the shape on the left?

Number of **reflections**: ____

Reflect the Figure

Work out which option would look like the figure on the left if it was reflected over the line.

Example:

Reflect

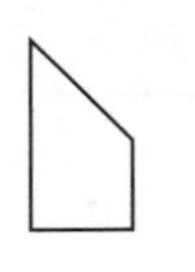

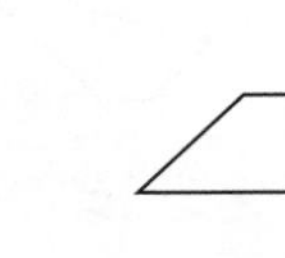 a

 b

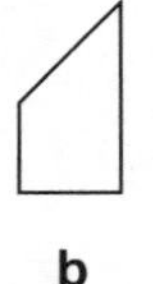 c

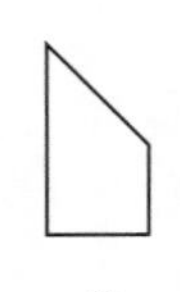 d

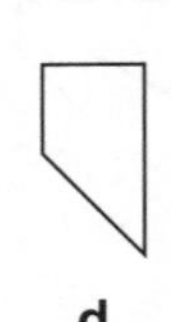

(b)

Options A and D are rotations of the shape on the left. Option C has not been reflected.

4.

Reflect

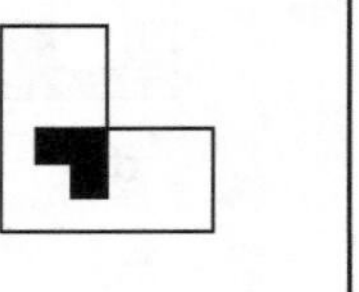

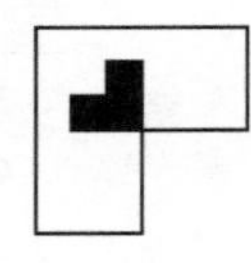 a

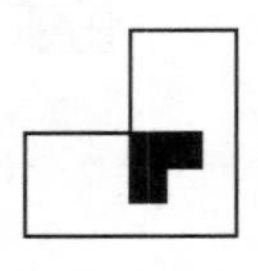 b

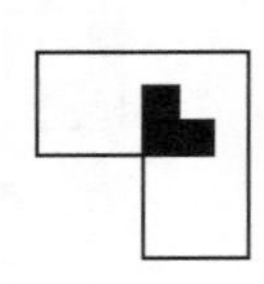 c

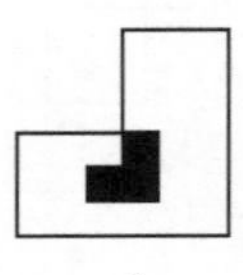 d

(____)

5.

Reflect

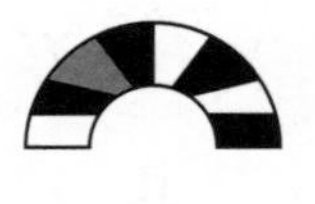

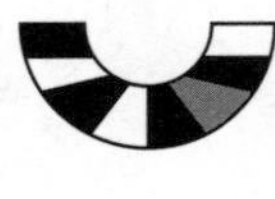 a

 b

 c

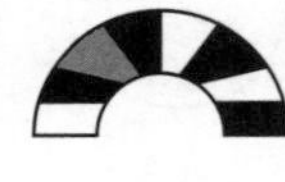 d

(____)

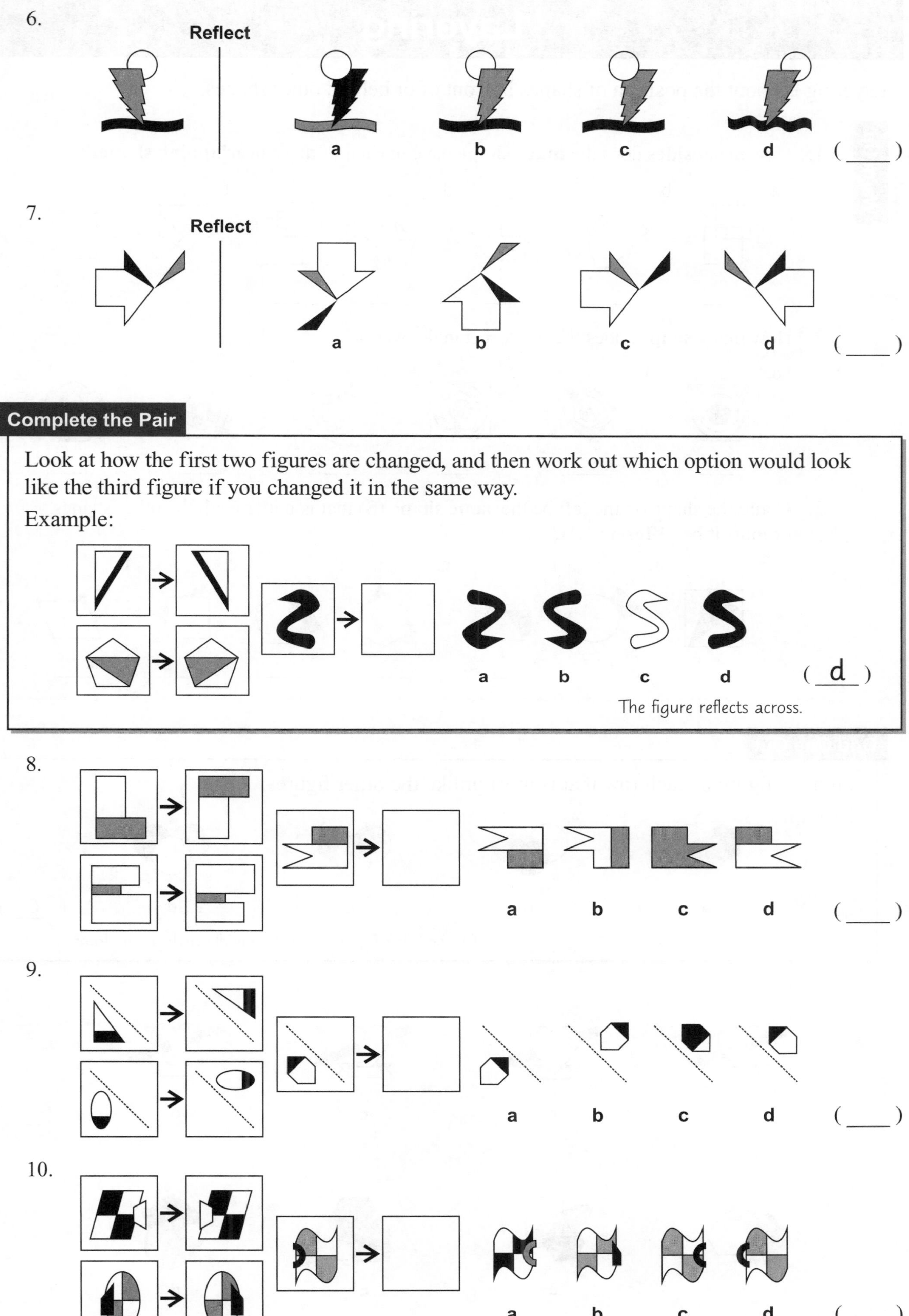
6.
Reflect
a
b
c
d
(___)
7.
Reflect
a
b
c
d
(___)
Complete the Pair
Look at how the first two figures are changed, and then work out which option would look like the third figure if you changed it in the same way.
Example:
a
b
c
d
(d)
The figure reflects across.
8.
a
b
c
d
(___)
9.
a
b
c
d
(___)
10.
a
b
c
d
(___)

Layering

Layering is about the position of shapes in front of or behind other shapes.

Warm Up

1. How many **sides** does the **inner shape** have in each of these **overlapping shapes**?

a. b. c. d. e. f. g.

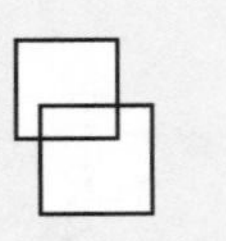
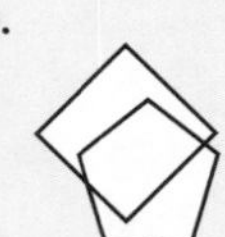

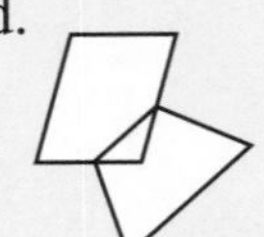
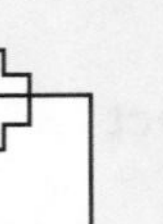

____ ____ ____ ____ ____ ____ ____

2. How many **shapes** does the black rectangle overlap?

a. b. c. d. e. f.

____ ____ ____ ____ ____ ____

3. Could the shape on the left be the **same shape** (S) that is underneath the other shapes, or must it be **different** (D)?

a. b. c. d. e. f.

____ ____ ____ ____ ____ ____

Odd One Out

Find the figure in each row that is most unlike the other figures.

Example:

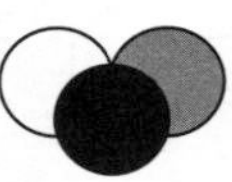
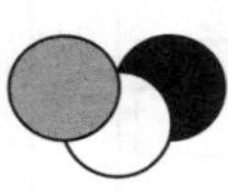
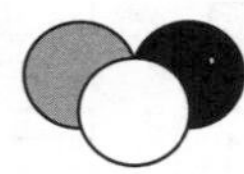

a b c d

(C)

All the other figures have the middle circle at the front.

4.

a b c d

(____)

5.

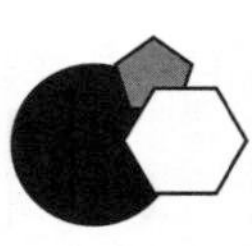
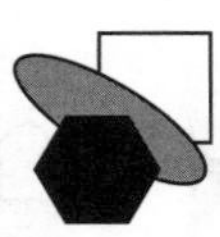

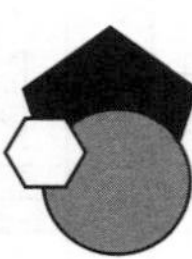

a b c d (____)

6.

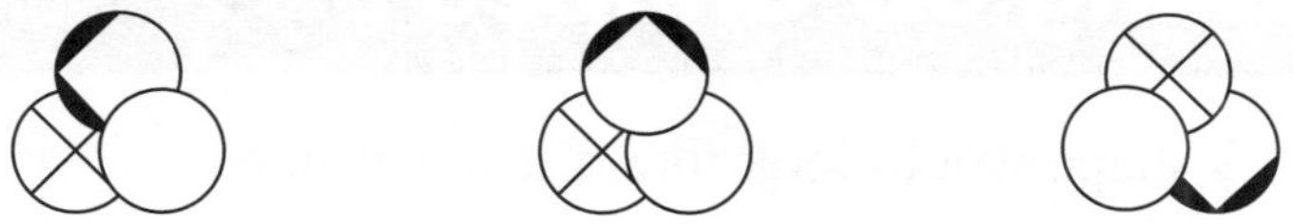

a b c d (____)

7.

a b c d (____)

Complete the Pair

Look at how the first two figures are changed, and then work out which option would look like the third figure if you changed it in the same way.

Example:

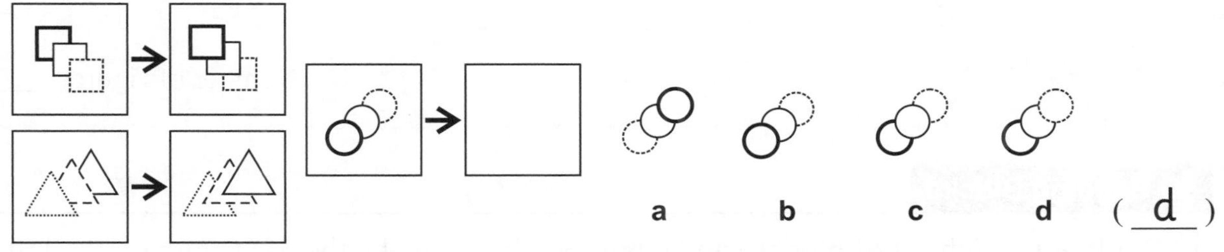

The front shape moves to the back, and the back shape moves to the front.

8.

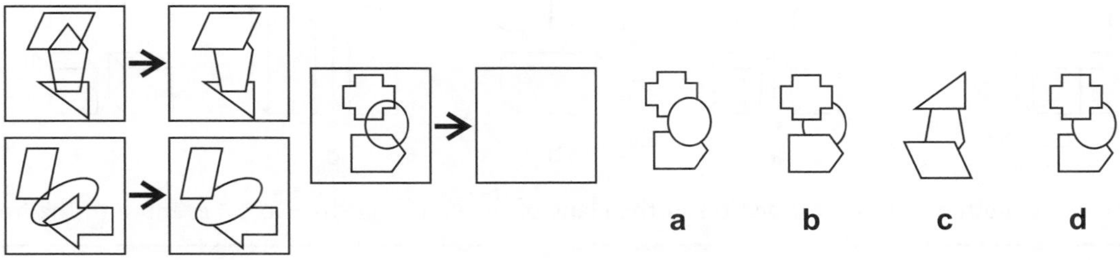

a b c d (____)

9.

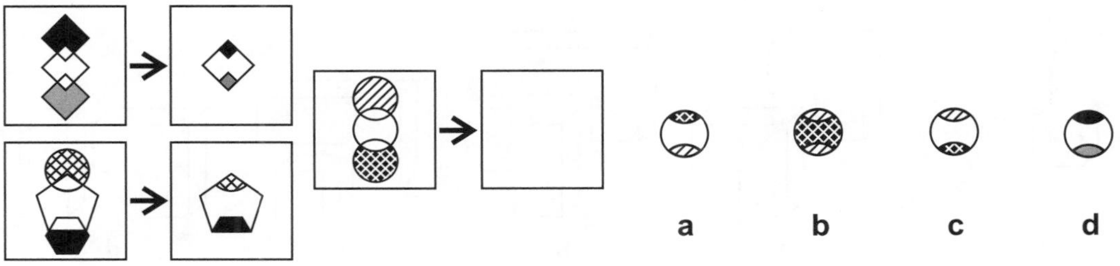

a b c d (____)

10.

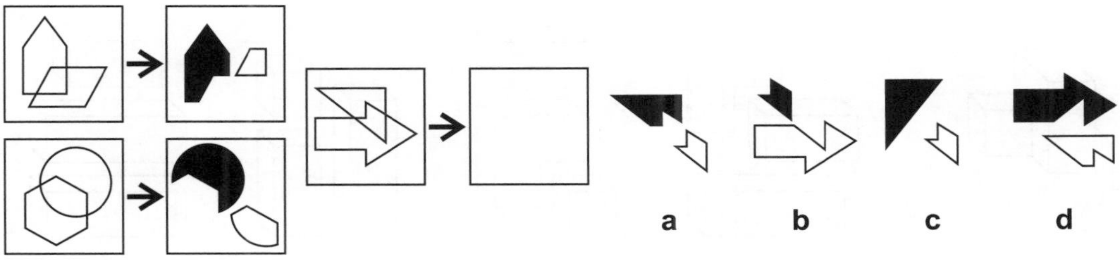

a b c d (____)

Rotating 3D Shapes

You might need to imagine what a 3D shape would look like if it was rotated.

Warm Up

1. How many blocks are each of the figures below made up of?

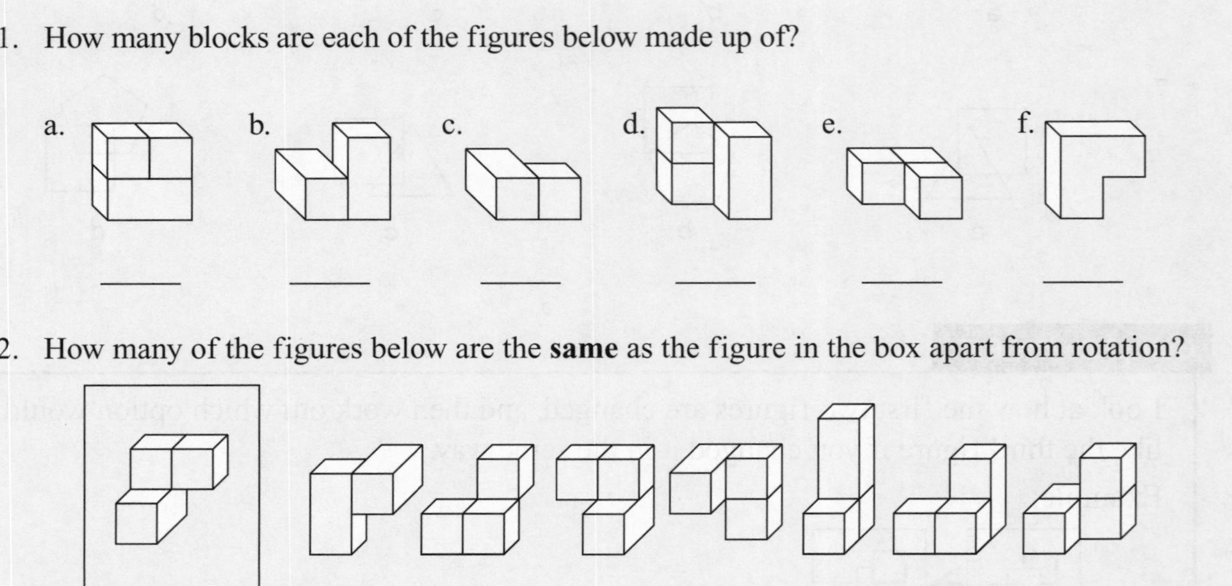

a. ____ b. ____ c. ____ d. ____ e. ____ f. ____

2. How many of the figures below are the **same** as the figure in the box apart from rotation?

Number of figures: ________

3D Building Blocks

Work out which set of blocks can be put together to make the 3D figure on the left.

Example:

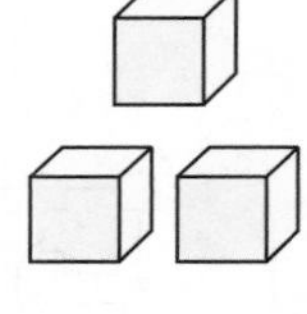

a

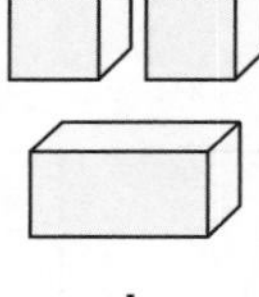

b

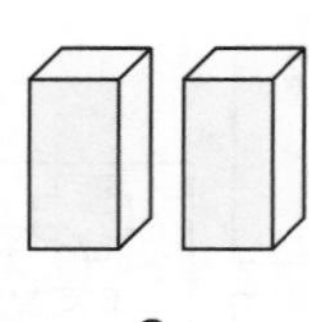

c

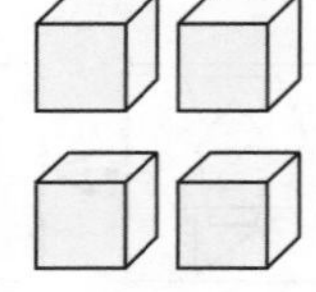

d

(b)

The block at the bottom rotates 90 degrees in the plane of the page and the two cubes move to the front.

3.

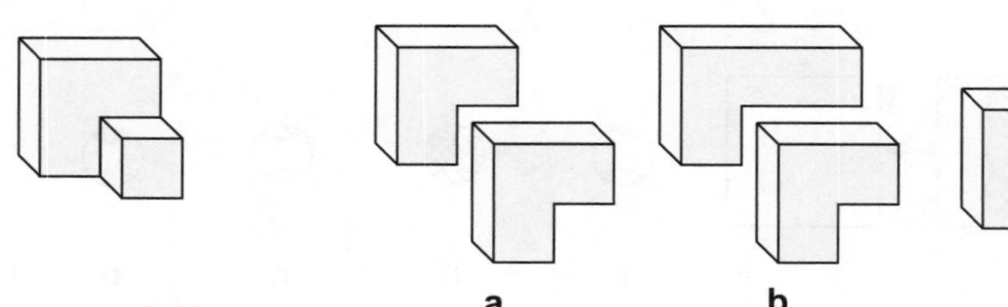

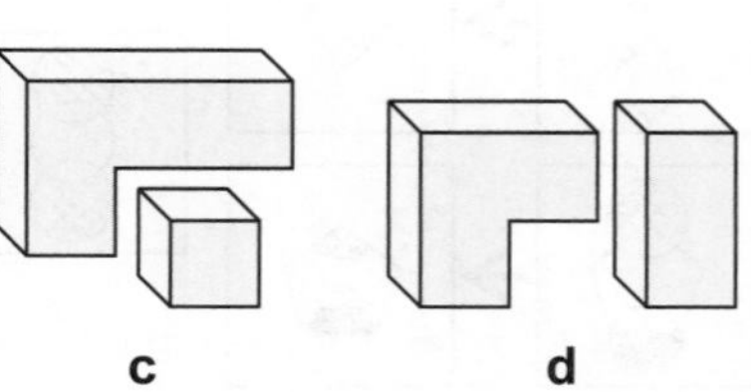

a b c d (____)

4.

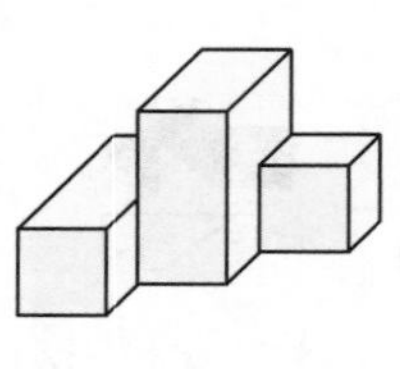

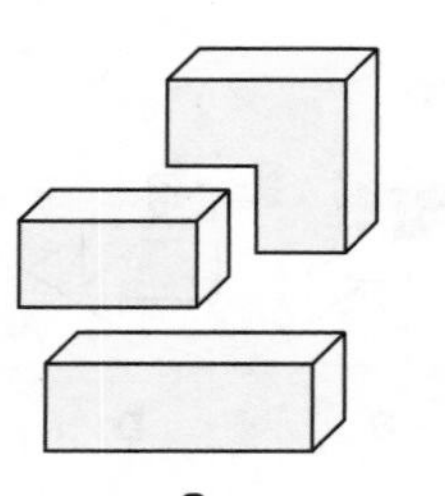

a

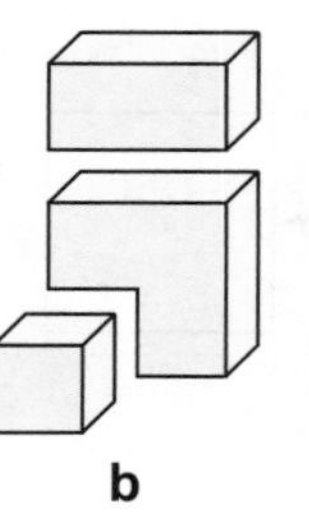

b

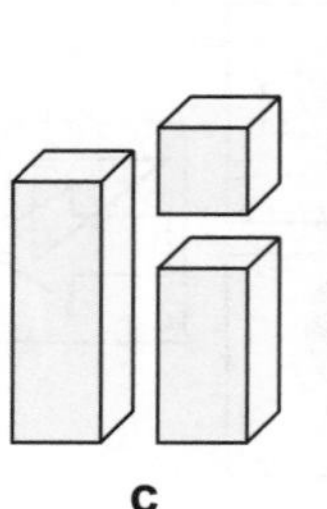

c

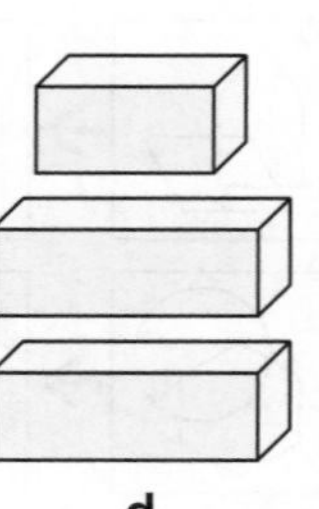

d

(____)

5.

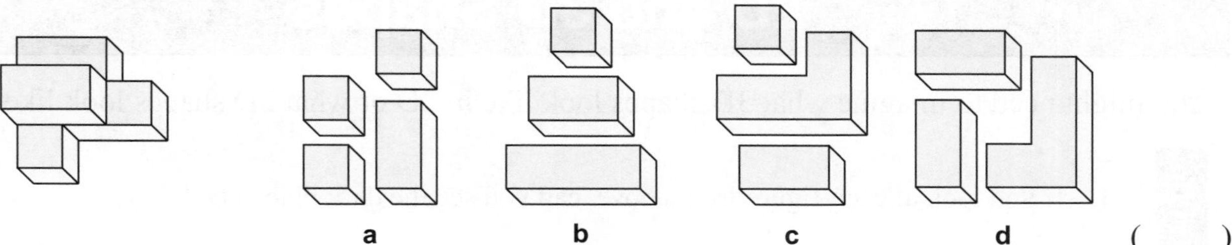

(____)

3D Rotation

Work out which 3D figure in the grey box has been rotated to make the new 3D figure.

Example:

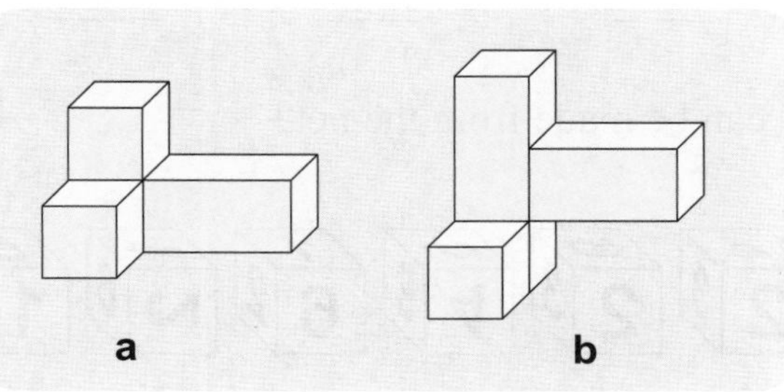

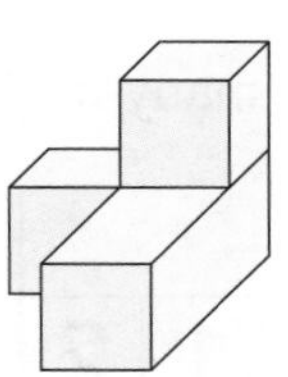

(a)

Figure A has been rotated 90 degrees right-to-left.

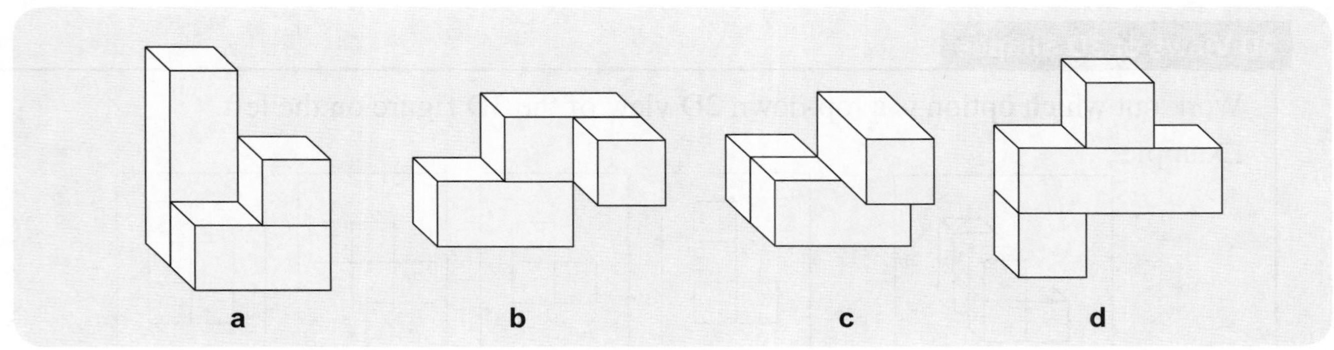

6.

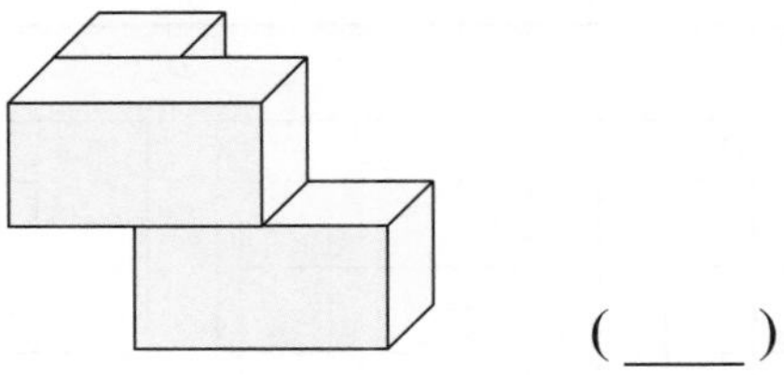

(____)

7.

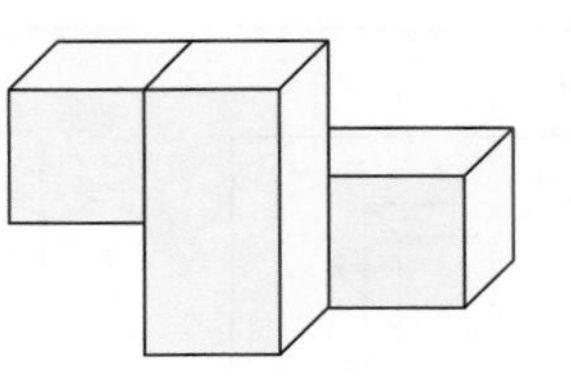

(____)

8.

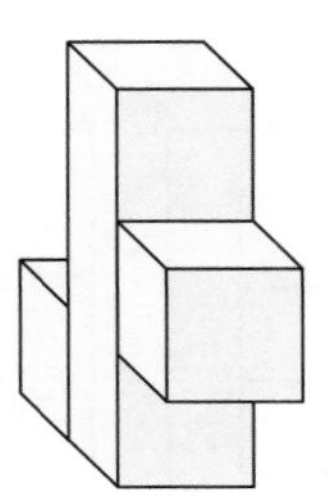

(____)

9.

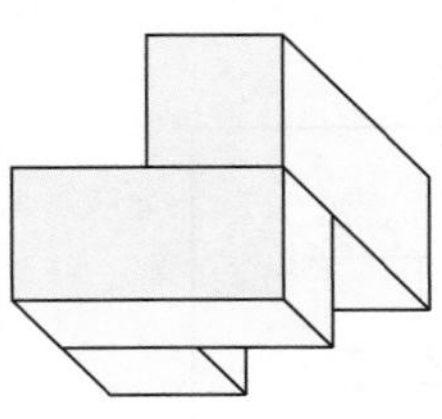

(____)

2D and 3D Shapes

You might need to imagine what 3D shapes look like in 2D or what 2D shapes look like in 3D.

Warm Up

1. If you look at each figure from above, can you see the dark blue cube?

a. 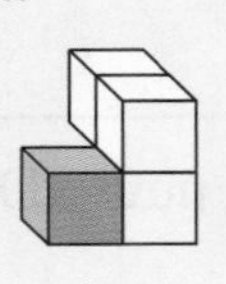 ______

b. 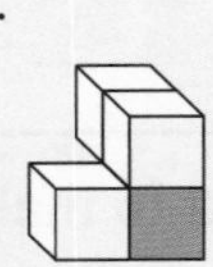 ______

c. 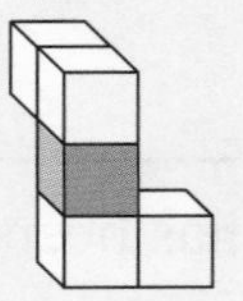 ______

d. 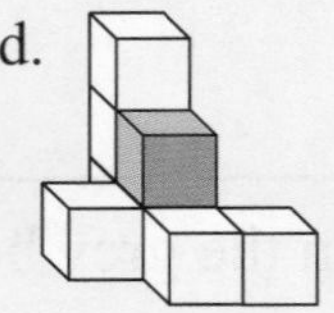 ______

e. 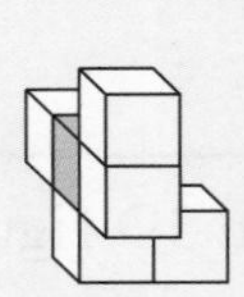 ______

f. 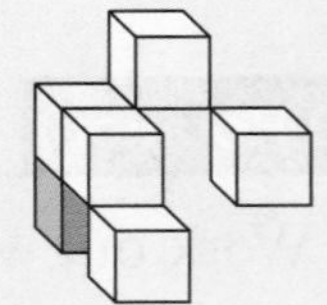 ______

2. How many of the cubes below can be made from the net?

Number of cubes made from the net: _____

2D Views of 3D Shapes

Work out which option is a top-down 2D view of the 3D figure on the left.

Example:

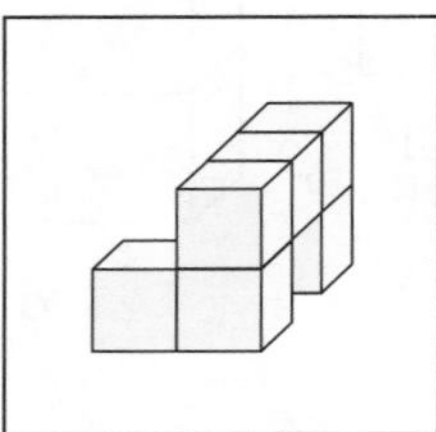

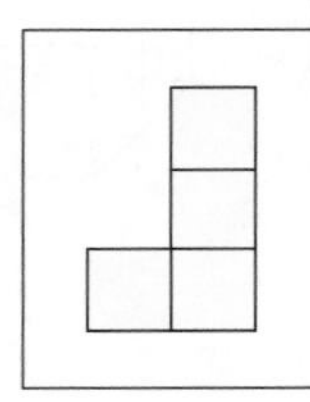 a

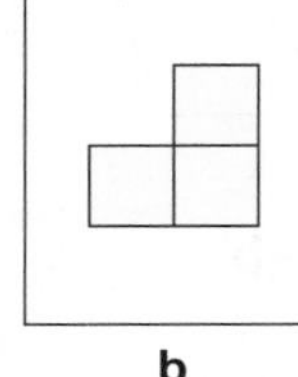 b

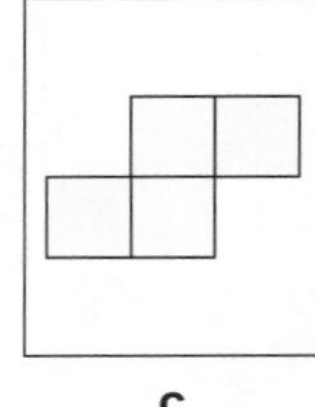 c

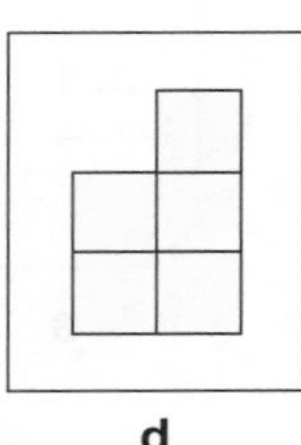 d

(a)

There are four blocks visible from above, which rules out options B and D. There is a line of three blocks on the right-hand side of the shape, which rules out option C.

3. 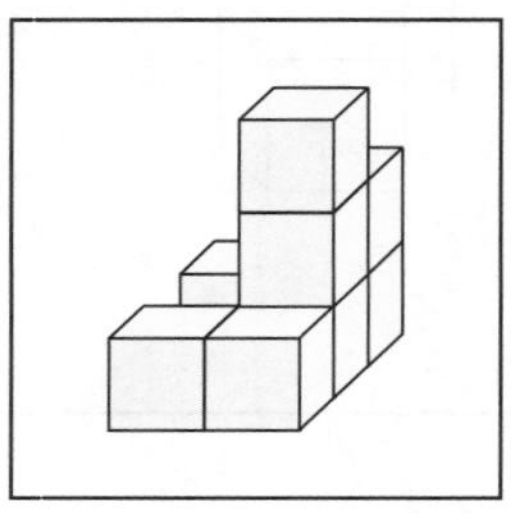

a

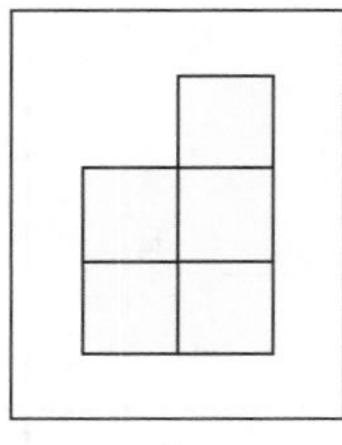 b

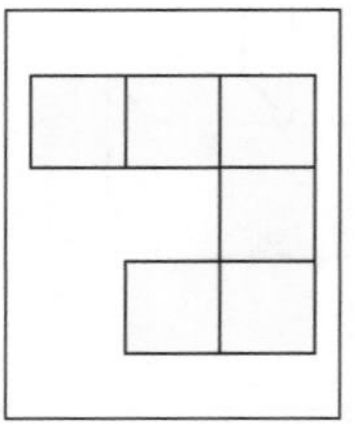 c

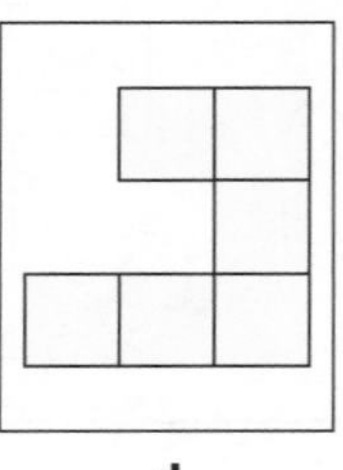 d

(____)

4. 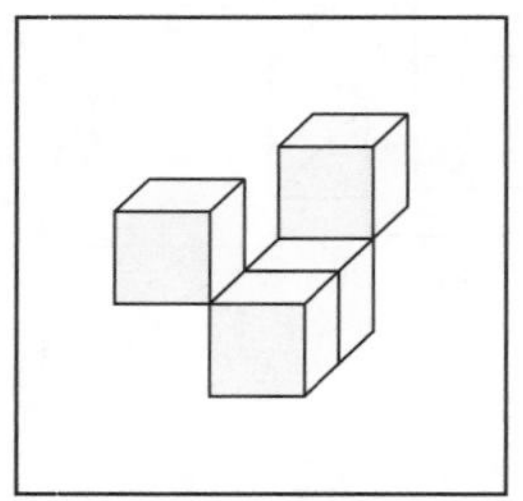

a

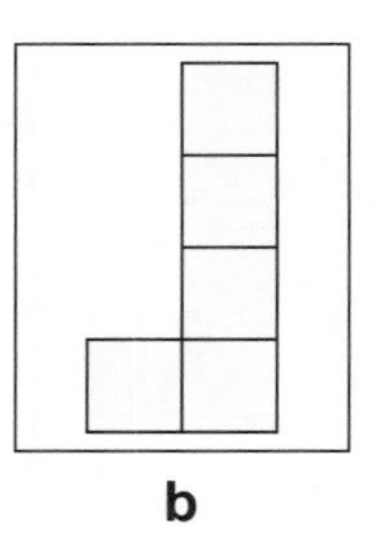 b

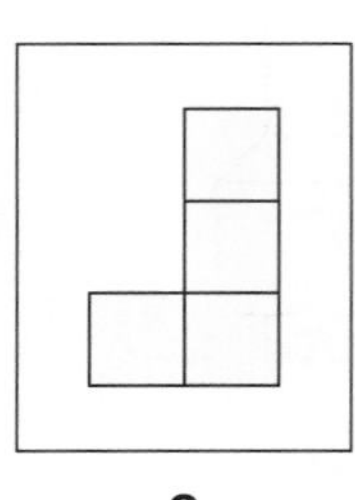 c

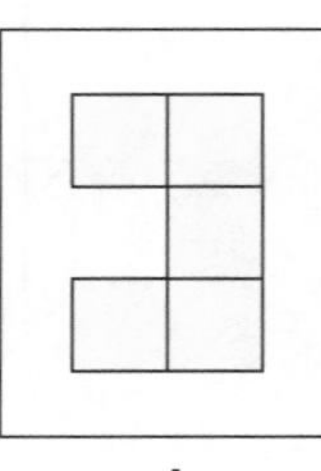 d

(____)

5.

a b c d (____)

Cubes and Nets

Work out which of the four cubes can be made from the net.

Example:

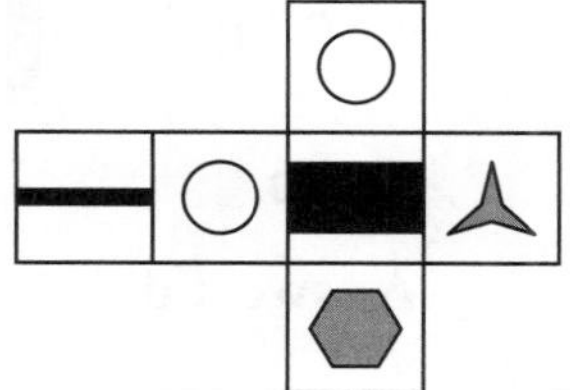

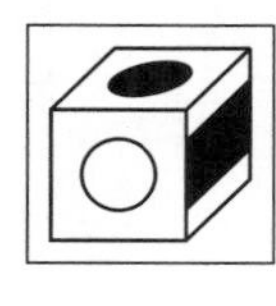

a

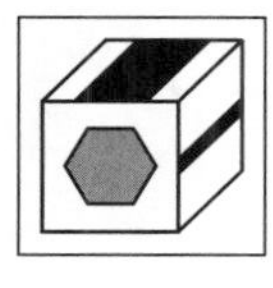

b

c

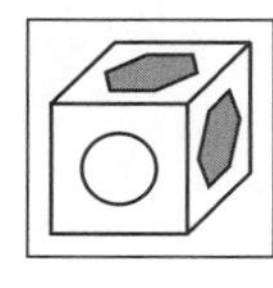

d

(C)

There is no black circle, which rules out option A. The thick black line and the thin black line must be on opposite sides, which rules out option B. There is only one grey hexagon, which rules out option D.

6.

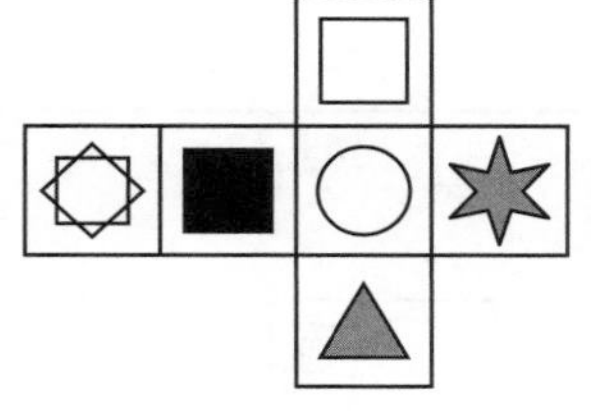

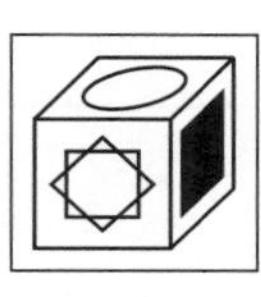

a

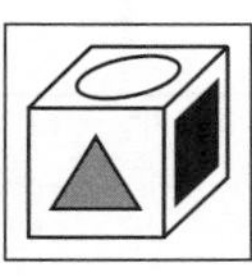

b

c

d (____)

7.

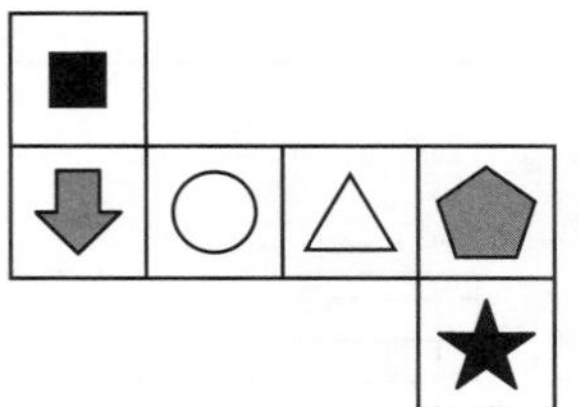

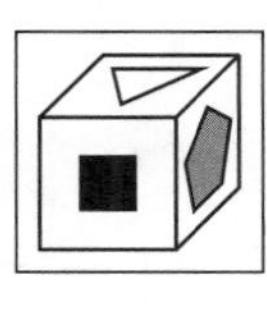

a

b c d (____)

8.

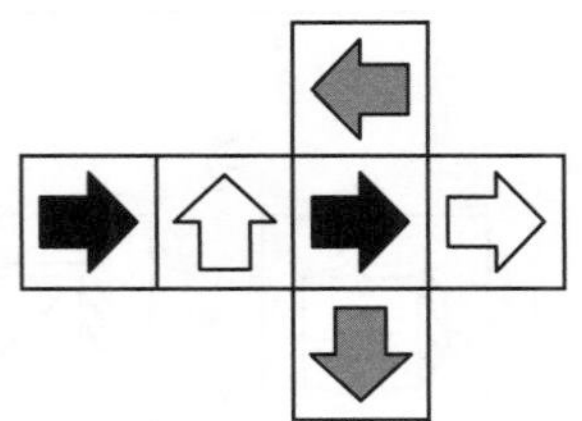

a

b

c d (____)

Assessment Test 1

You can print **multiple-choice answer sheets** for these questions from our website — go to www.cgplearning.co.uk/11+. If you'd prefer to answer them in standard write-in format, just circle the letter underneath the answer. The test should take around 20 minutes.

Section 1 — Complete the Series

Work out which of the options best fits in place of the missing square in the series.

Example:

a b c d

Answer: d

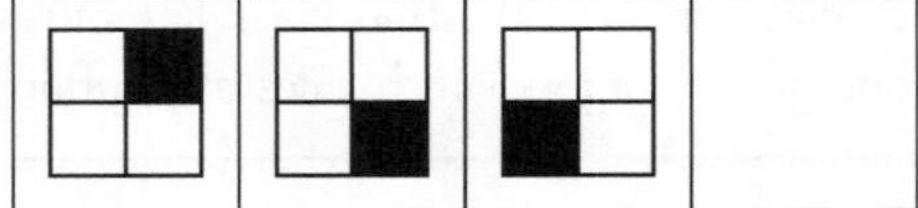

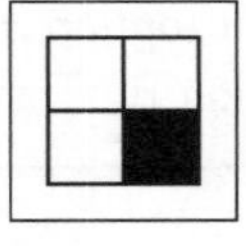
a

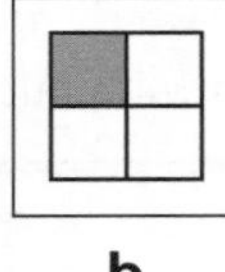
b

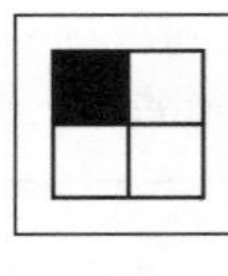
c

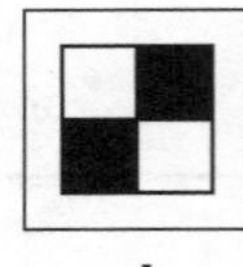
d

2

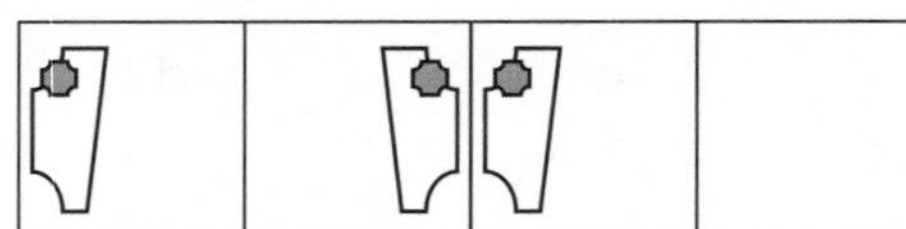

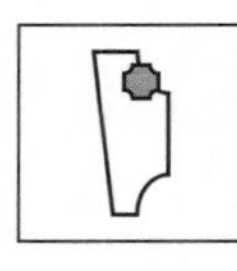
a

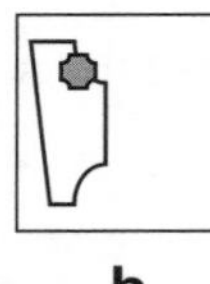
b

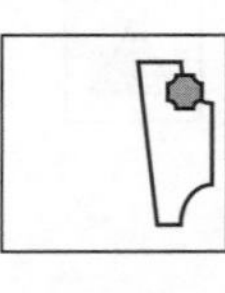
c

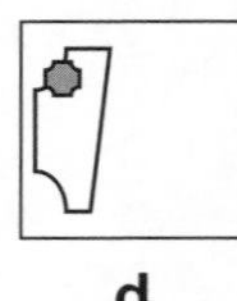
d

3

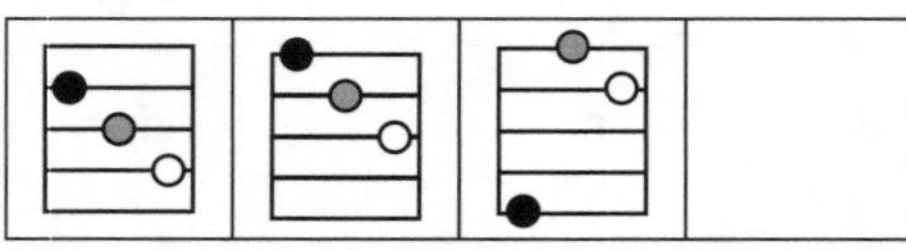

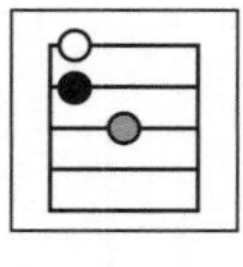
a

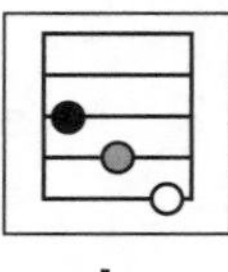
b

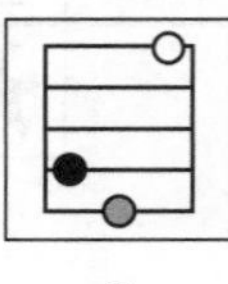
c

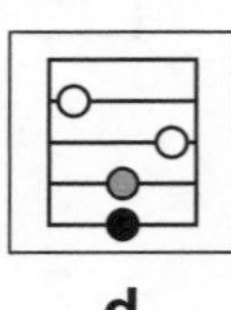
d

4

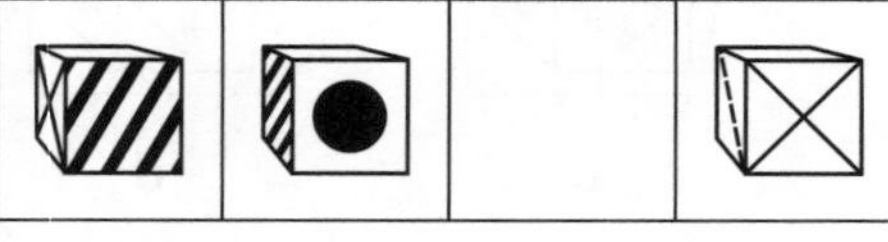

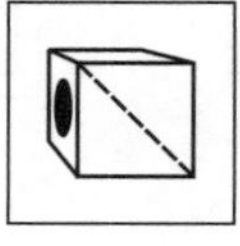
a

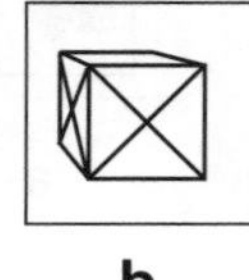
b

c

d

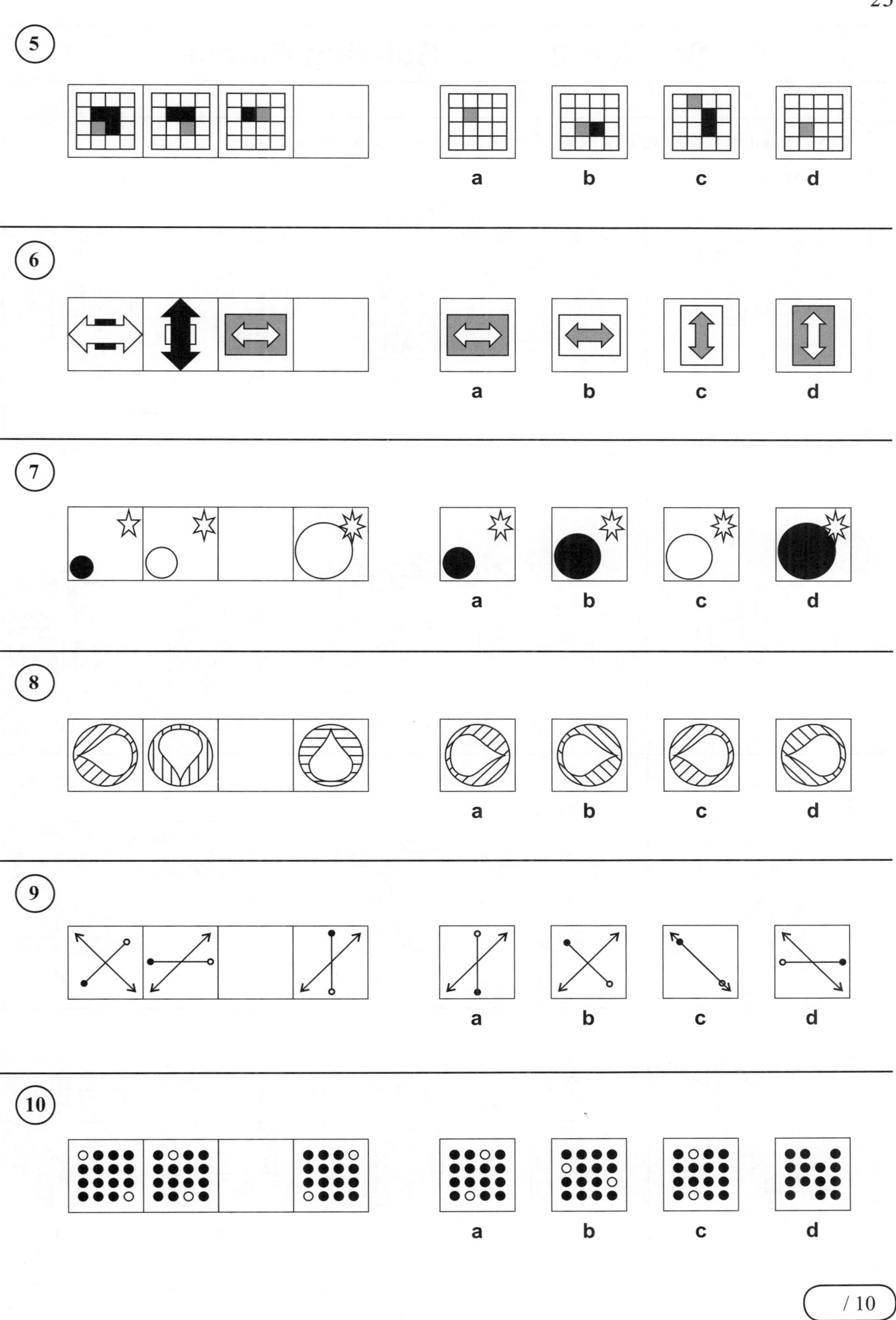

/ 10

Section 2 — 3D Building Blocks

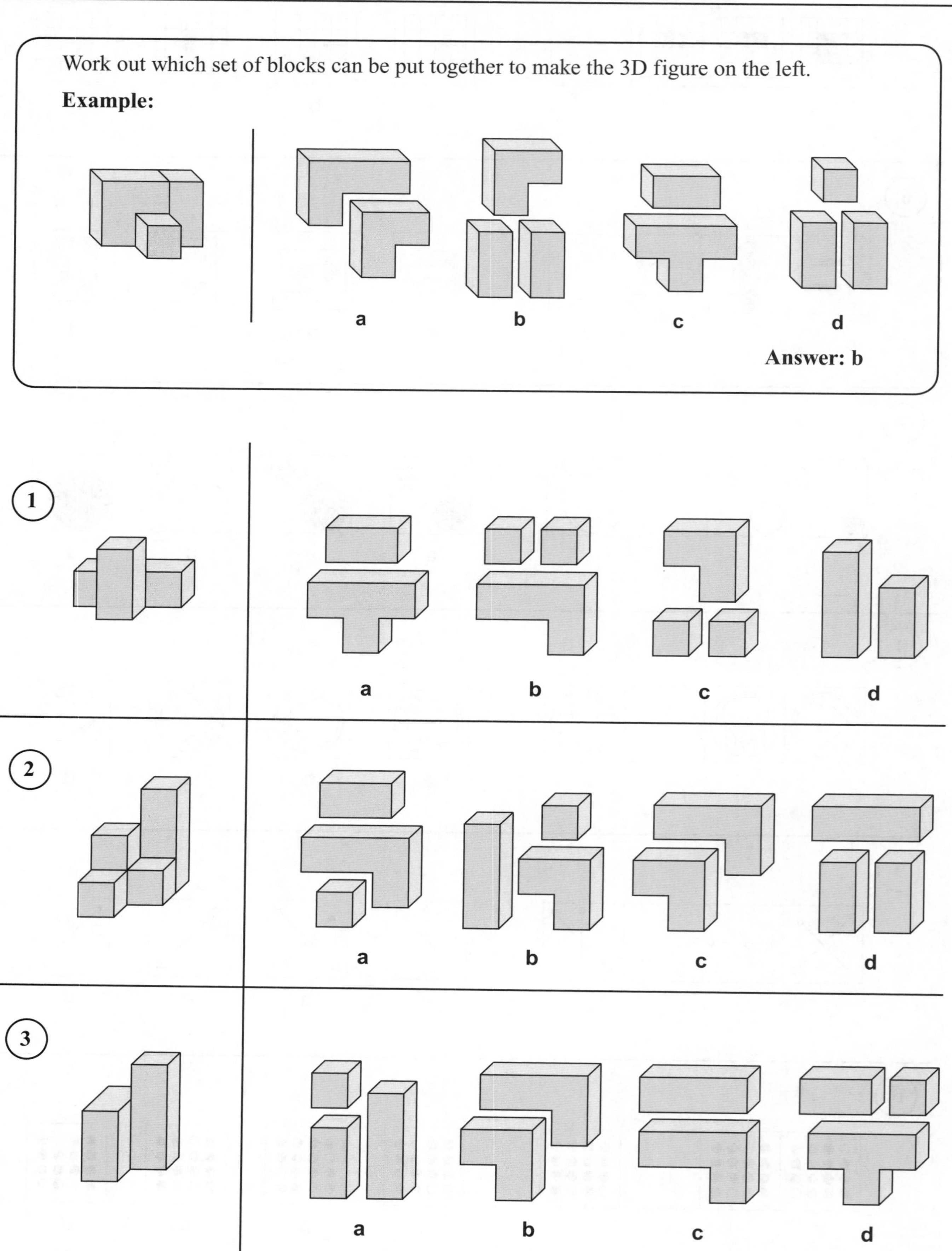

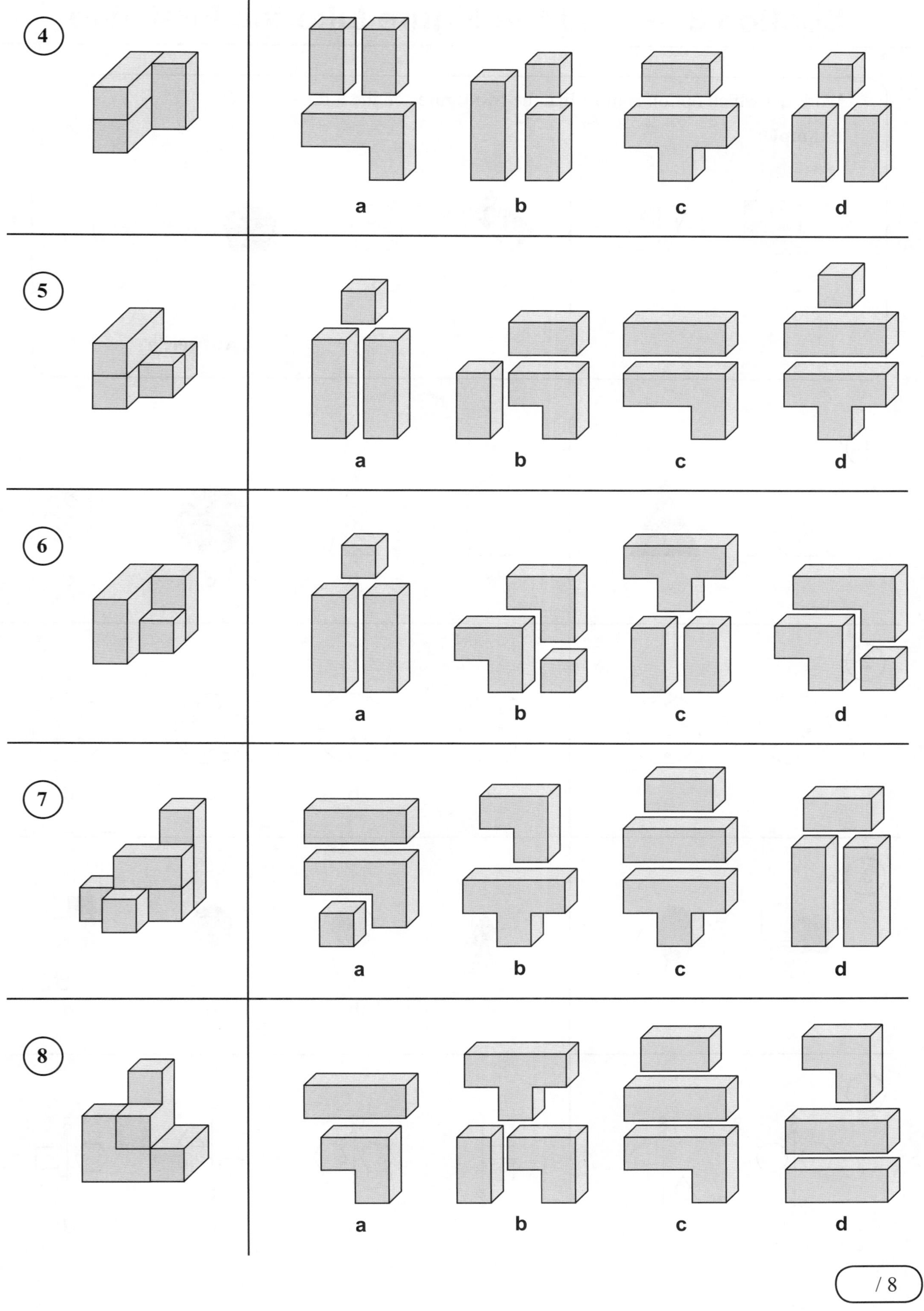

/ 8

Section 3 — Find the Figure Like the First Two

Work out which option is most like the two figures on the left.

Example:

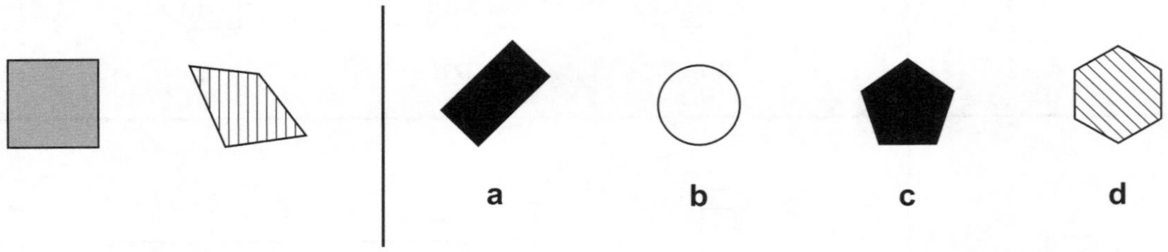

a b c d

Answer: a

1

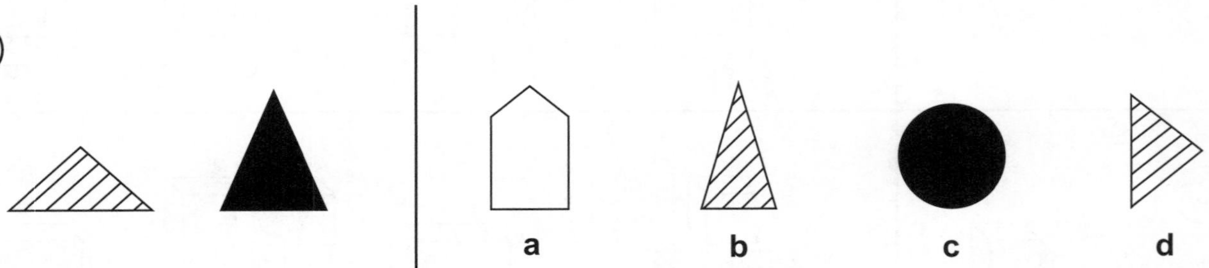

a b c d

2

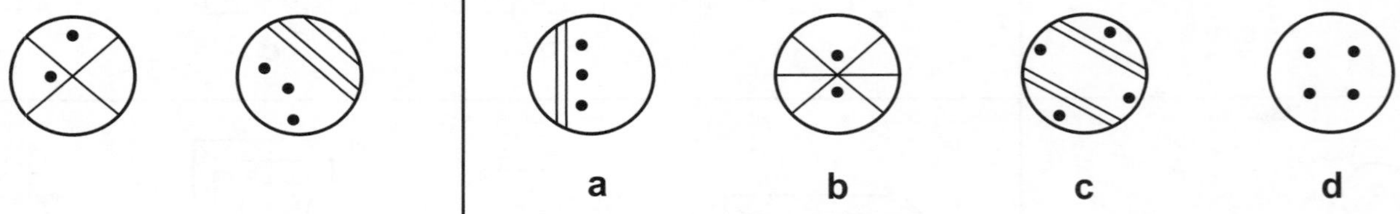

a b c d

3

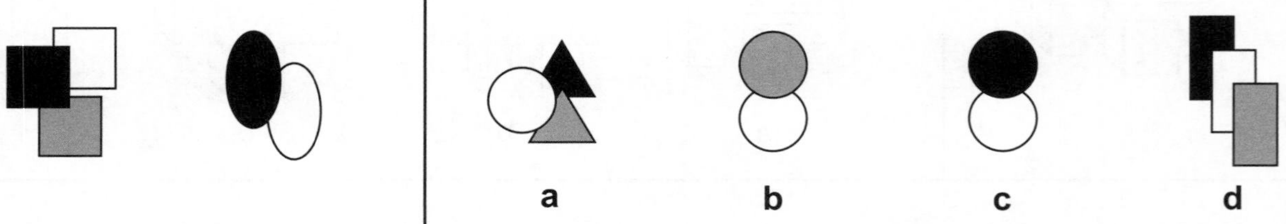

a b c d

4

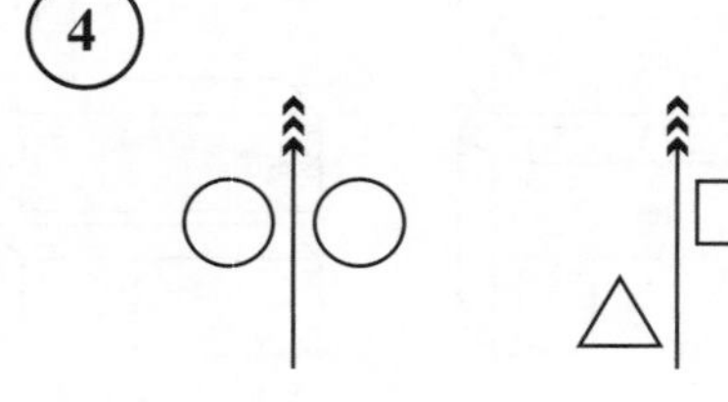

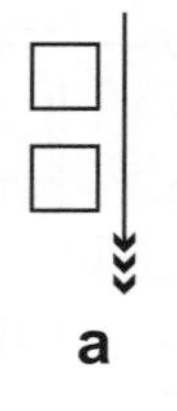

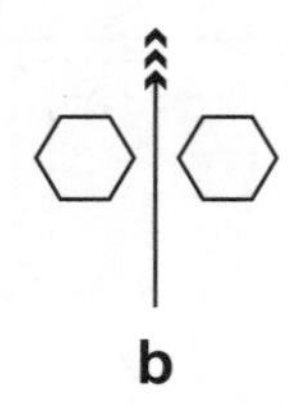

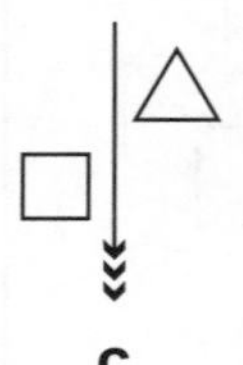

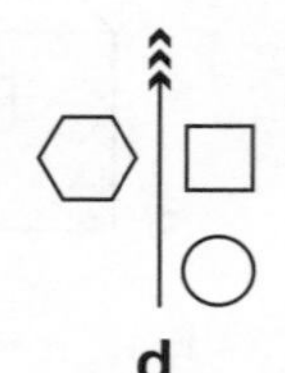

a b c d

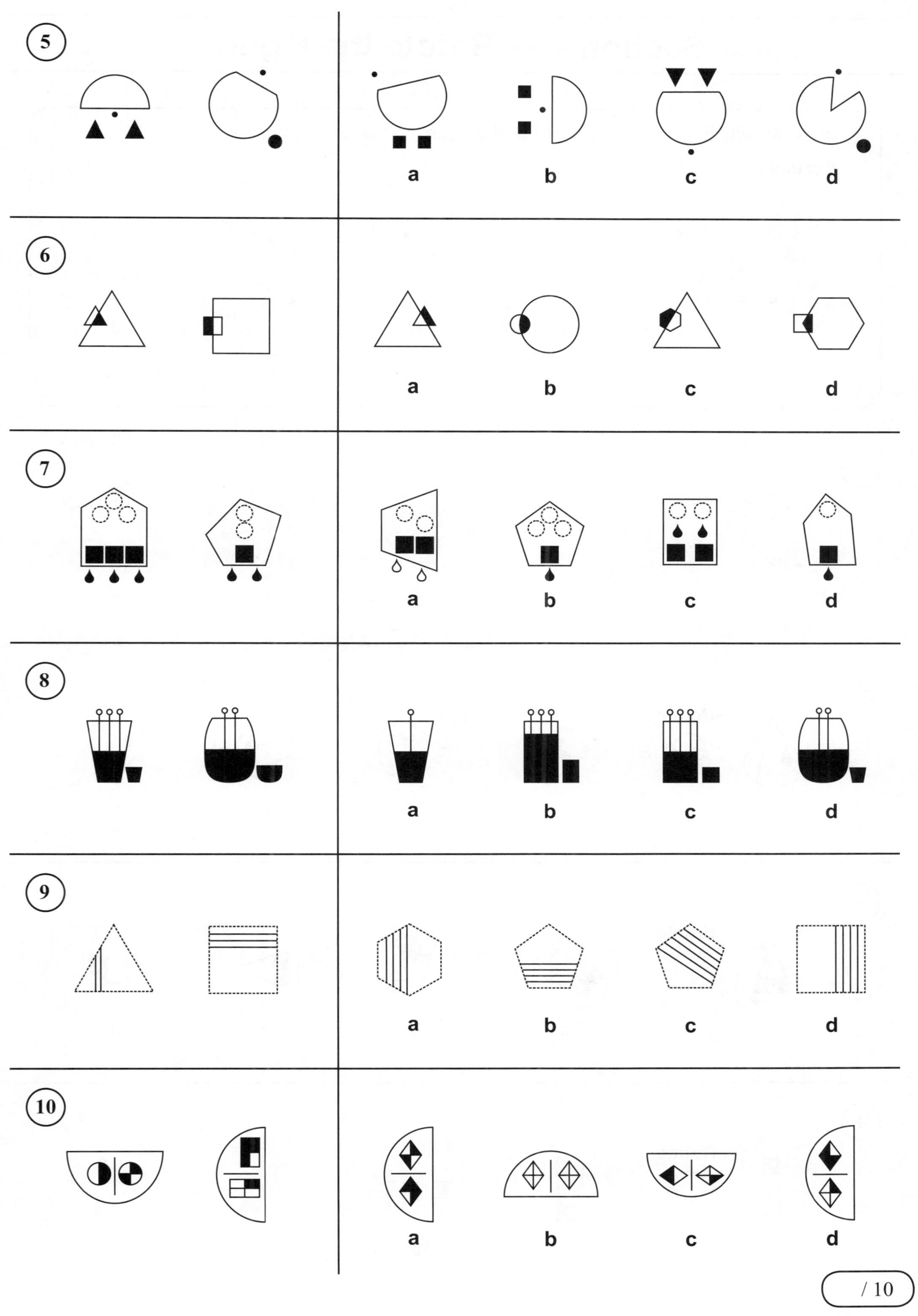

/ 10

Section 4 — Rotate the Figure

Work out which option would look like the figure on the left if it was rotated.

Example:

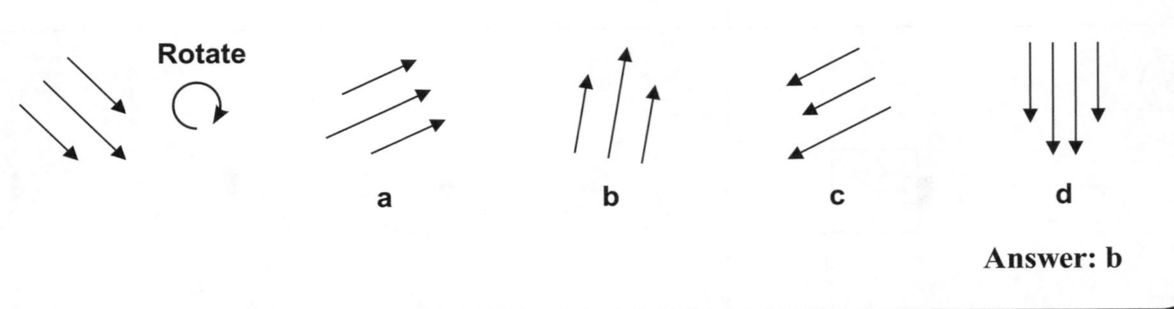

Answer: b

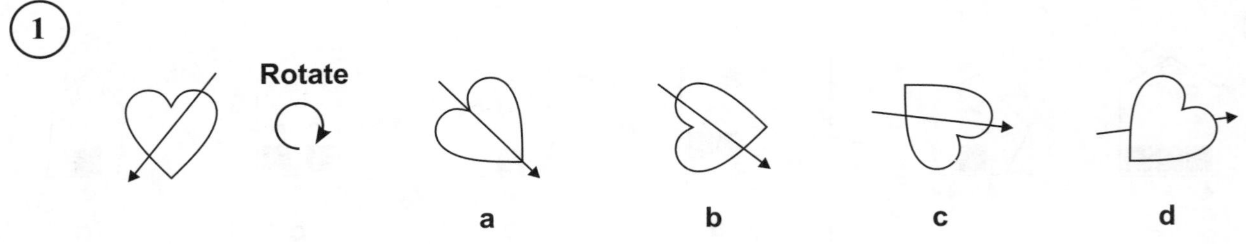

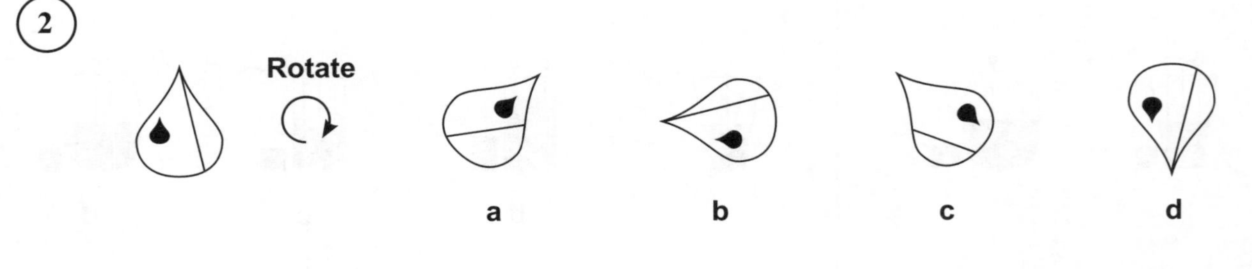

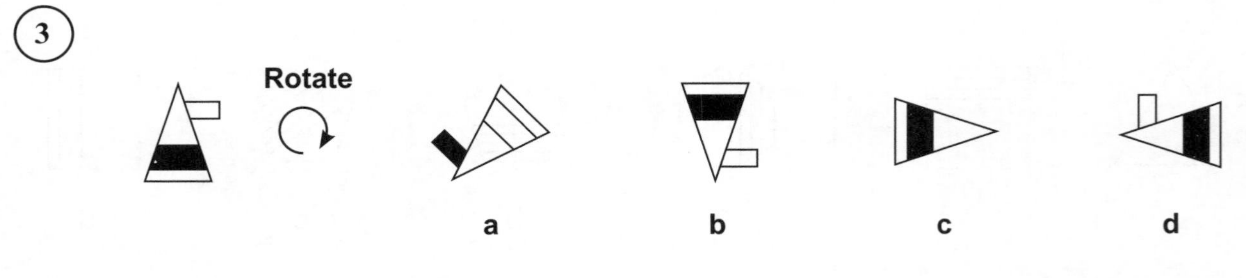

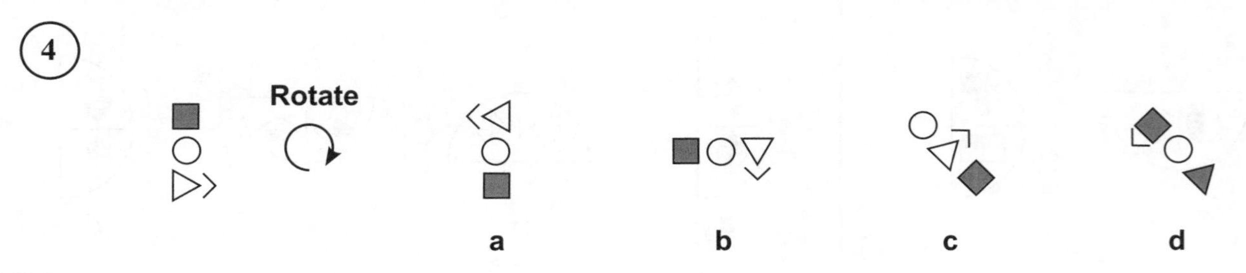

5

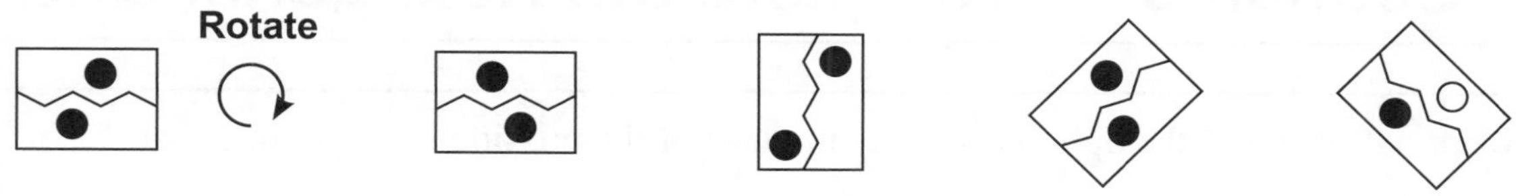

Rotate

a b c d

6

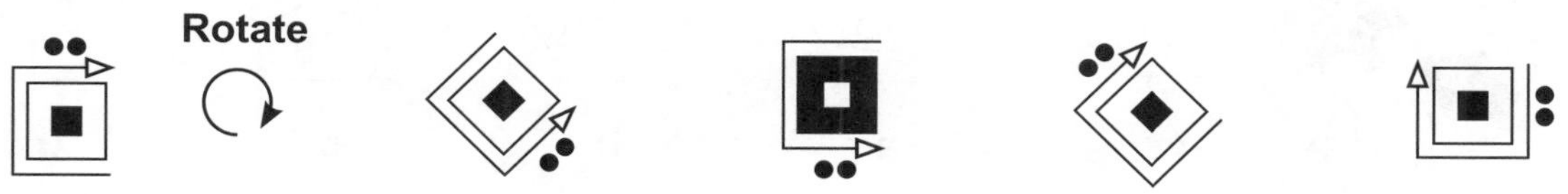

Rotate

a b c d

7

Rotate

a b c d

8

Rotate

a b c d

9

Rotate

a b c d

10

Rotate

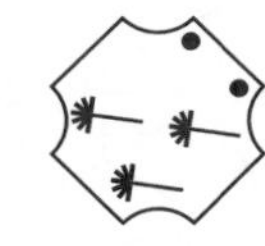

a b c d

/ 10

Section 5 — Complete the Hexagonal Grid

Work out which of the options best fits in place of the missing hexagon in the grid.

Example:

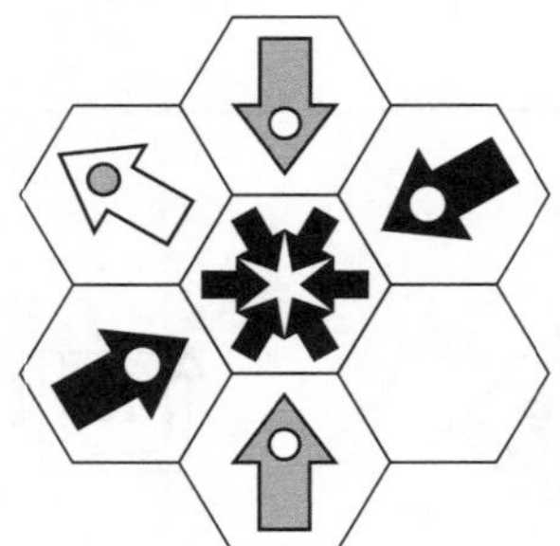

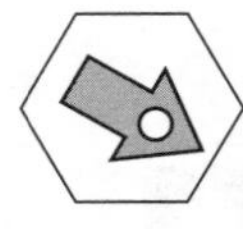

a b c d

Answer: b

1

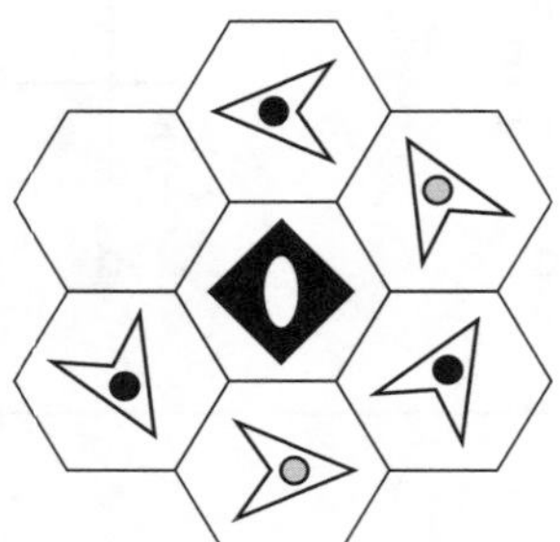

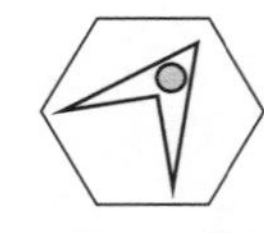

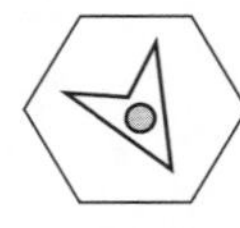

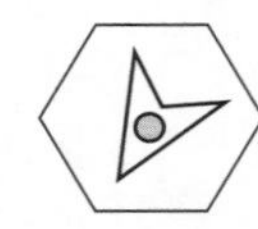

a b c d

2

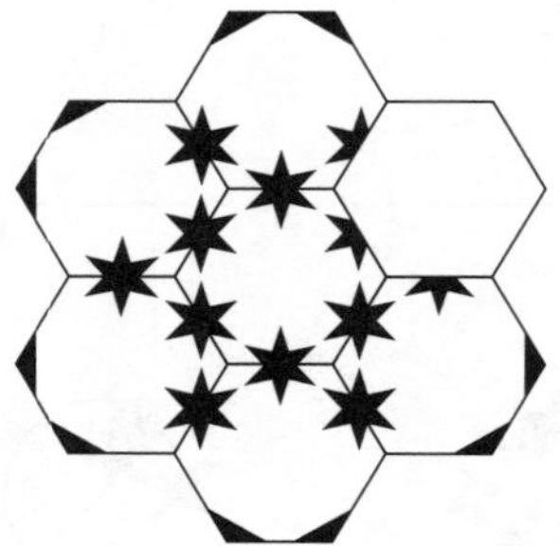

a b c d

3

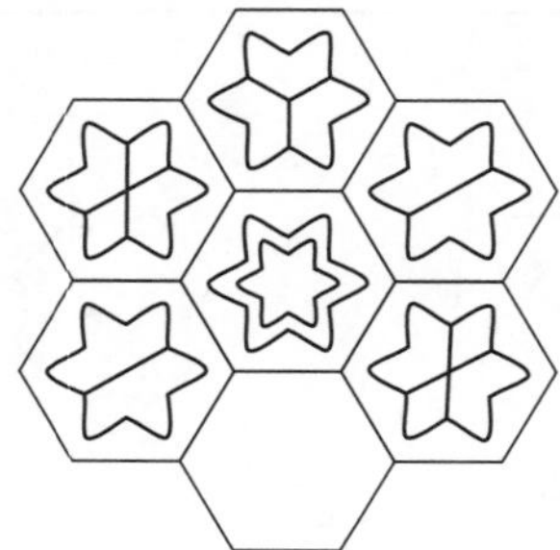

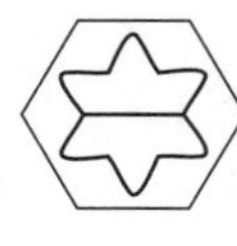

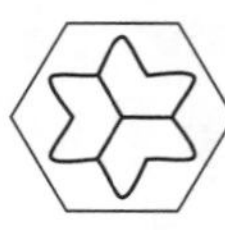

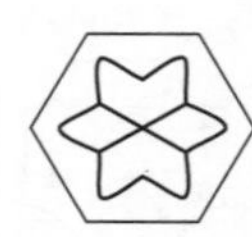

a b c d

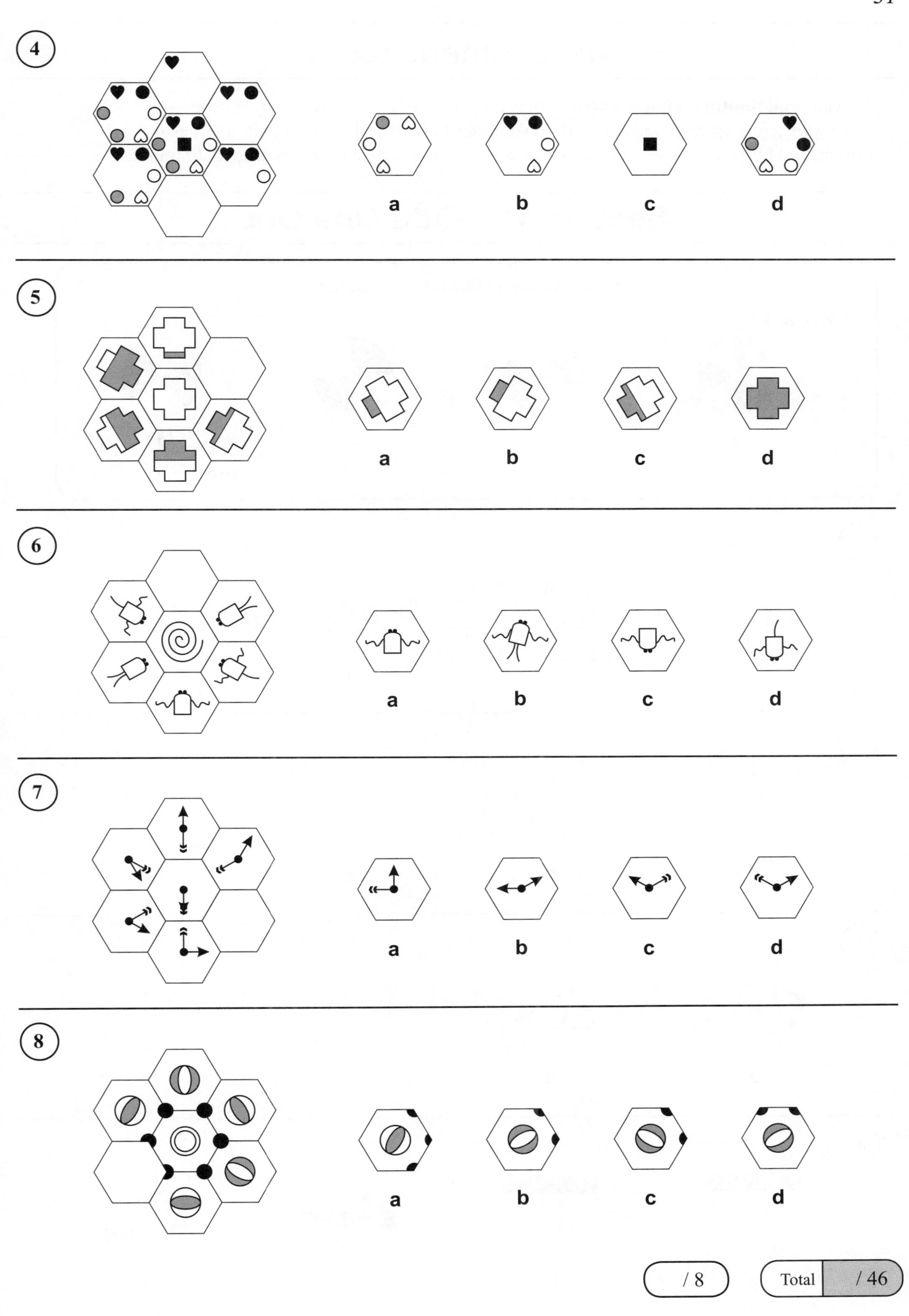

/ 8

Total / 46

END OF TEST

Assessment Test 2

You can print **multiple-choice answer sheets** for these questions from our website — go to www.cgplearning.co.uk/11+. If you'd prefer to answer them in standard write-in format, just circle the letter underneath the answer. The test should take around 20 minutes.

Section 1 — Odd One Out

Find the figure in each row that is most unlike the other figures.

Example:

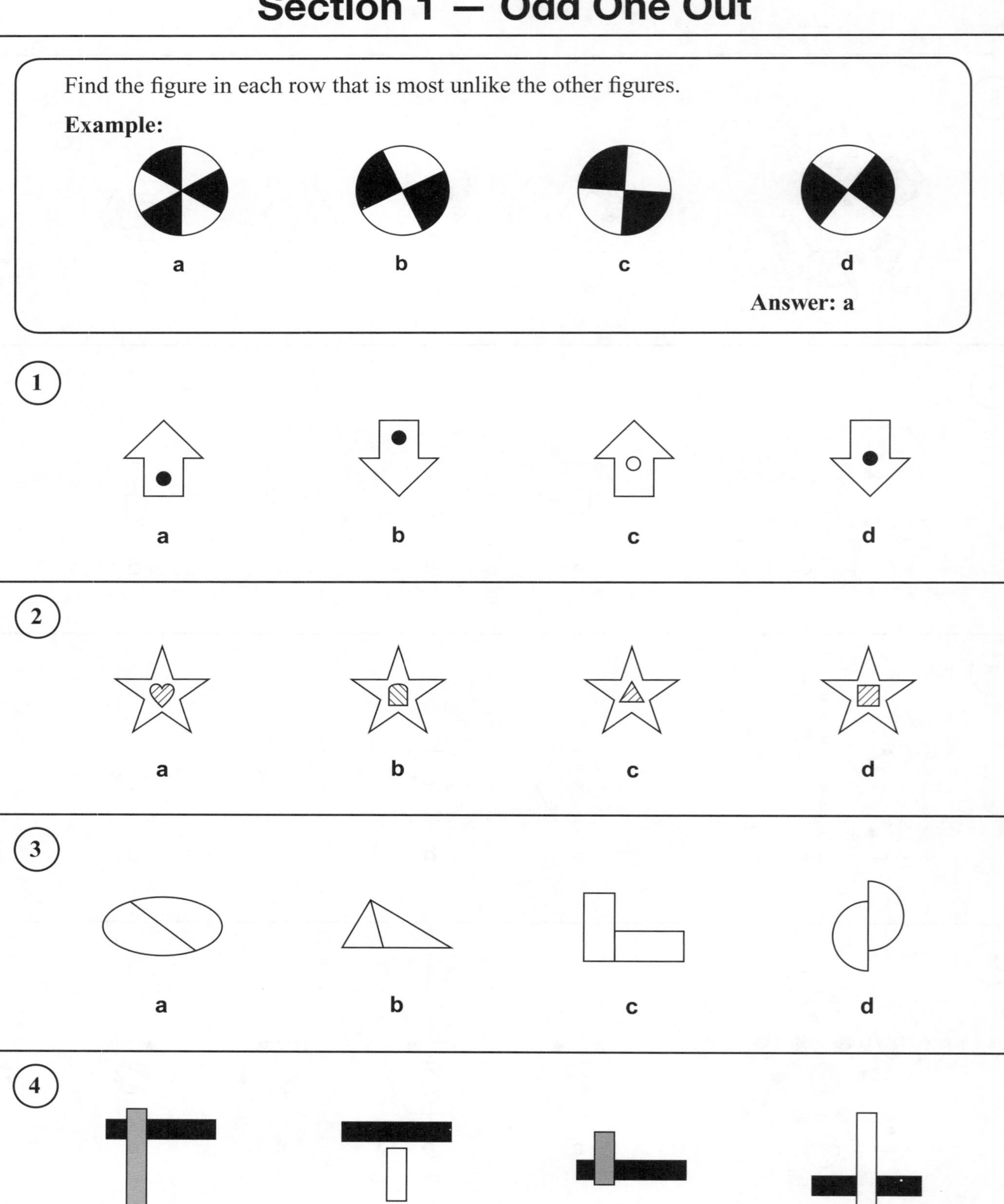

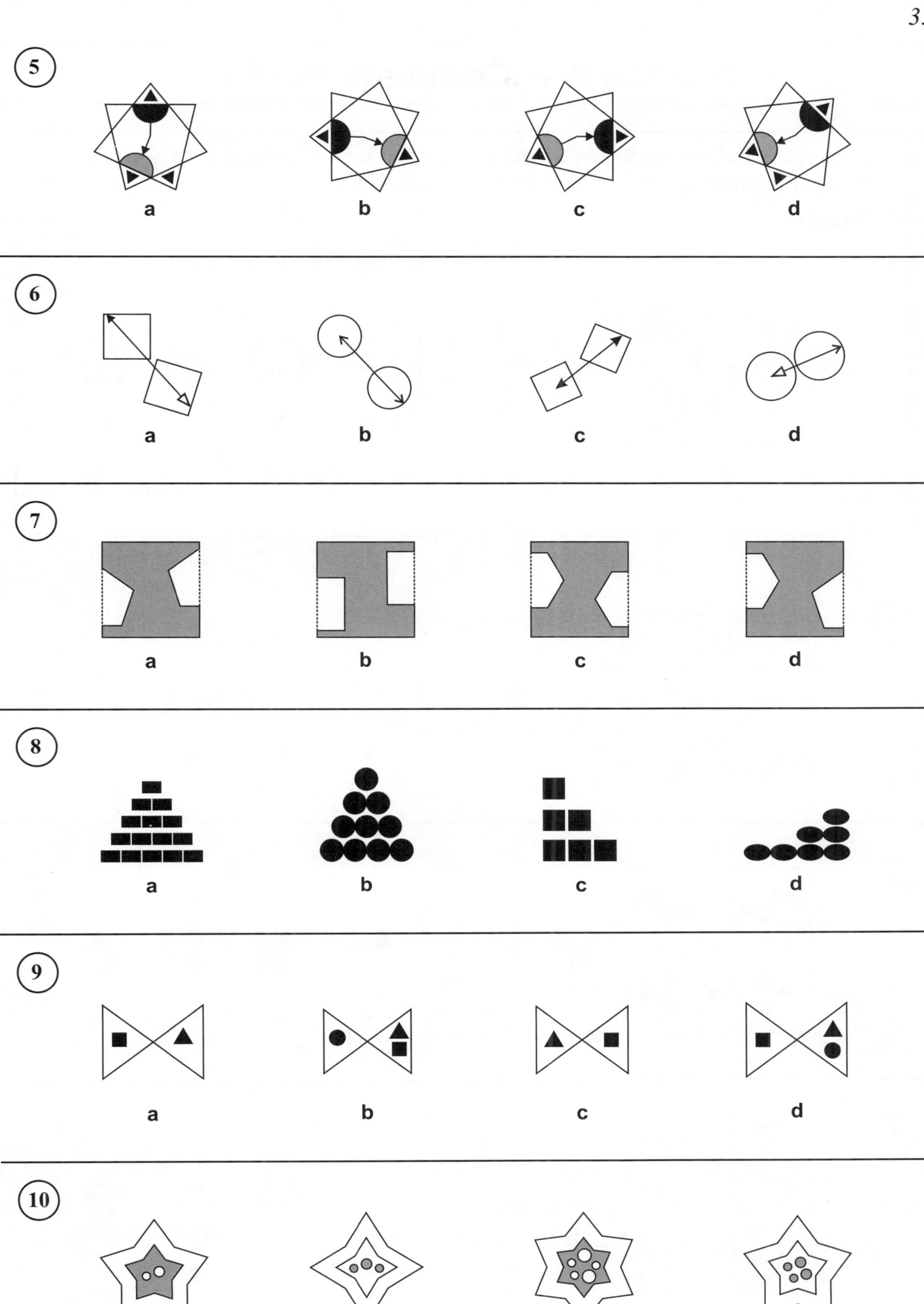

/ 10

Section 2 — Complete the Pair

Look at how the first two figures are changed, and then work out which option would look like the third figure if you changed it in the same way.

Example:

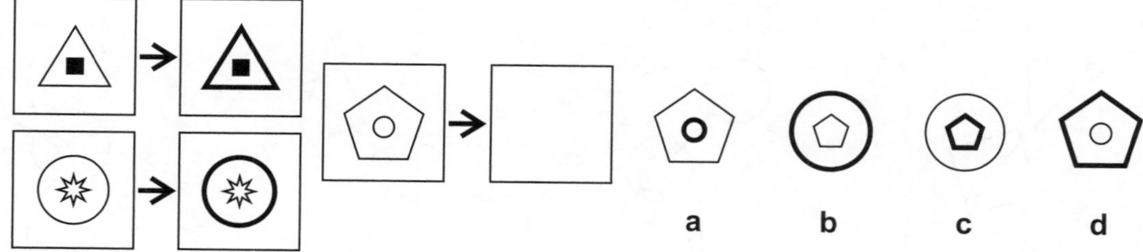

Answer: d

(1)

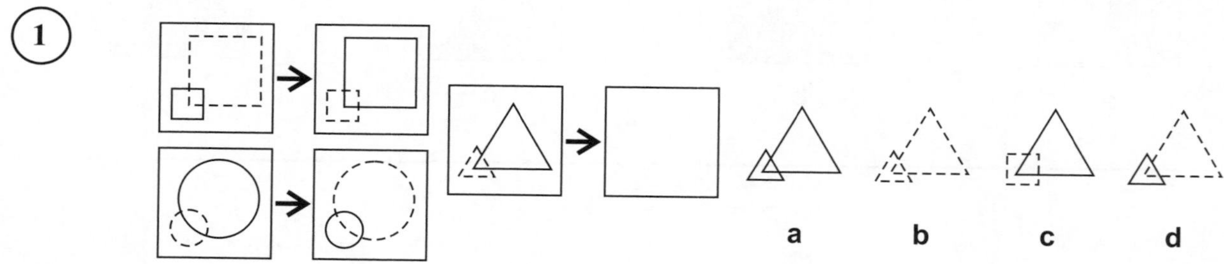

(2)

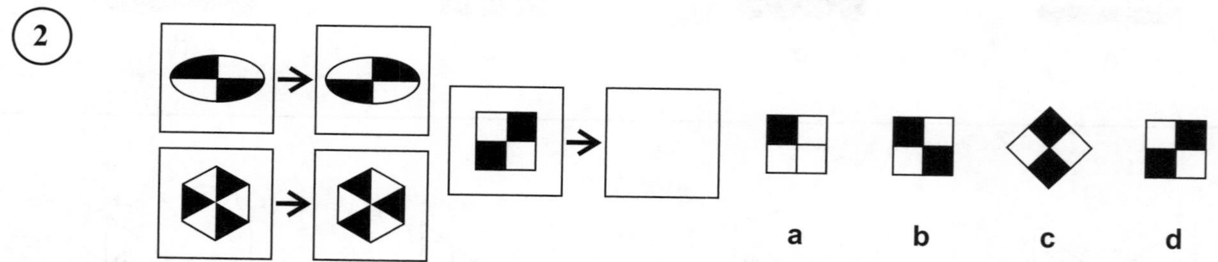

(3)

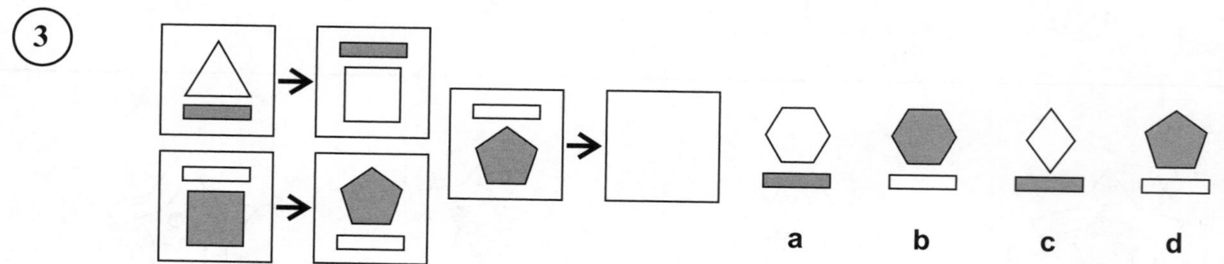

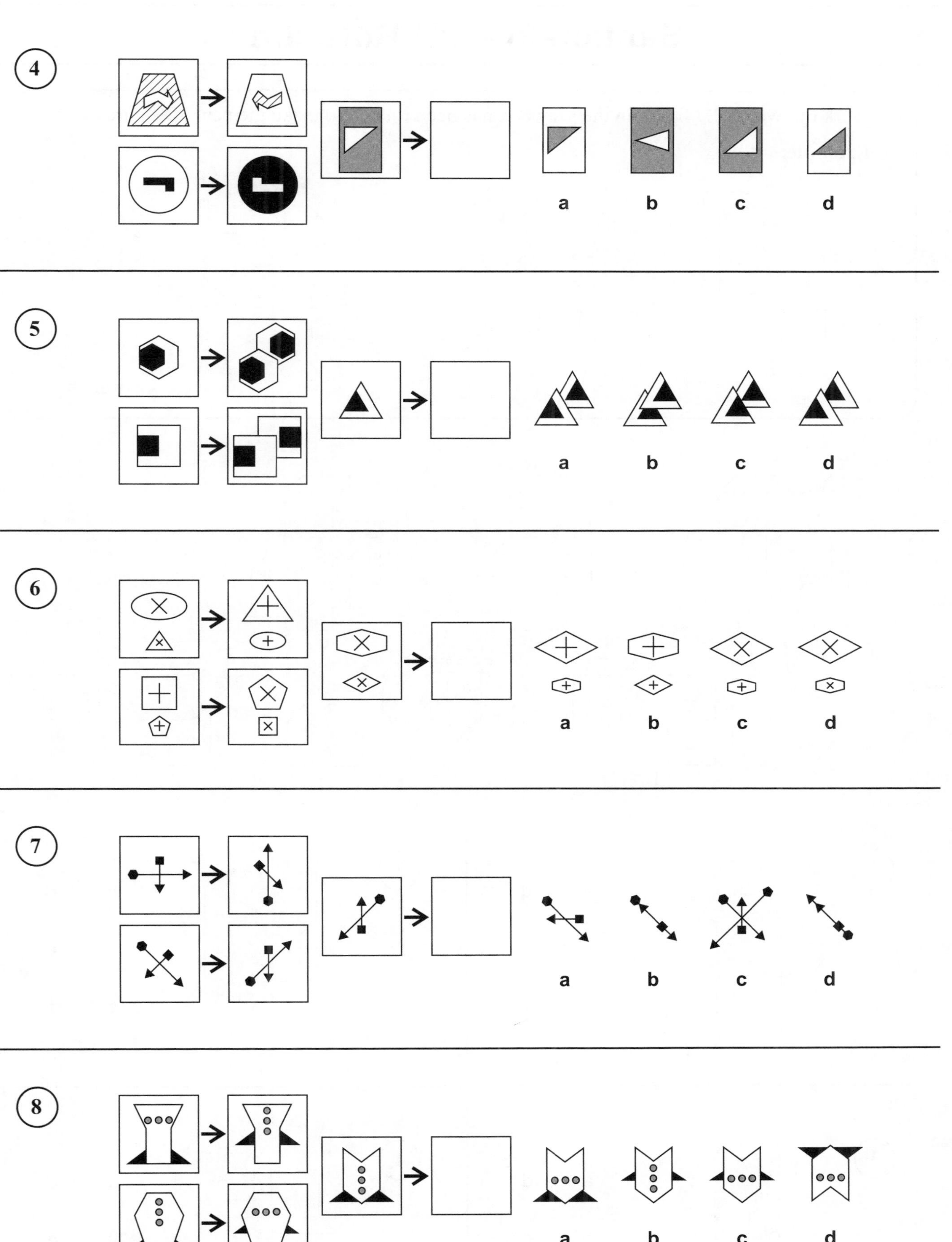

/ 8

Section 3 — 3D Rotation

Work out which 3D figure in the grey box has been rotated to make the new 3D figure.

Example:

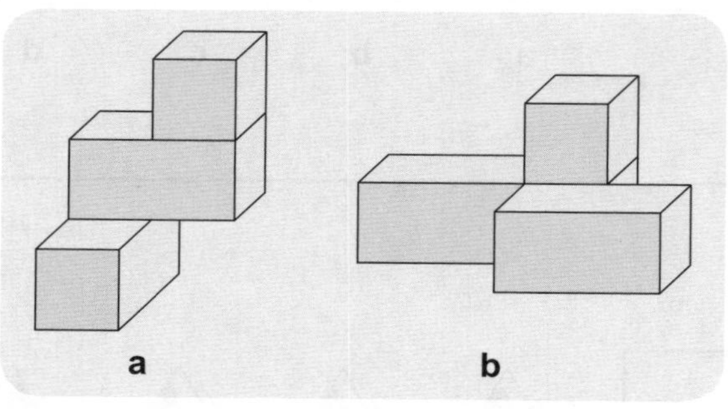

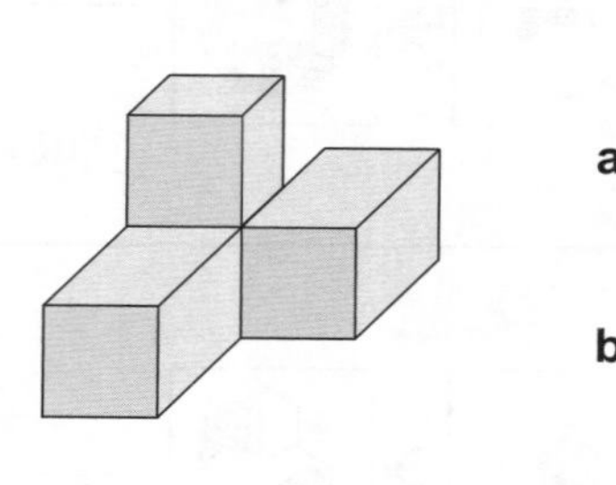

a

b

Answer: b

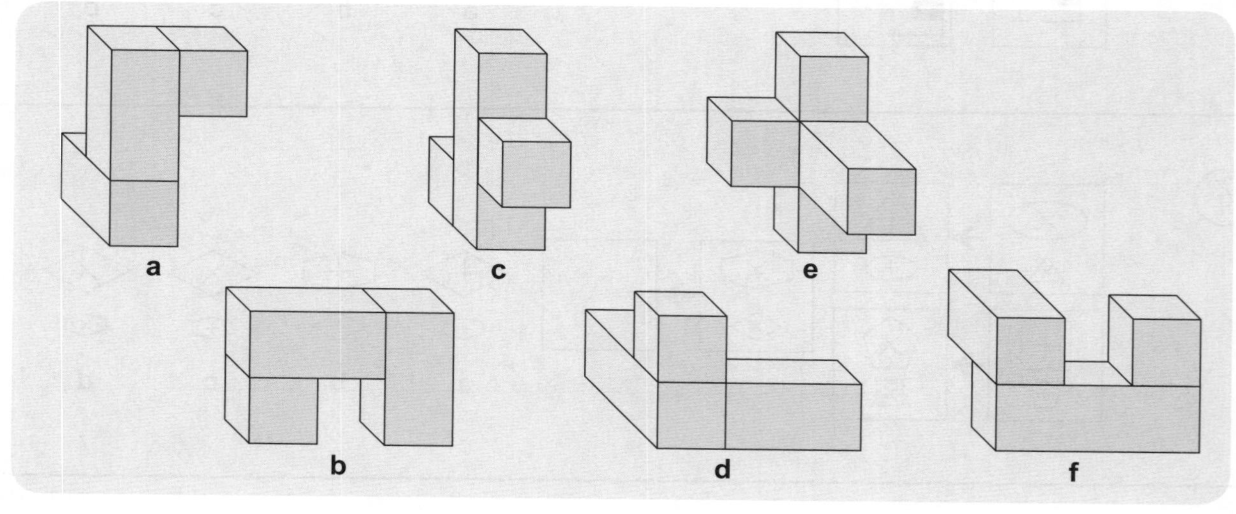

1

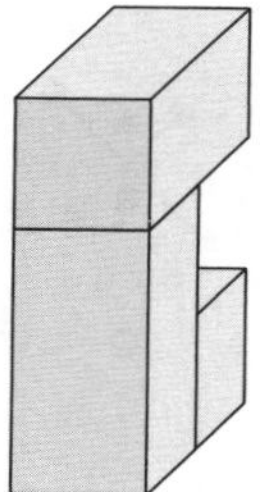

a d

b e

c f

2

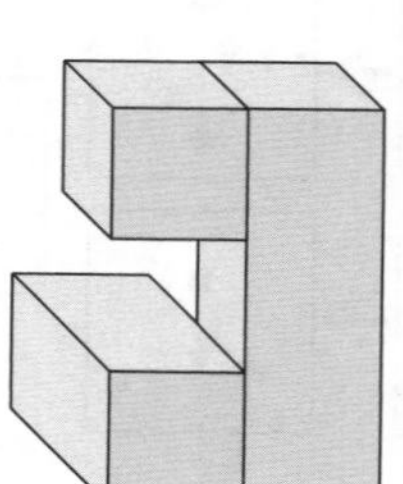

a d

b e

c f

3

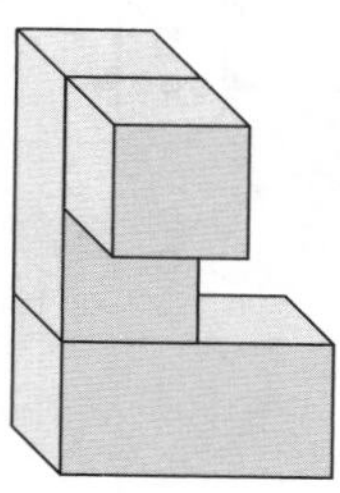

a d

b e

c f

4

a d

b e

c f

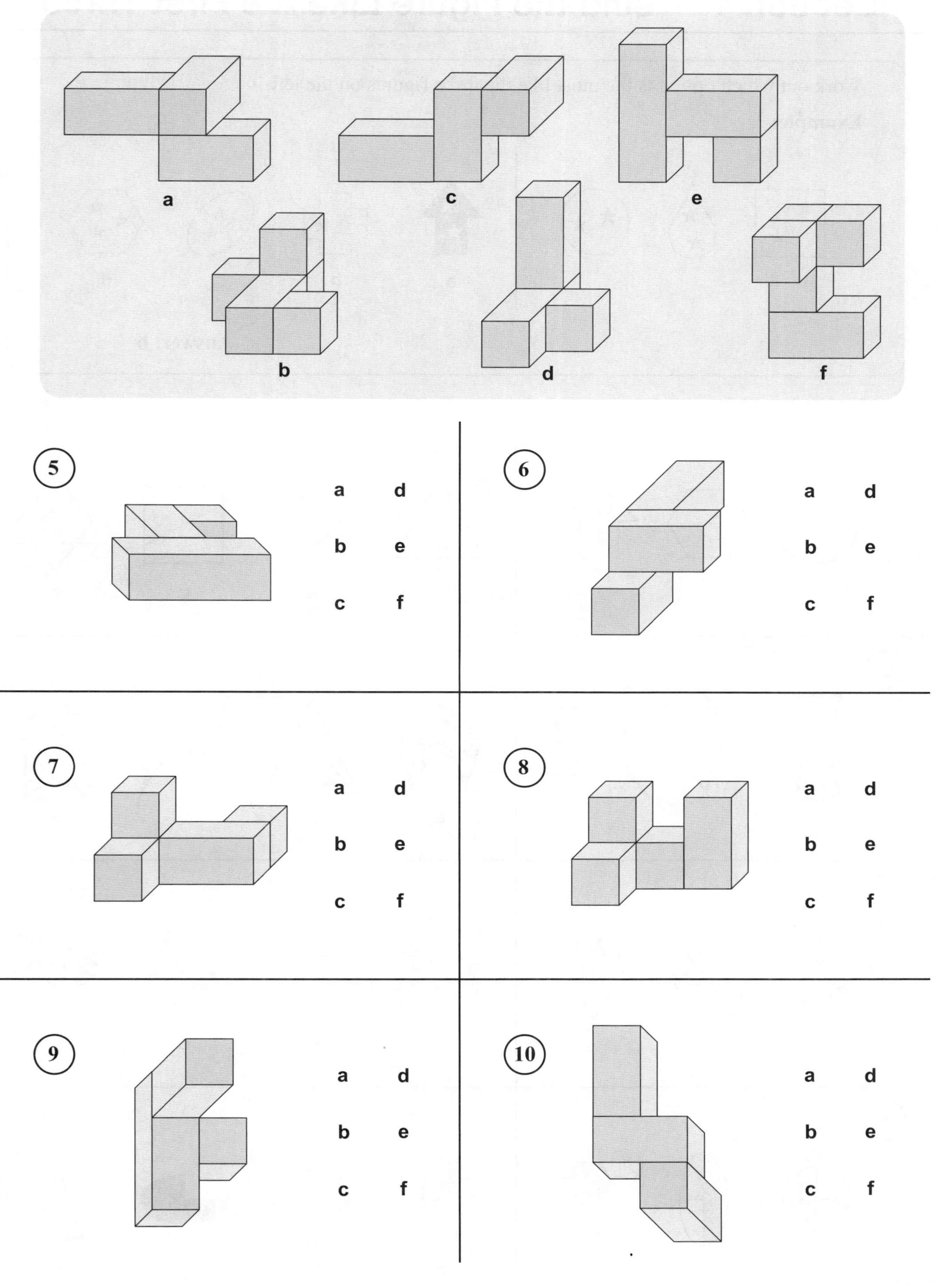

/ 10

Section 4 — Find the Figure Like the First Three

Work out which option is the most like the three figures on the left.

Example:

a b c d

Answer: b

1

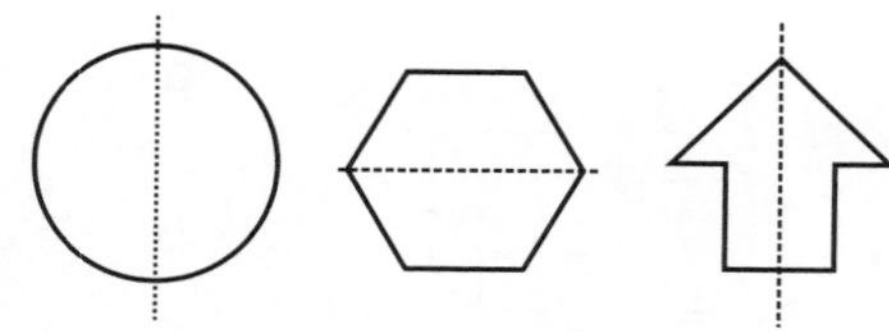

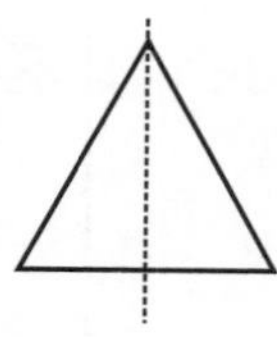 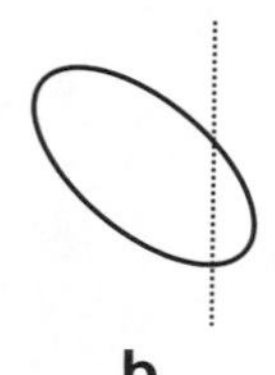 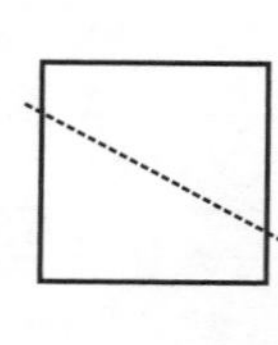 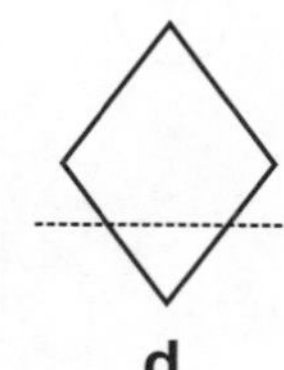

a b c d

2

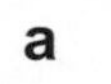

a b c d

3

a b c d

4

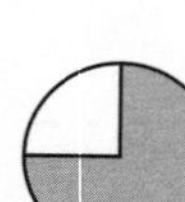 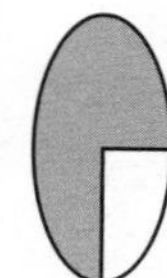 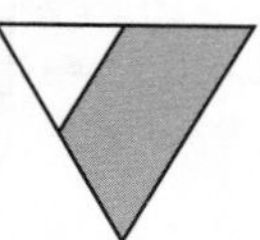

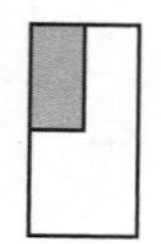 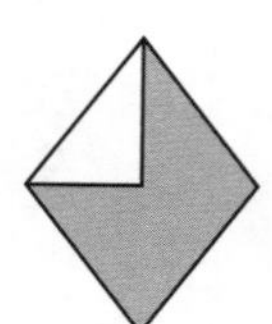 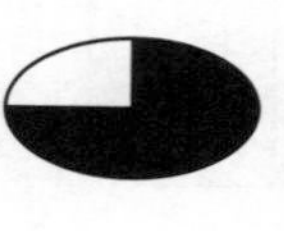 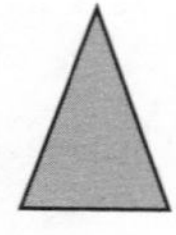

a b c d

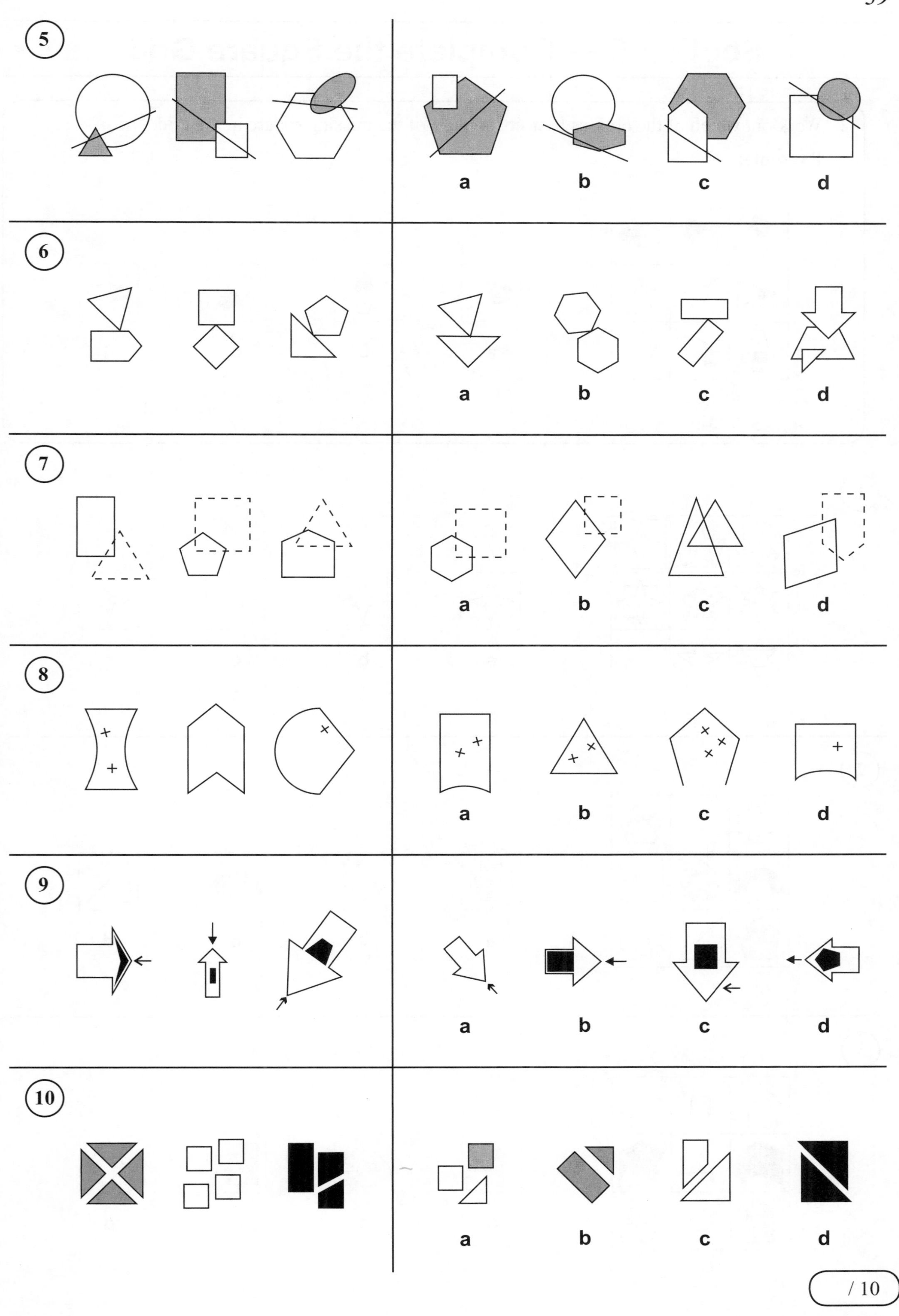

/ 10

Section 5 — Complete the Square Grid

Work out which of the options best fits in place of the missing square in the grid.

Example:

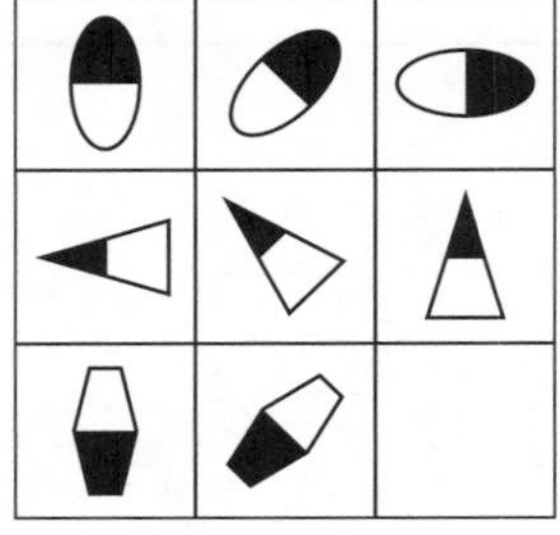

a b c d

Answer: d

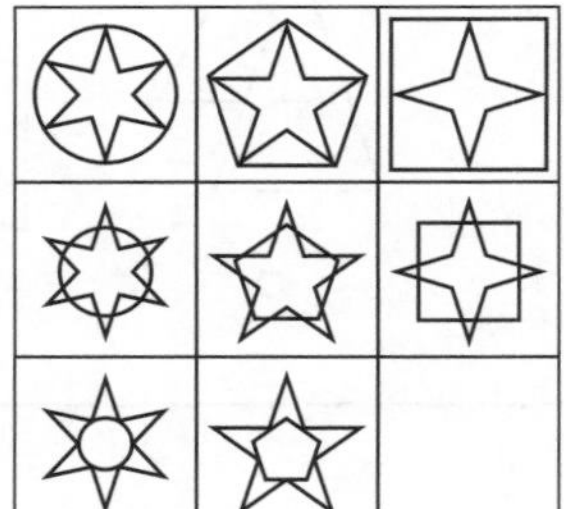

a b c d

(2)

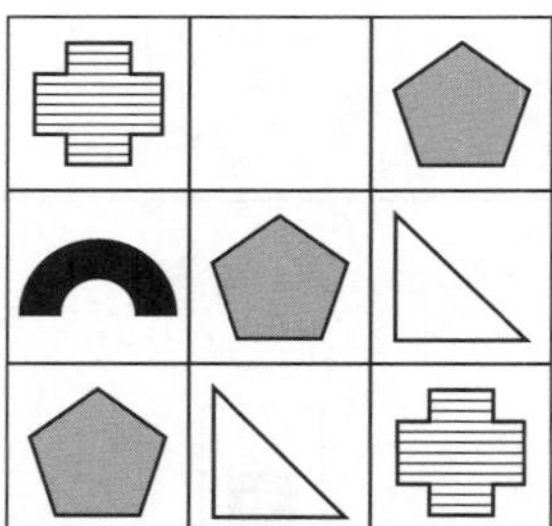

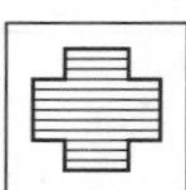 

a b c d

(3)

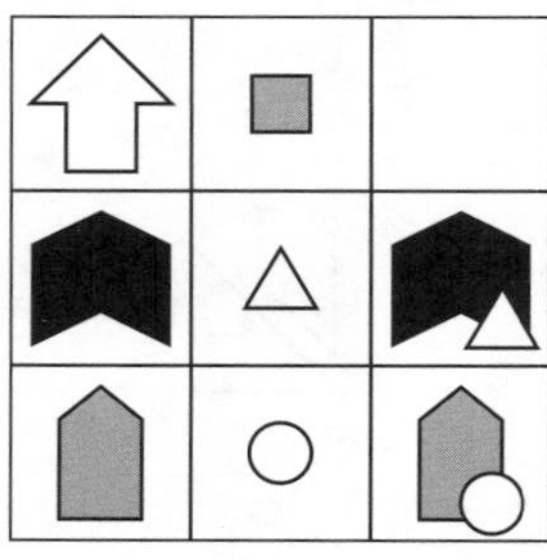

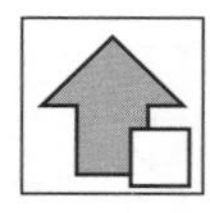 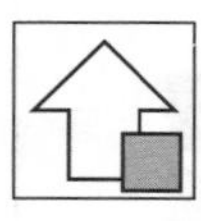 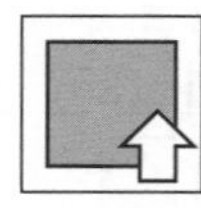 

a b c d

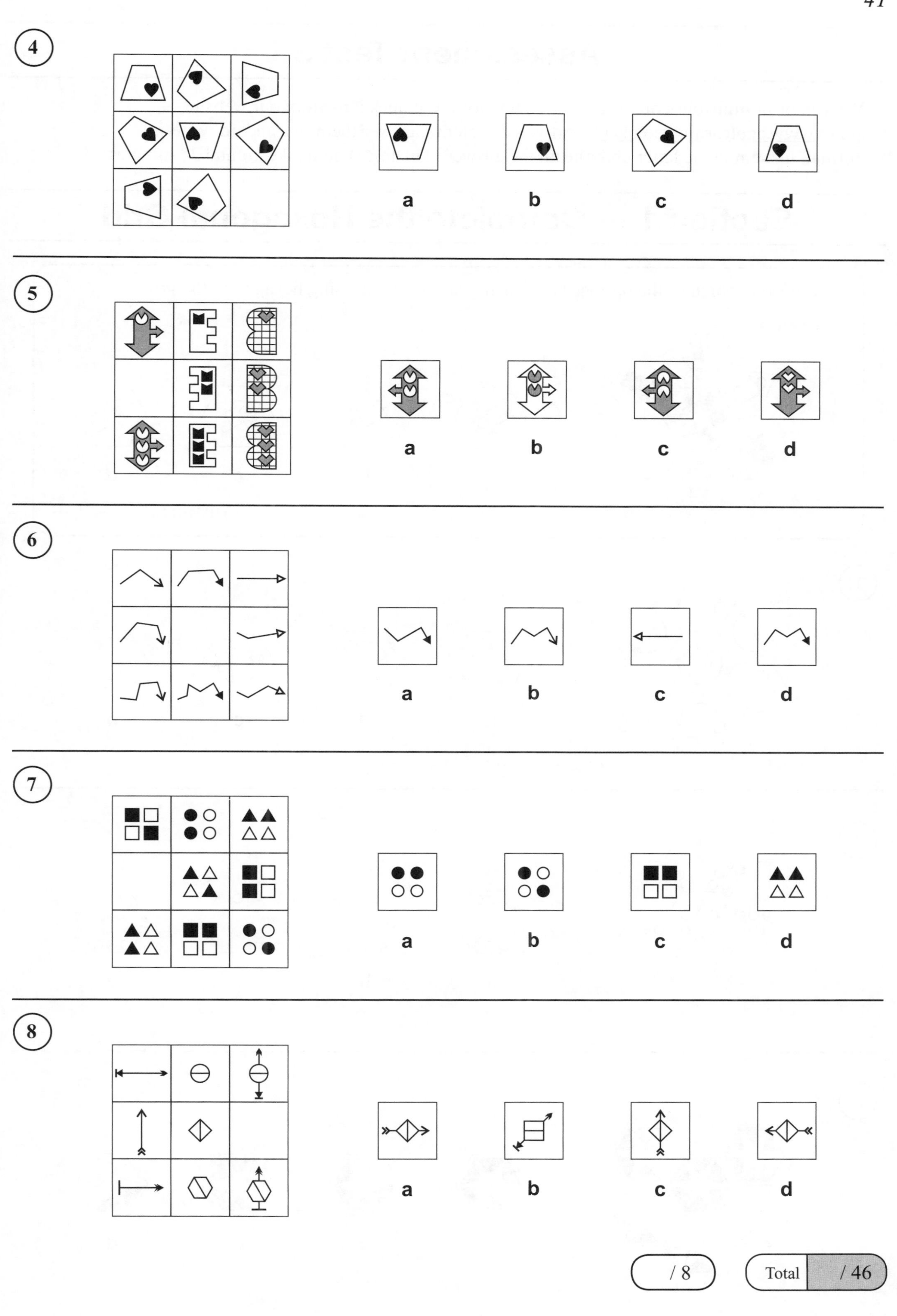

/ 8

Total / 46

END OF TEST

Assessment Test 3

You can print **multiple-choice answer sheets** for these questions from our website — go to www.cgplearning.co.uk/11+. If you'd prefer to answer them in standard write-in format, just circle the letter underneath the answer. The test should take around 20 minutes.

Section 1 — Complete the Hexagonal Grid

Work out which of the options best fits in place of the missing hexagon in the grid.

Example:

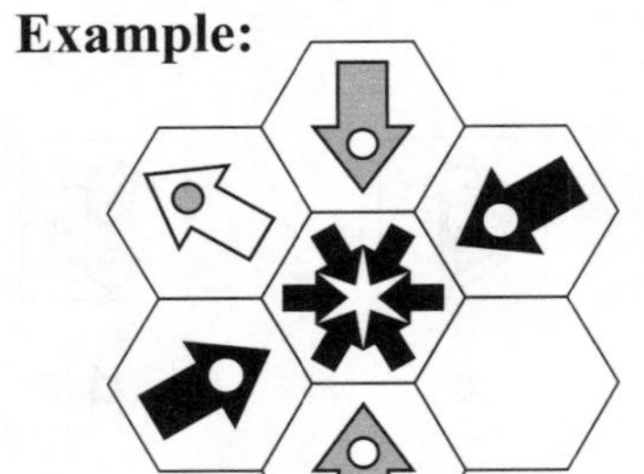

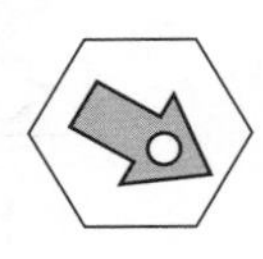  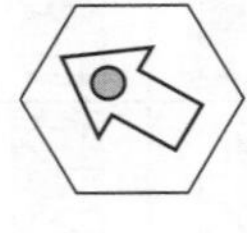 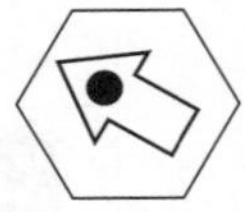

a b c d

Answer: b

1

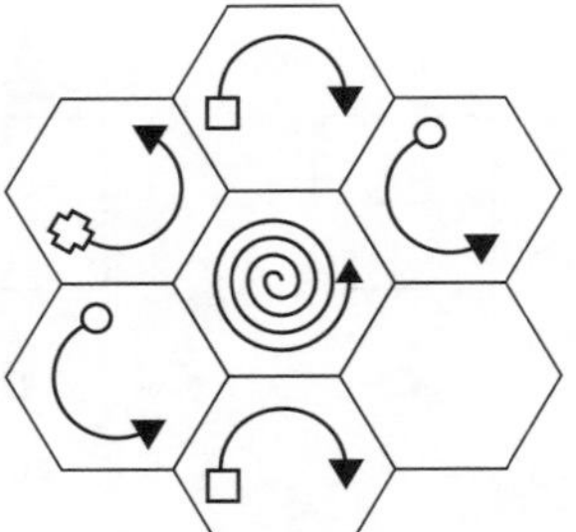

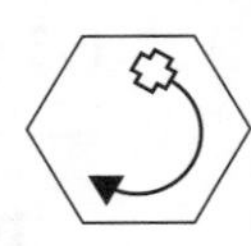

a b c d

2

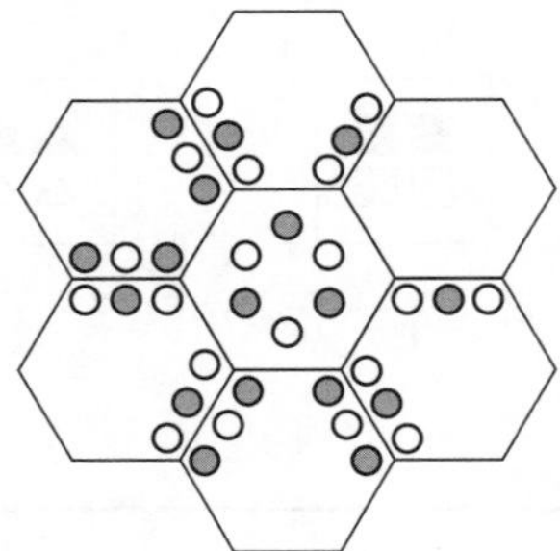

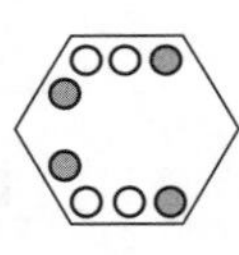 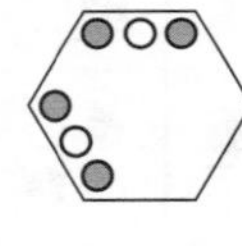 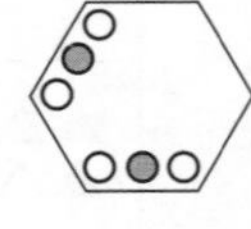

a b c d

3

a b c d

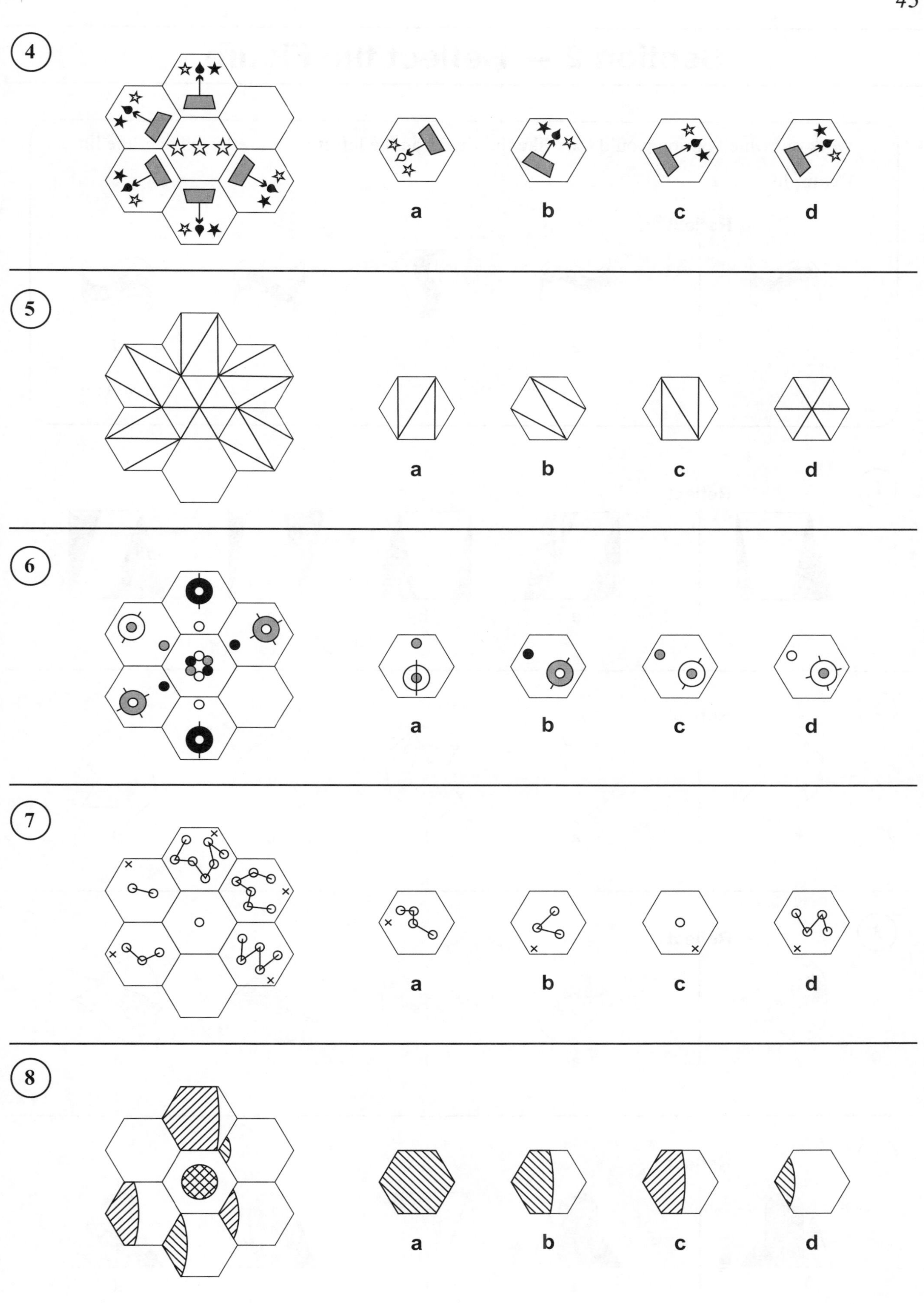

/ 8

Section 2 — Reflect the Figure

Work out which option would look like the figure on the left if it was reflected over the line.

Example:

Reflect

a

b

c

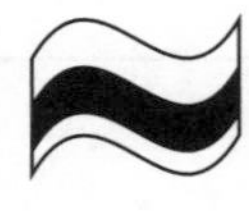
d

Answer: a

1

Reflect

a

b

c

d

2

Reflect

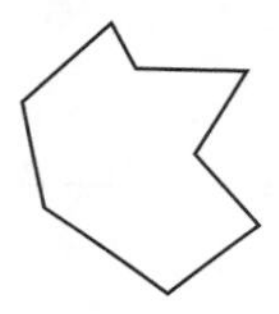

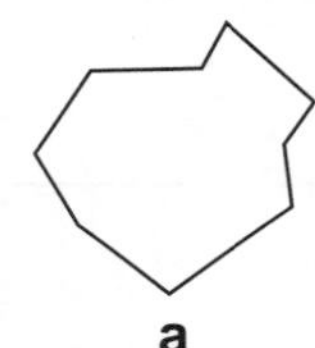
a

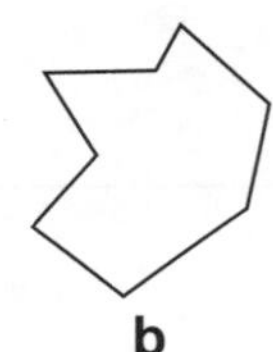
b

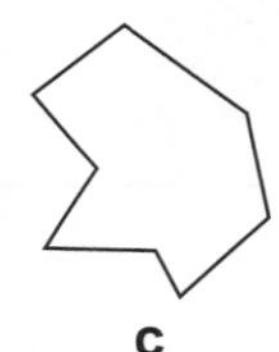
c

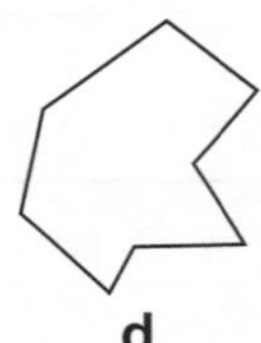
d

3

Reflect

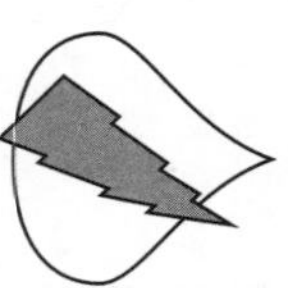

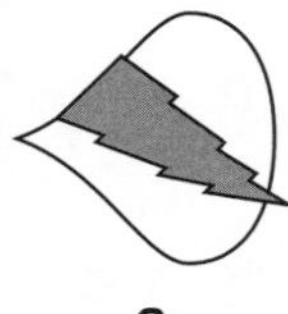
a

b

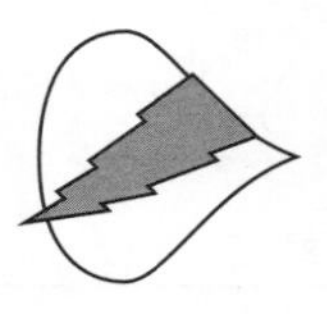
c

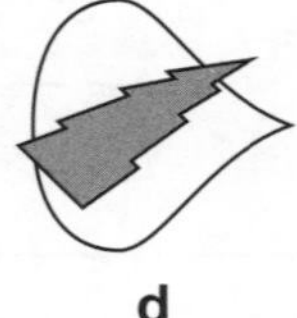
d

4

Reflect

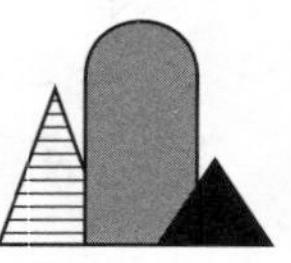

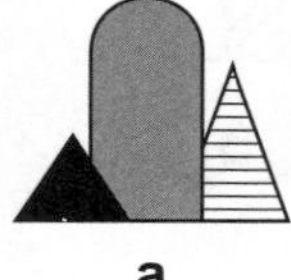
a

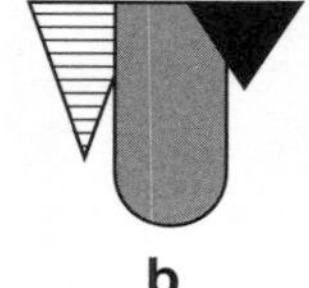
b

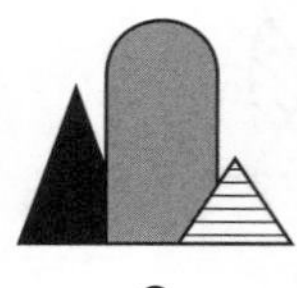
c

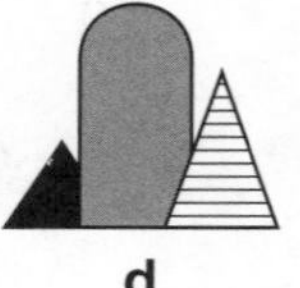
d

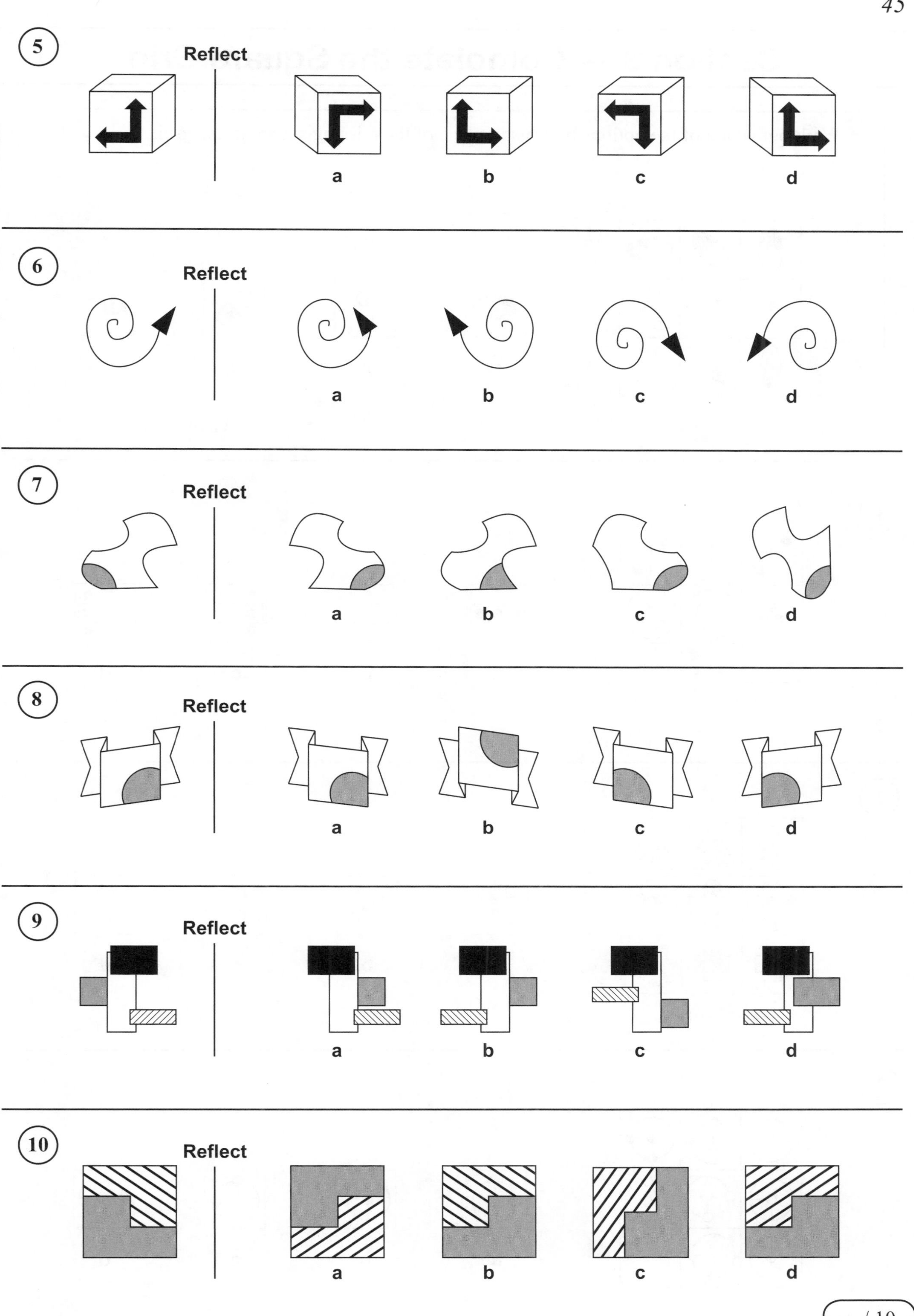
5
Reflect
a
b
c
d
6
Reflect
a
b
c
d
7
Reflect
a
b
c
d
8
Reflect
a
b
c
d
9
Reflect
a
b
c
d
10
Reflect
a
b
c
d

/ 10

Section 3 — Complete the Square Grid

Work out which of the options best fits in place of the missing square in the grid.

Example:

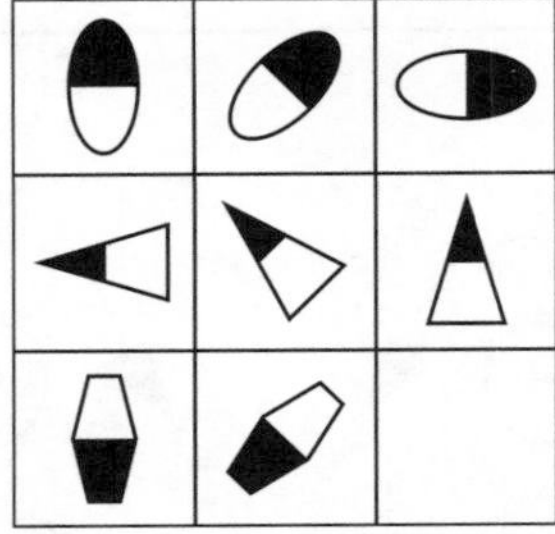

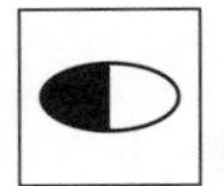
a

b

c

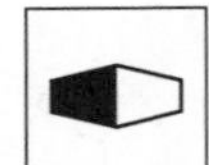
d

Answer: d

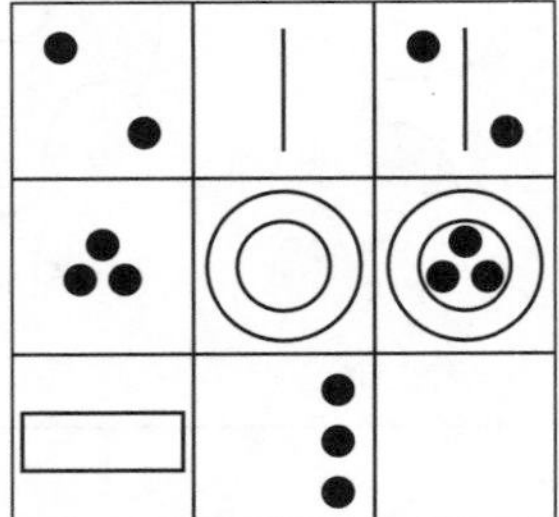

a

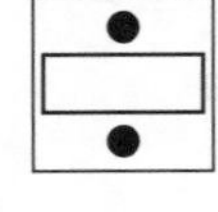
b

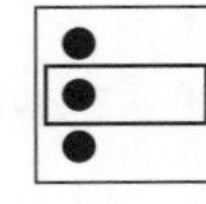
c

d

2

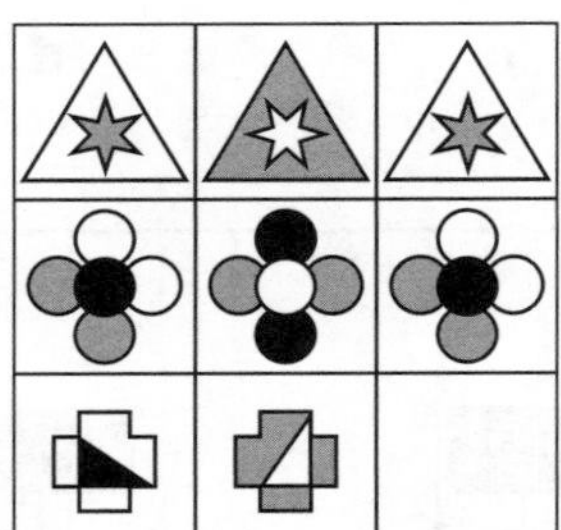

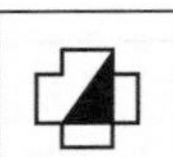
a

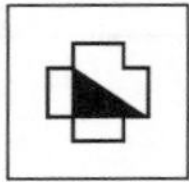
b

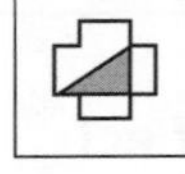
c

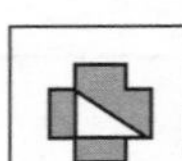
d

3

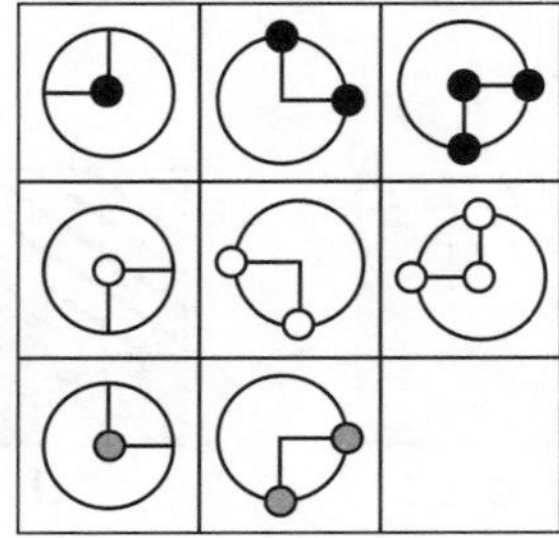

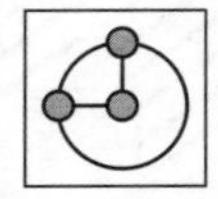
a

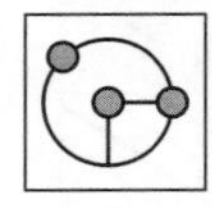
b

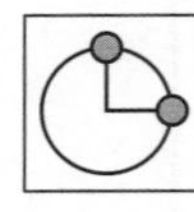
c

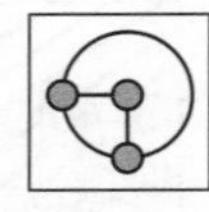
d

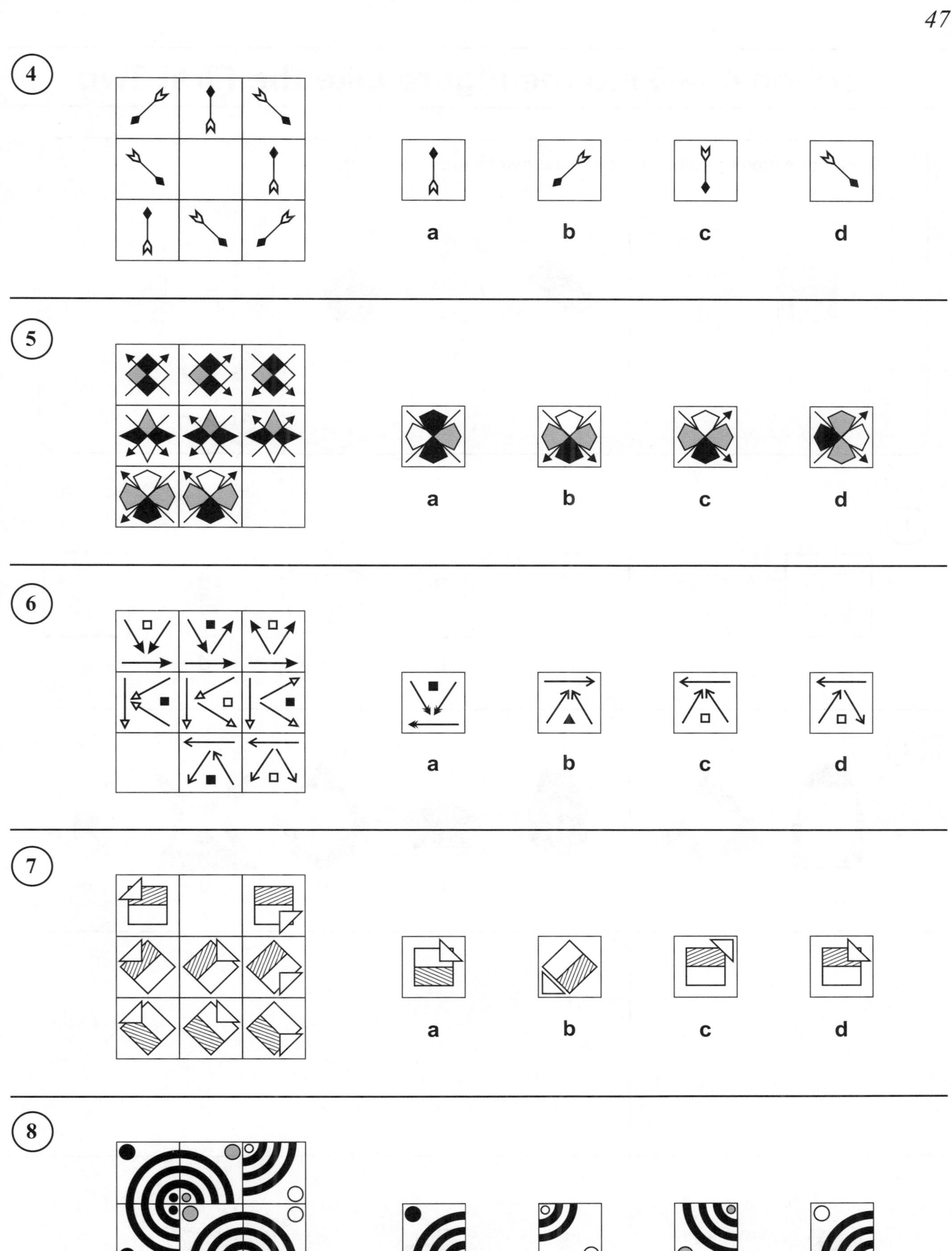

/ 8

Section 4 — Find the Figure Like the First Two

Work out which option is most like the two figures on the left.

Example:

a b c d e

Answer: a

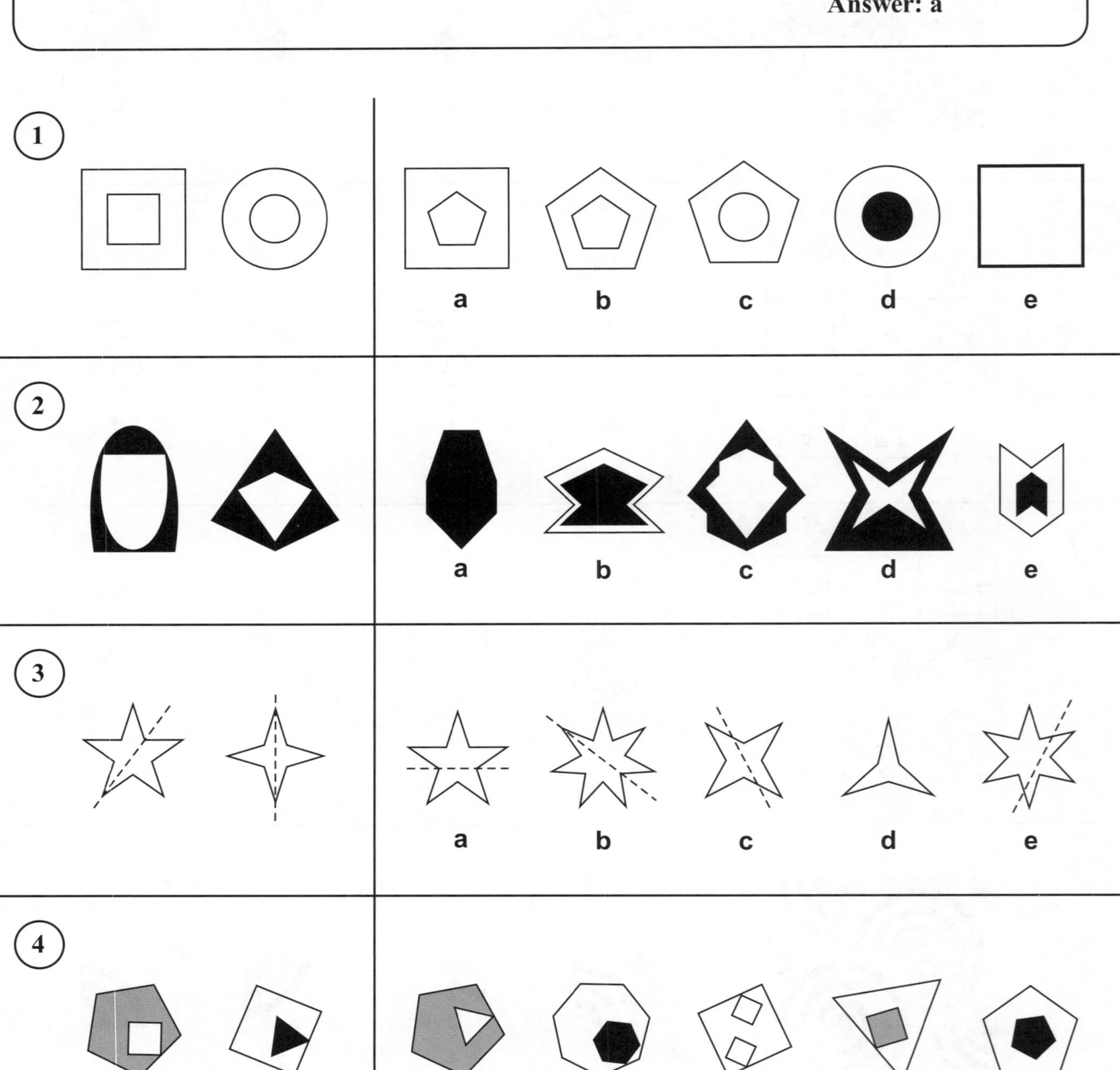

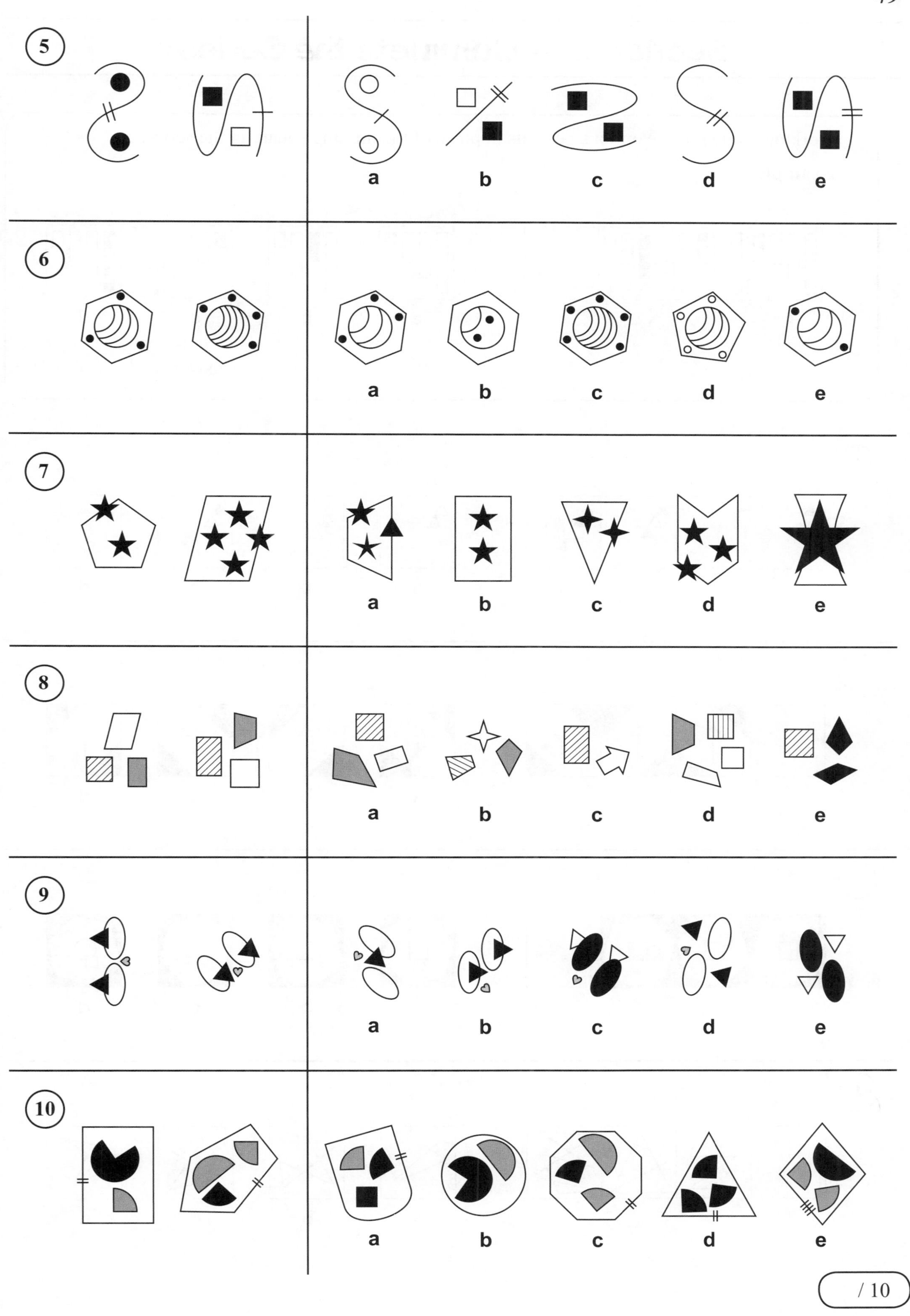

/ 10

Section 5 — Complete the Series

Work out which of the options best fits in place of the missing square in the series.

Example:

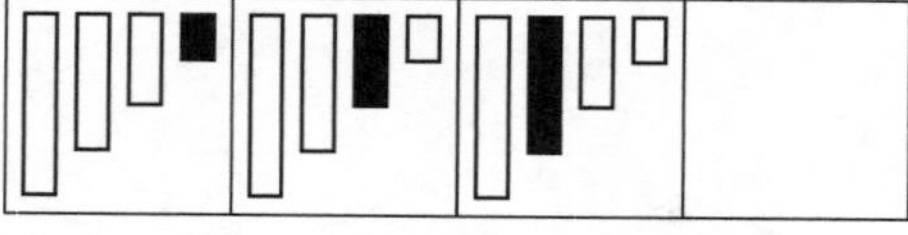

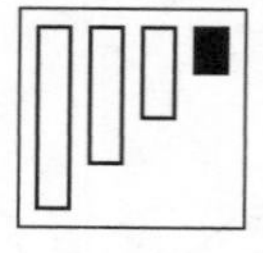
a

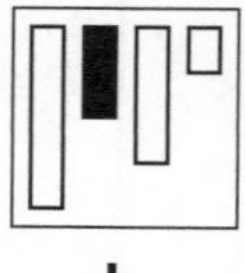
b

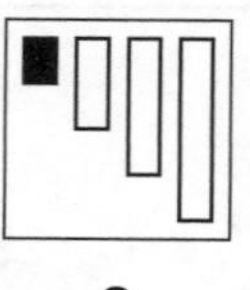
c

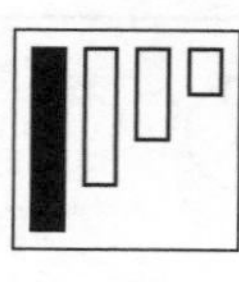
d

Answer: d

1

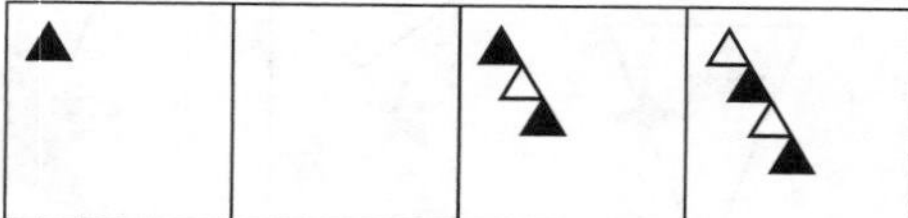

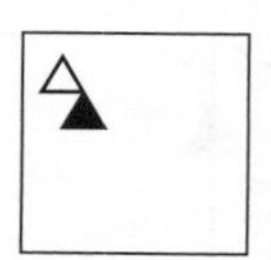
a

b

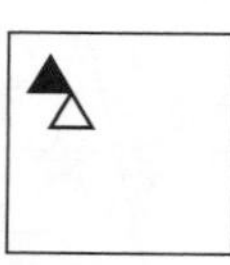
c

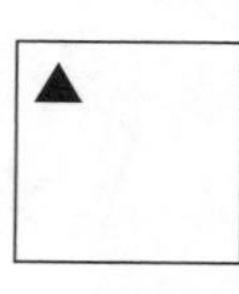
d

2

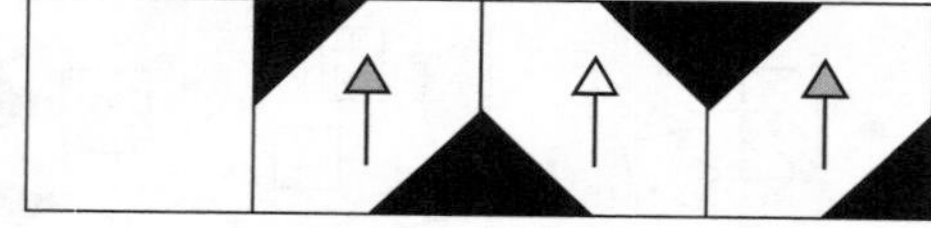

a

b

c

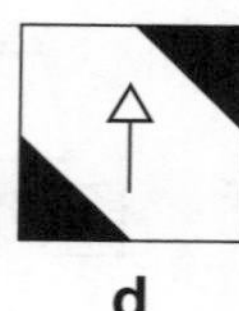
d

3

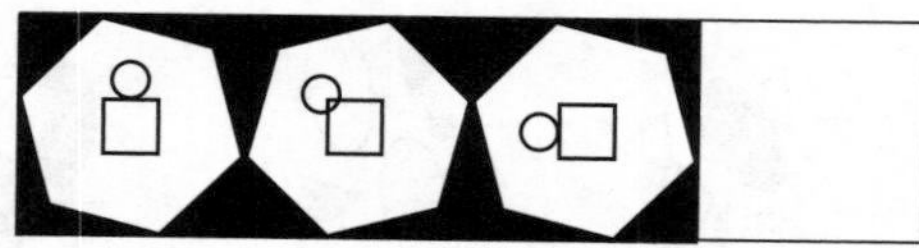

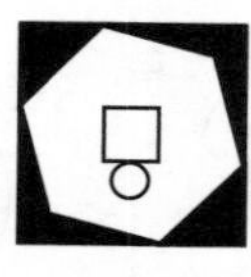
a

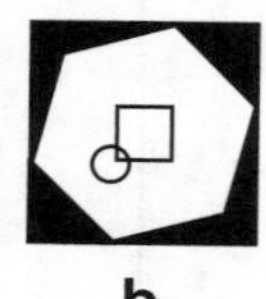
b

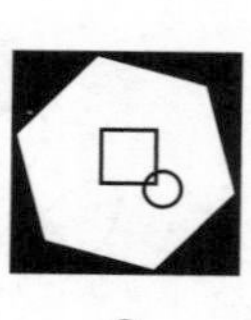
c

d

4

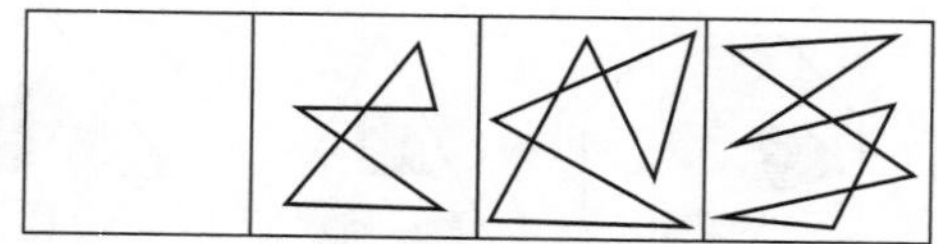

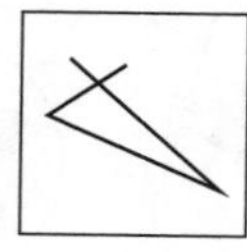
a

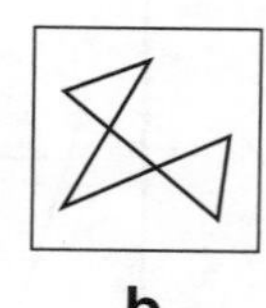
b

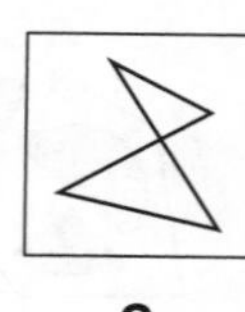
c

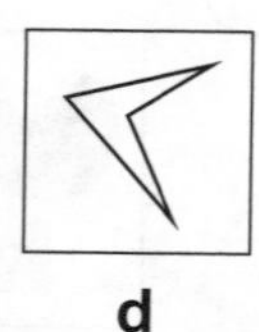
d

5

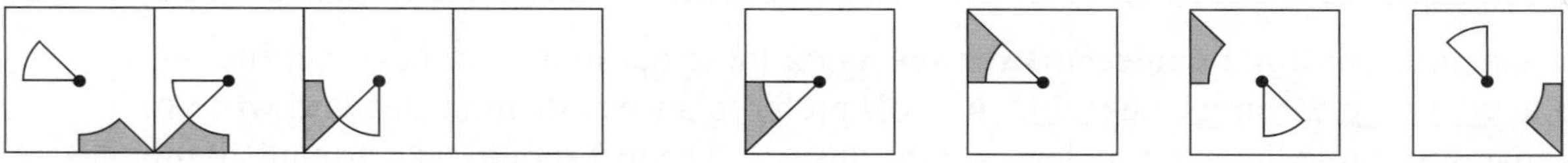

a b c d

6

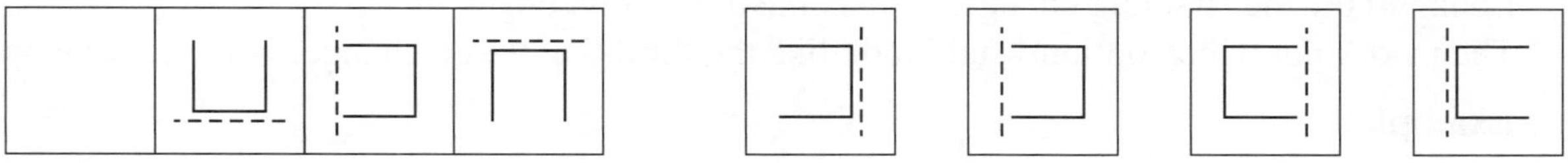

a b c d

7

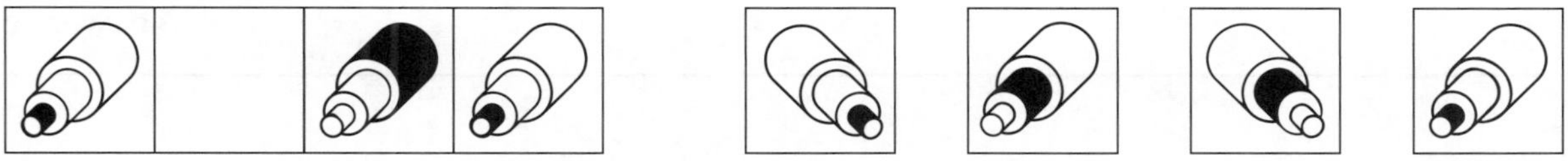

a b c d

8

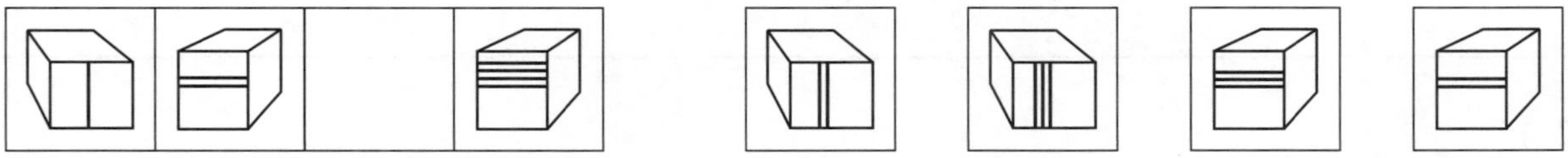

a b c d

9

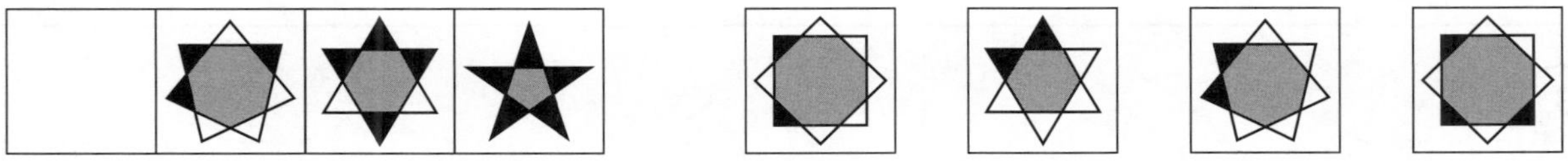

a b c d

10

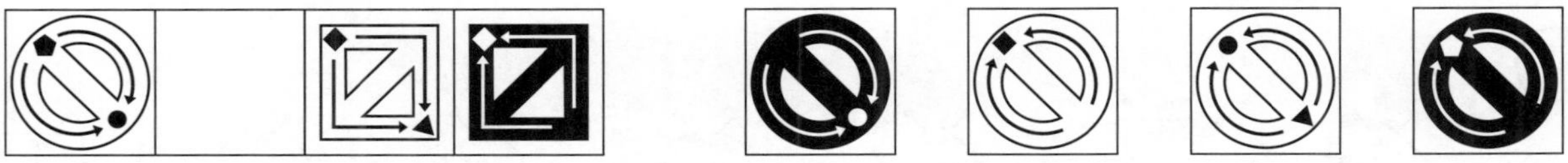

a b c d

/ 10 Total / 46

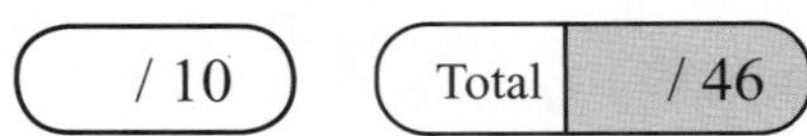

Assessment Test 4

You can print **multiple-choice answer sheets** for these questions from our website — go to www.cgplearning.co.uk/11+. If you'd prefer to answer them in standard write-in format, just circle the letter underneath the answer. The test should take around 20 minutes.

Section 1 — Changing Bugs

Look at how the first bug changes to become the second bug.
Then work out which option would look like the third bug if you changed it in the same way.

Example:

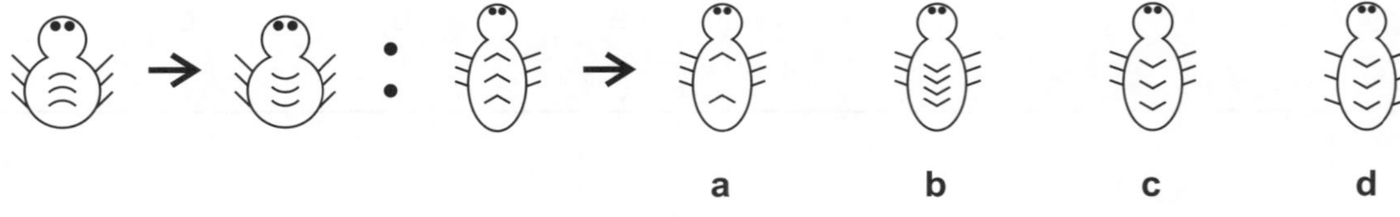

Answer: c

1

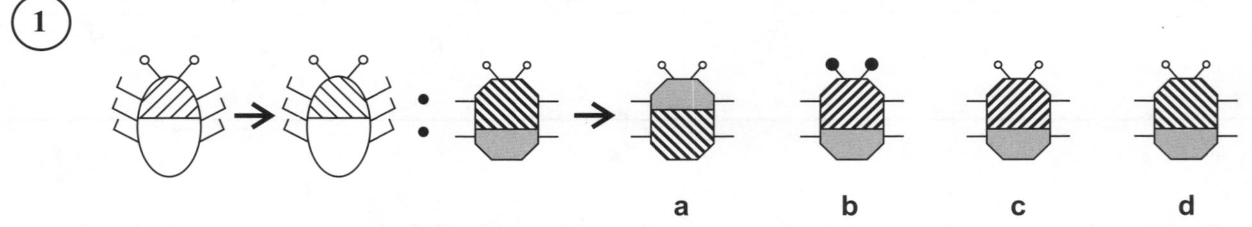

2

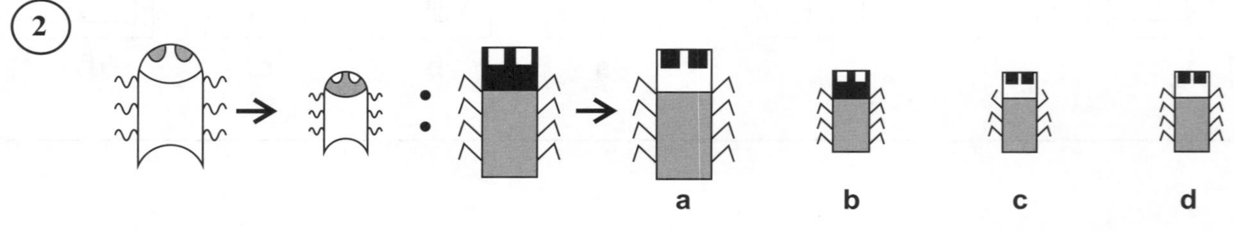

3

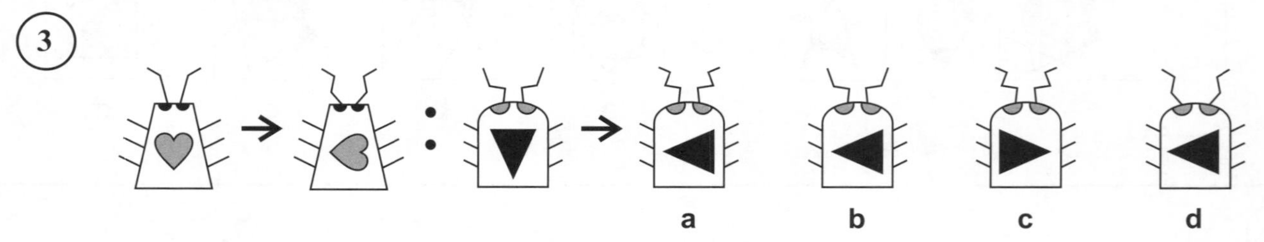

4

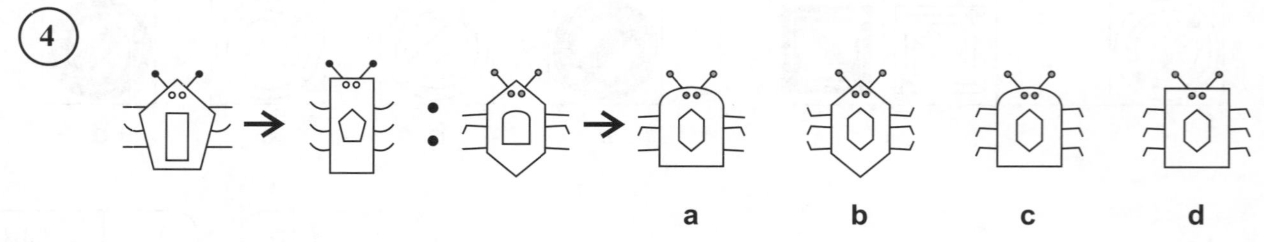

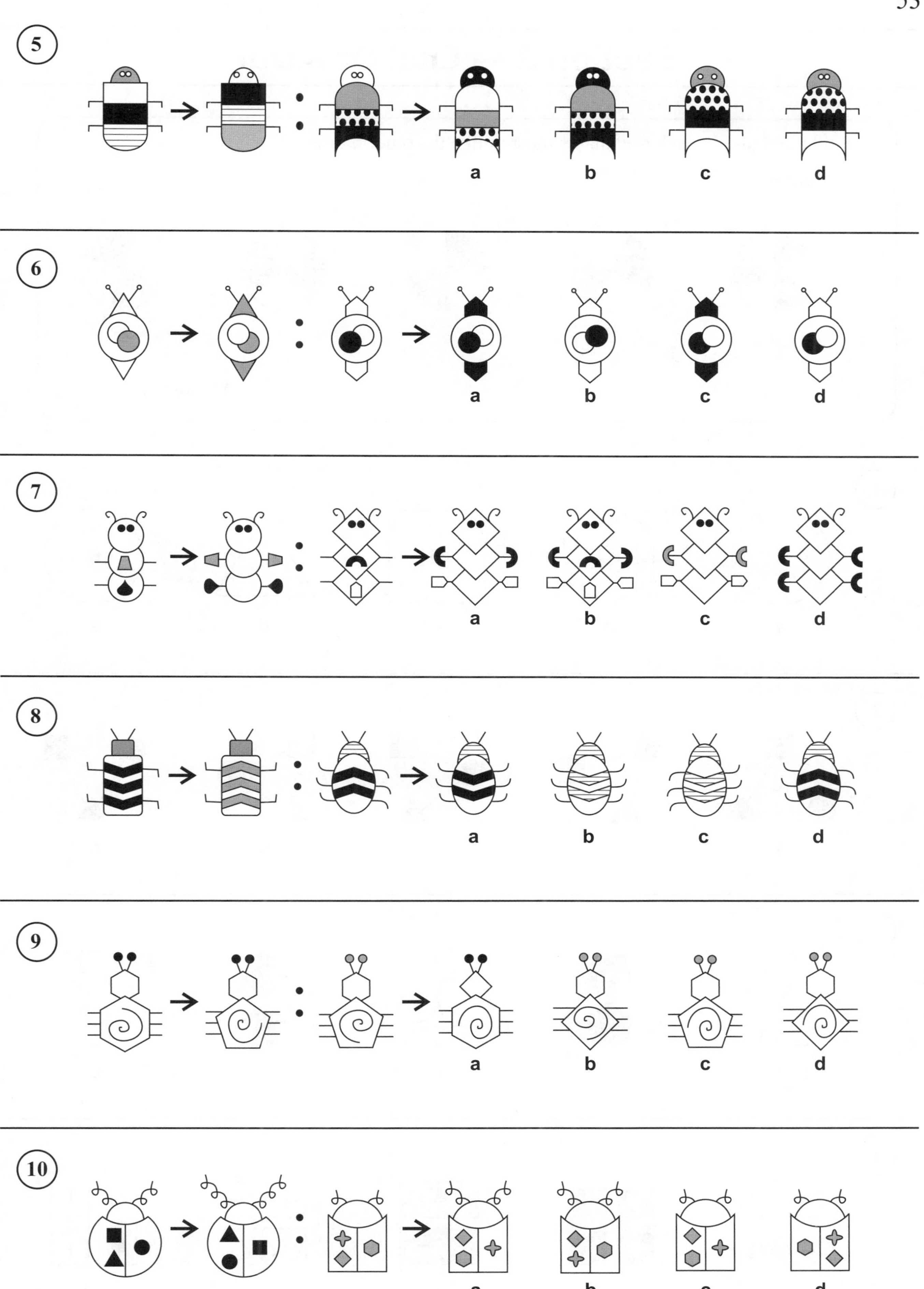

/ 10

Section 2 — Odd One Out

Find the figure in each row that is most unlike the other figures.

Example:

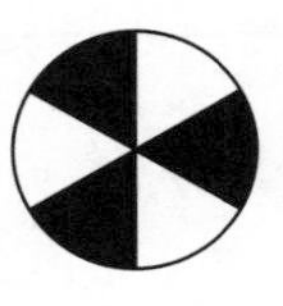

a

b

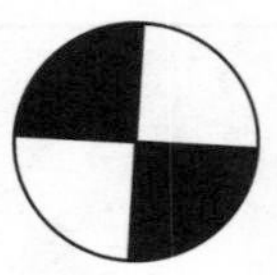

c

d

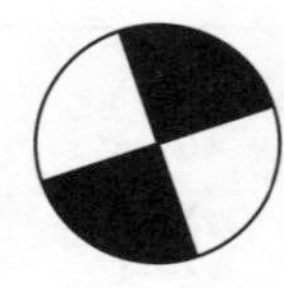

e

Answer: a

1

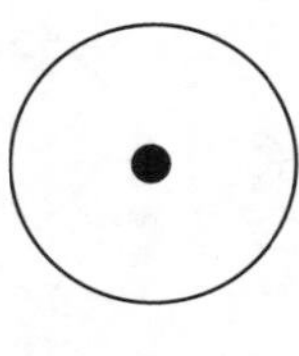

a

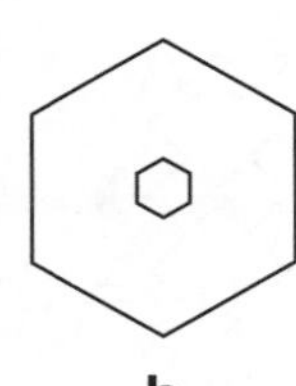

b

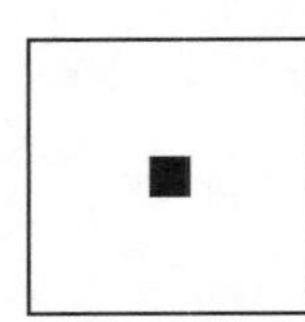

c

d

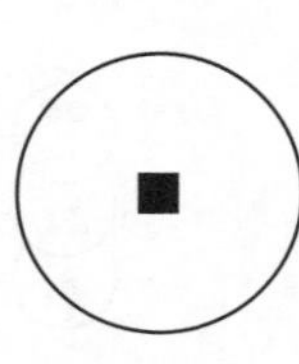

e

2

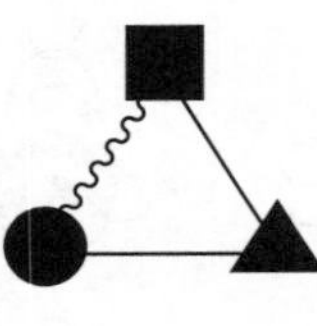

a

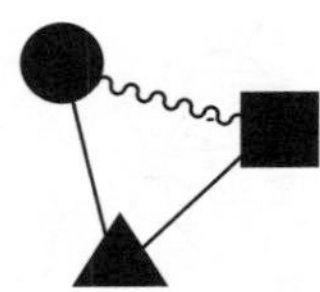

b

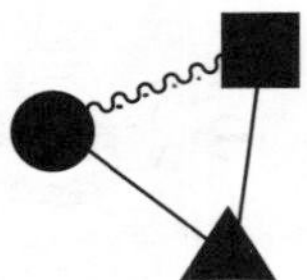

c

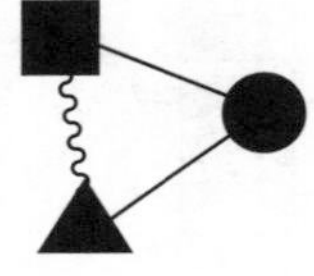

d

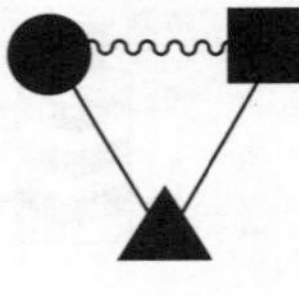

e

3

a

b

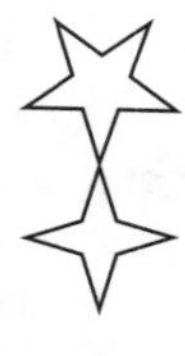

c

d

e

4

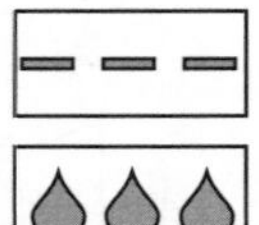

a

b

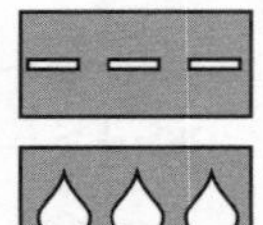

c

d

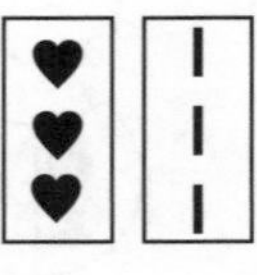

e

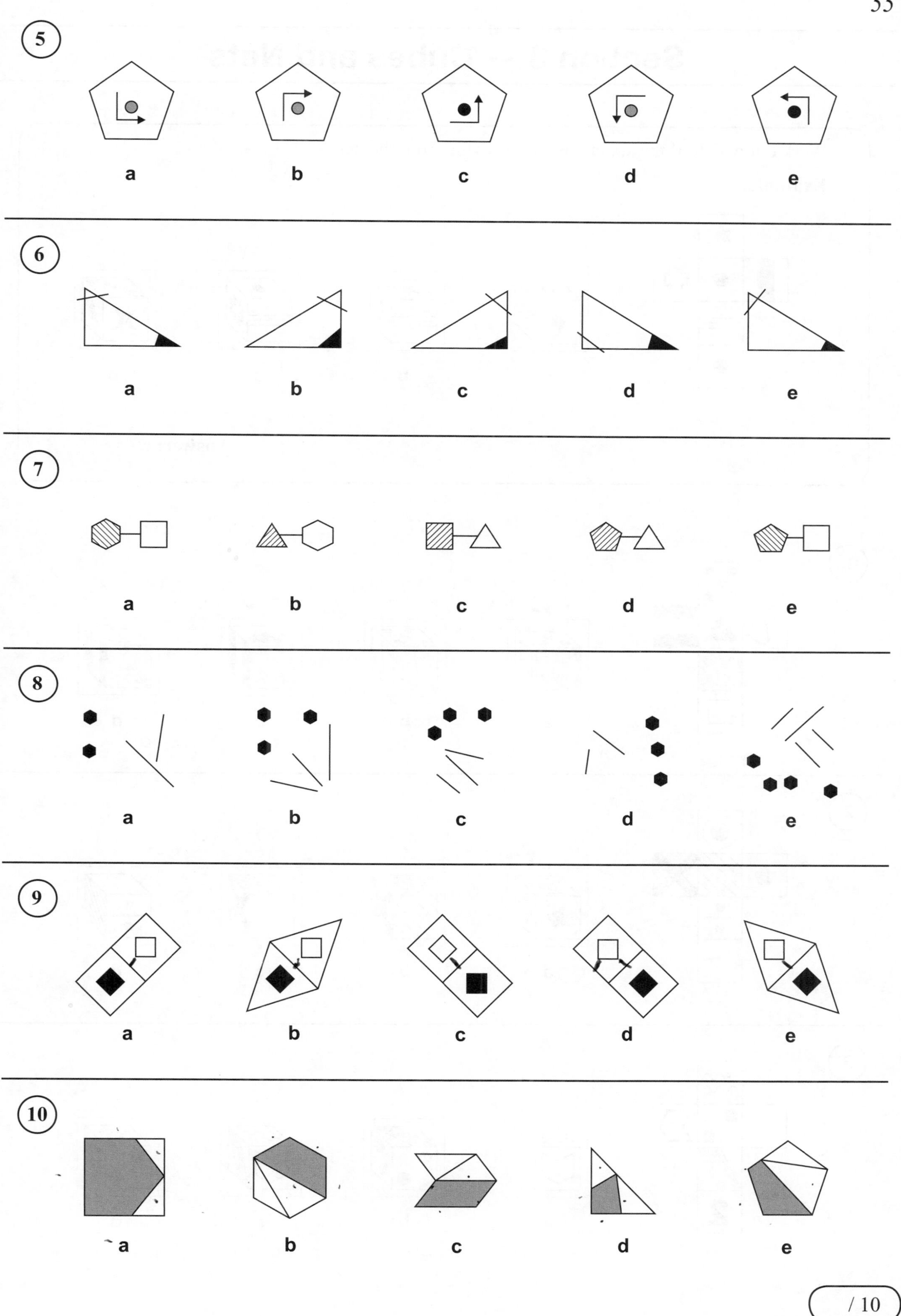

/ 10

Section 3 — Cubes and Nets

Work out which of the six cubes can be made from the net.

Example:

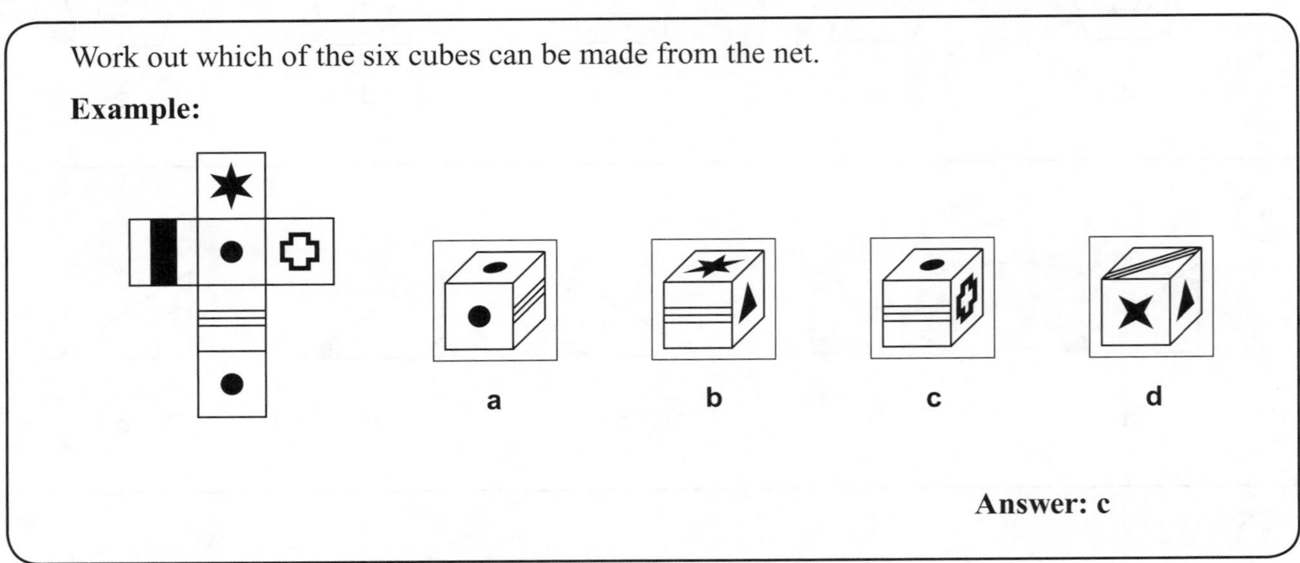

Answer: c

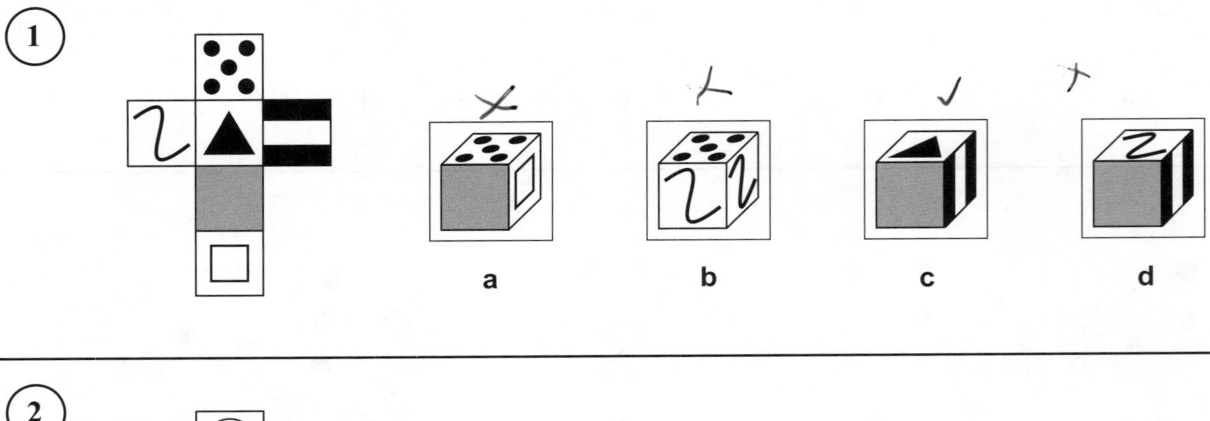

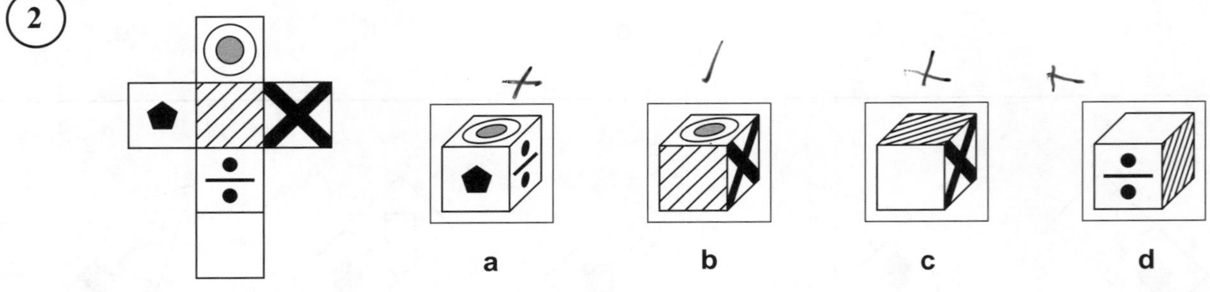

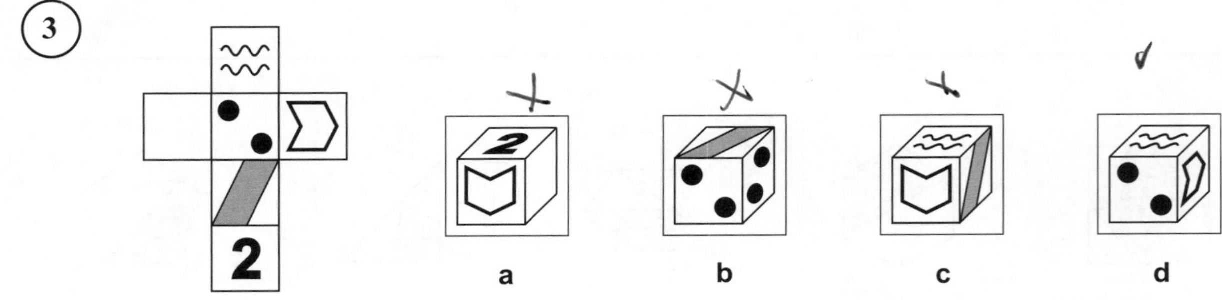

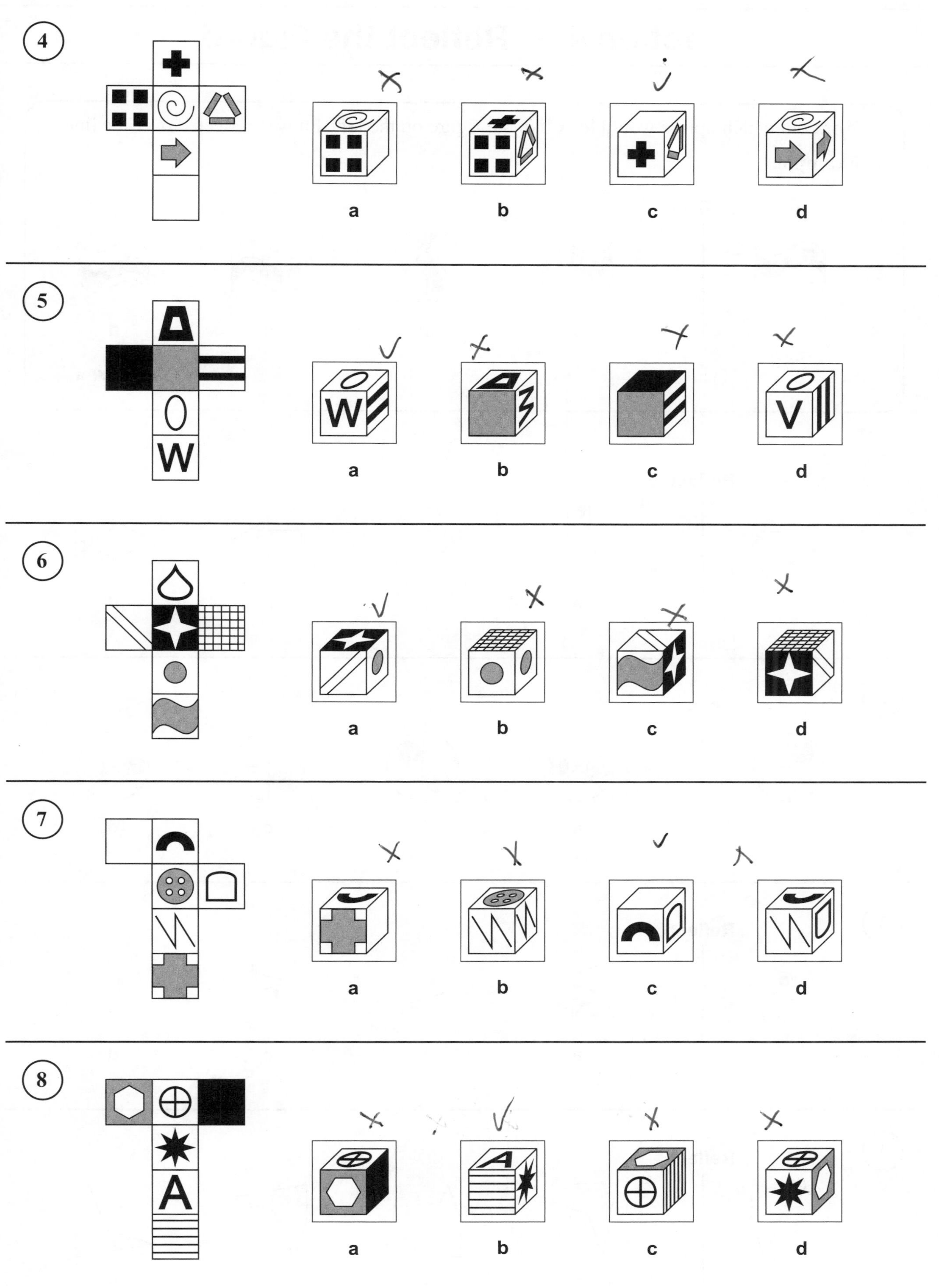

/ 8

Section 4 — Reflect the Figure

Work out which option would look like the figure on the left if it was reflected over the line.

Example:

Reflect

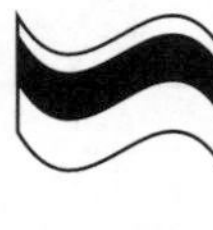
a

b

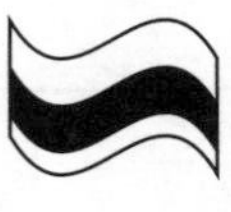
c

d

Answer: a

1

Reflect

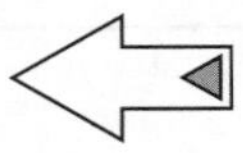

a

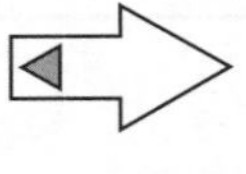
b

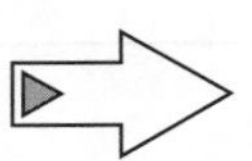
c

d

2

Reflect

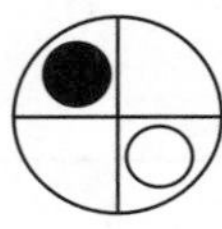

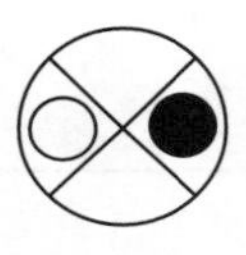
a

b

c

d

3

Reflect

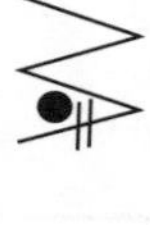
a

b

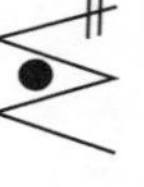
c

d

4

Reflect

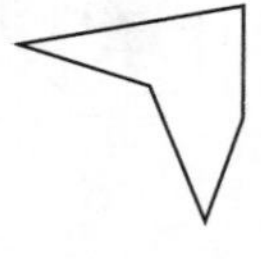

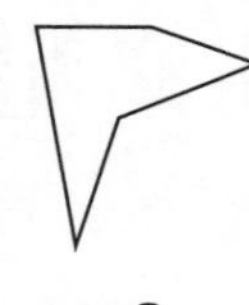
a

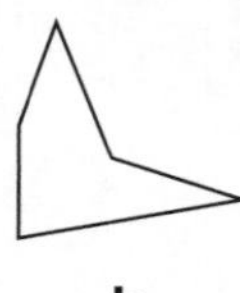
b

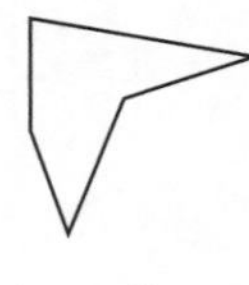
c

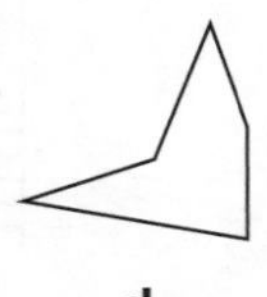
d

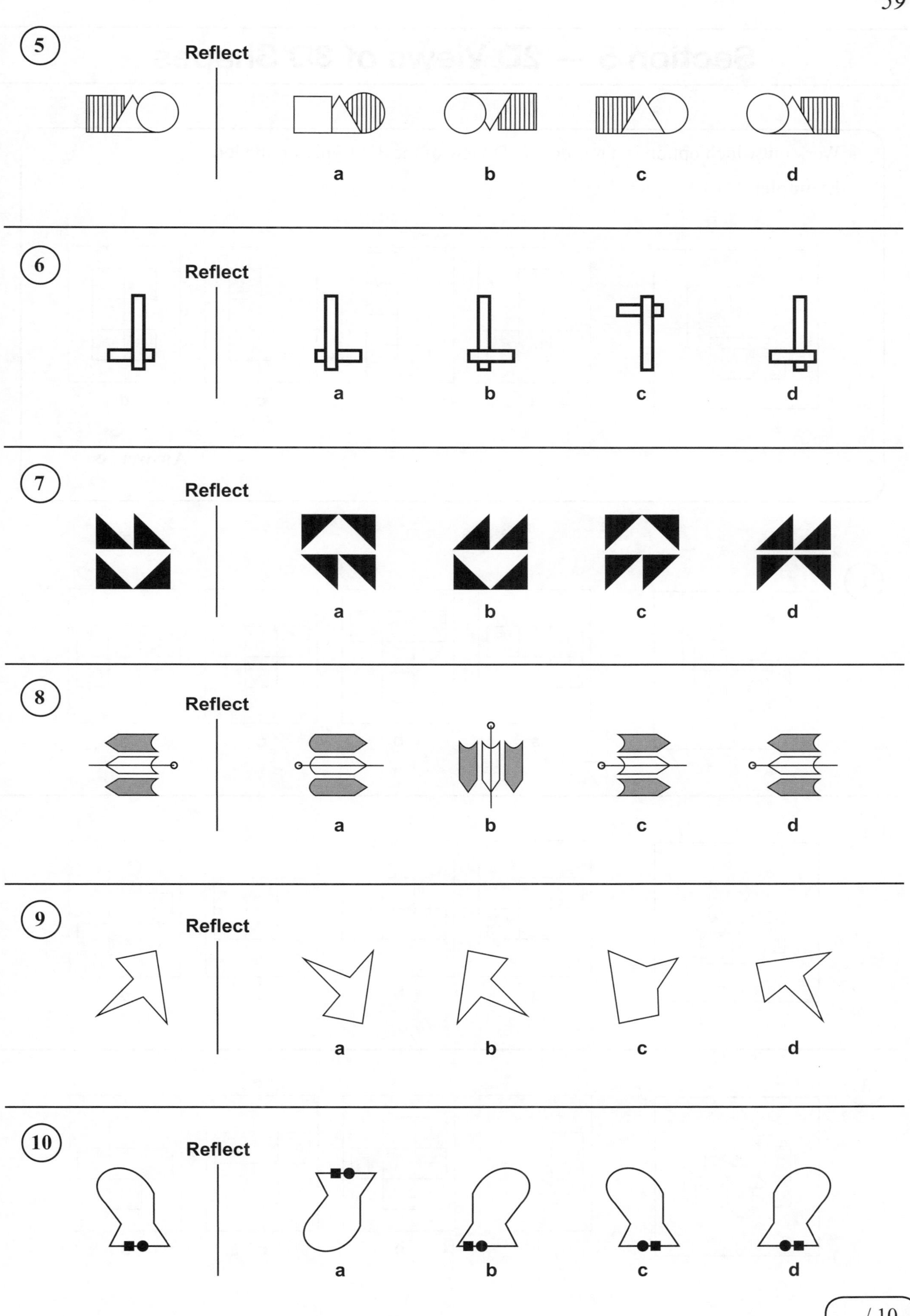
5
Reflect
a
b
c
d
6
Reflect
a
b
c
d
7
Reflect
a
b
c
d
8
Reflect
a
b
c
d
9
Reflect
a
b
c
d
10
Reflect
a
b
c
d

/ 10

Section 5 — 2D Views of 3D Shapes

Work out which option is a top-down 2D view of the 3D figure on the left.

Example:

a b c d

Answer: c

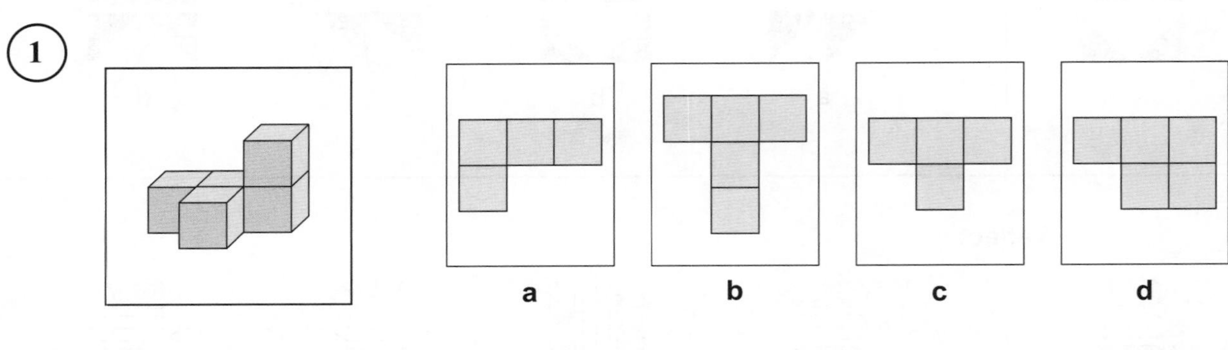

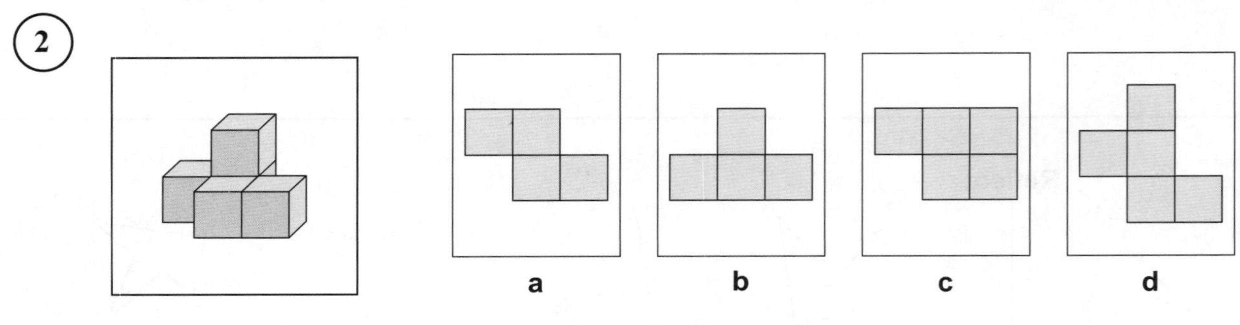

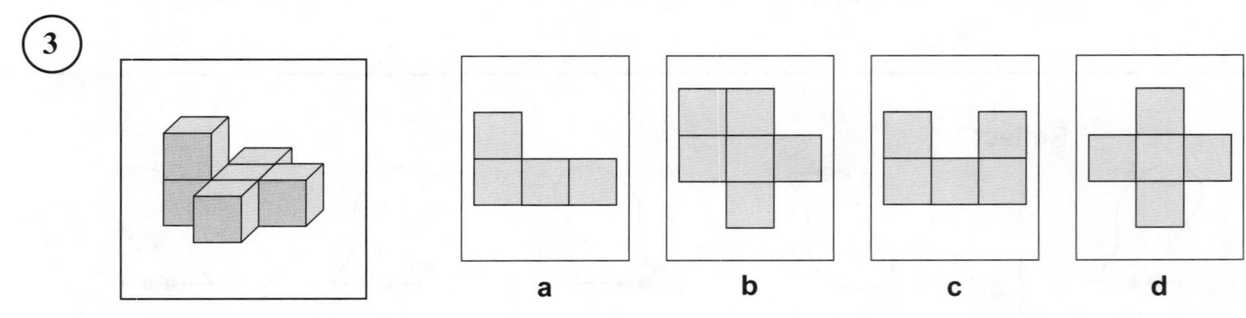

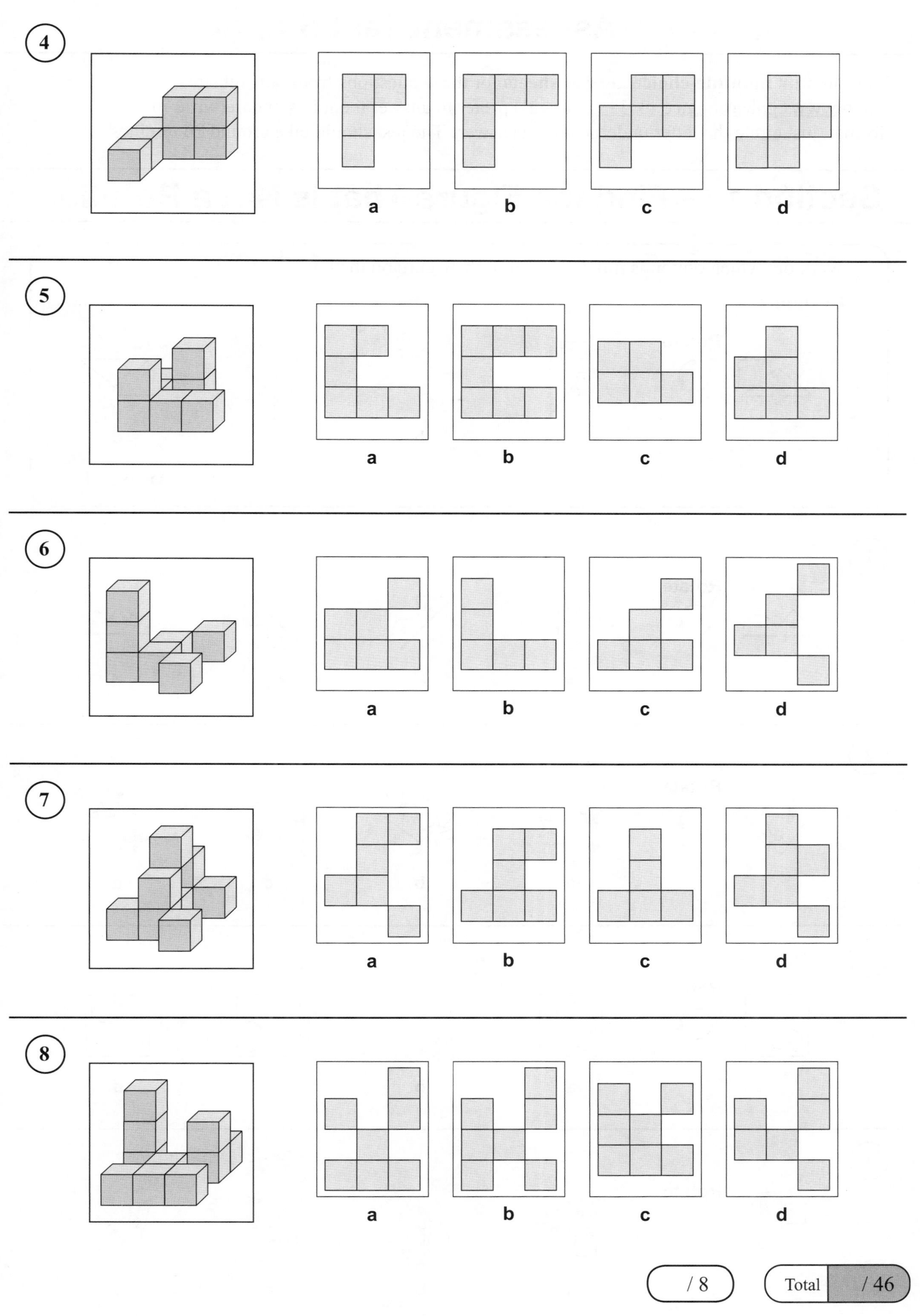

END OF TEST

Assessment Test 5

You can print **multiple-choice answer sheets** for these questions from our website — go to www.cgplearning.co.uk/11+. If you'd prefer to answer them in standard write-in format, just circle the letter underneath the answer. The test should take around 20 minutes.

Section 1 — Find the Figure That is Not a Rotation

Work out which option is **not** a rotation of the figure on the left.

Example:

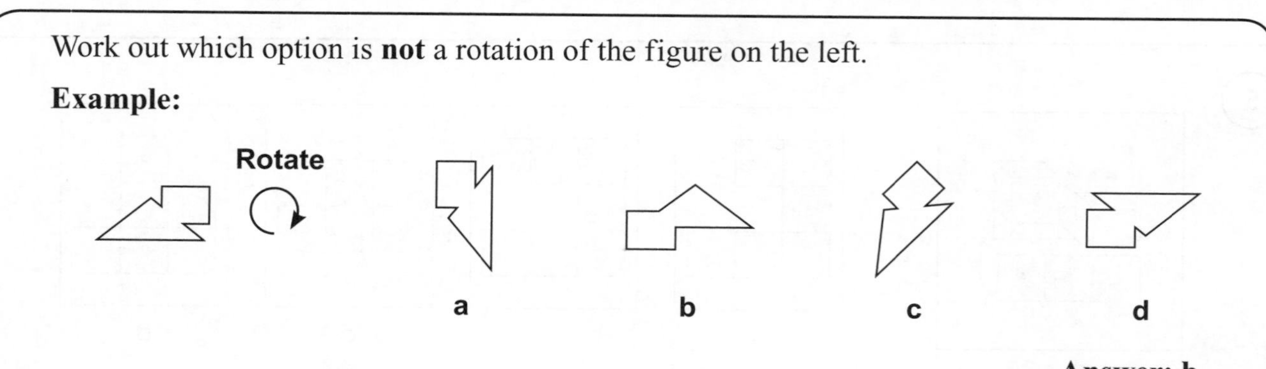

Answer: b

1

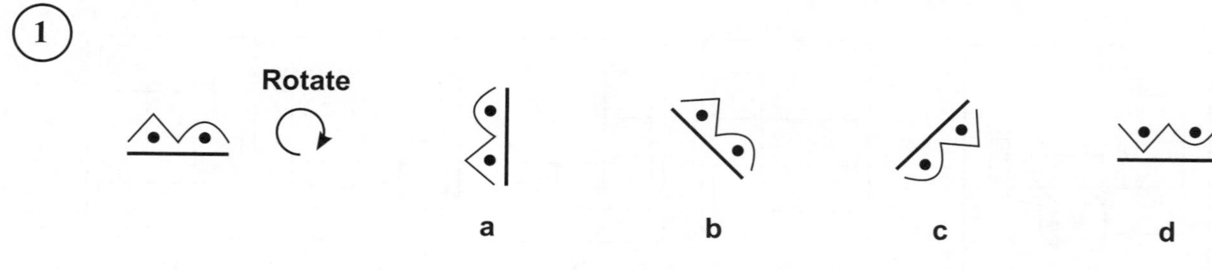

2

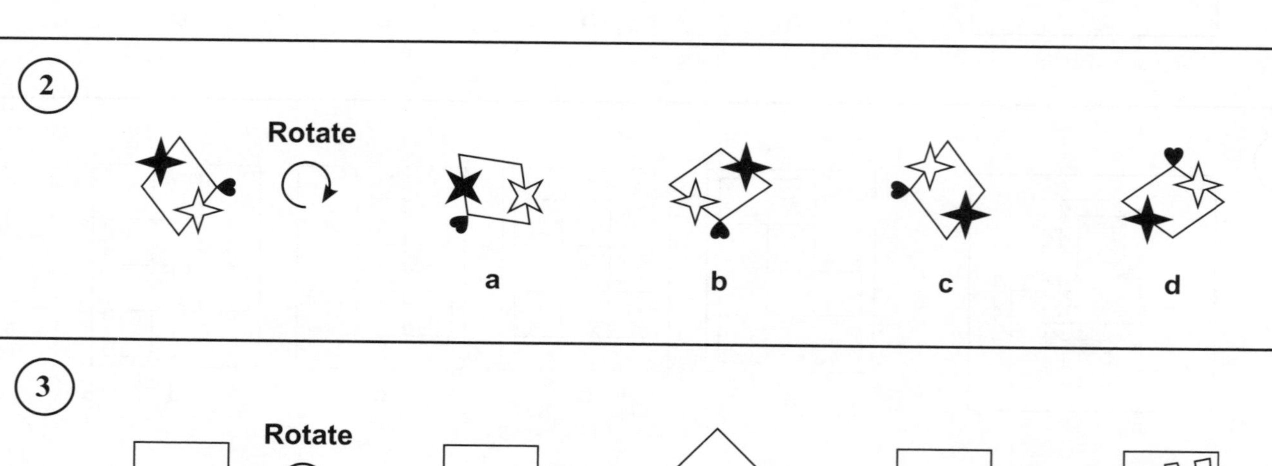

3

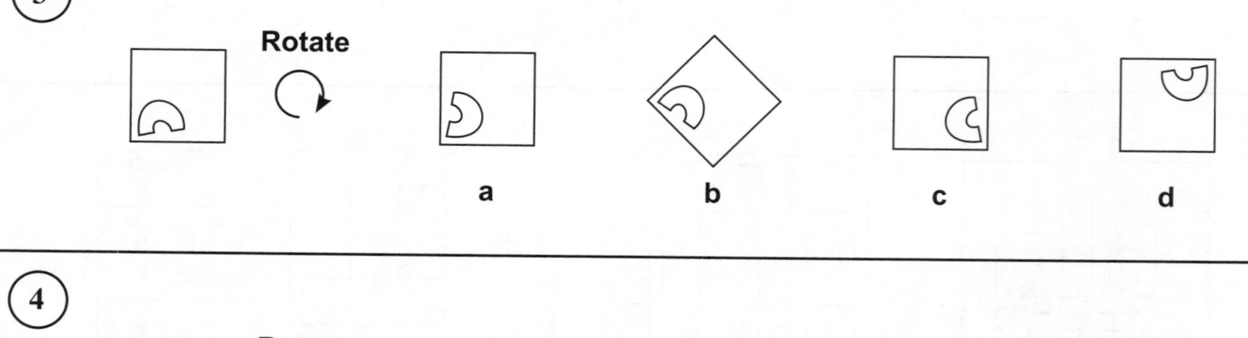

4

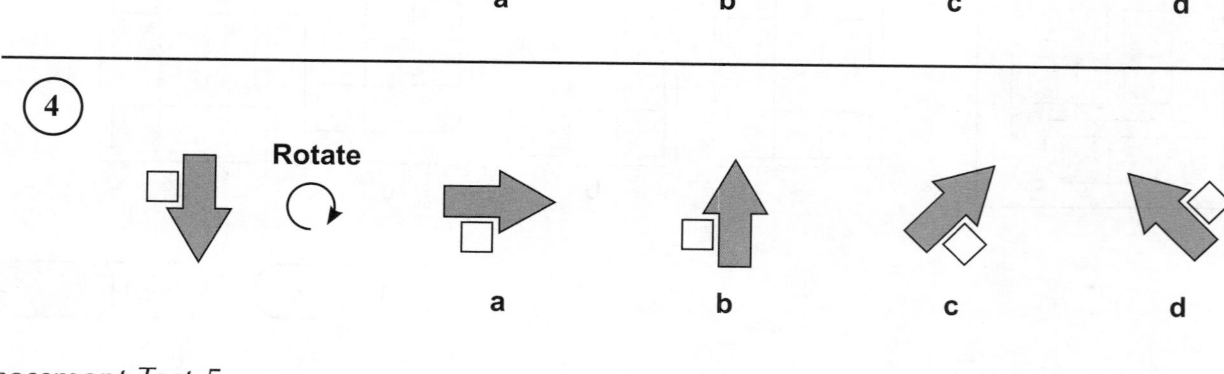

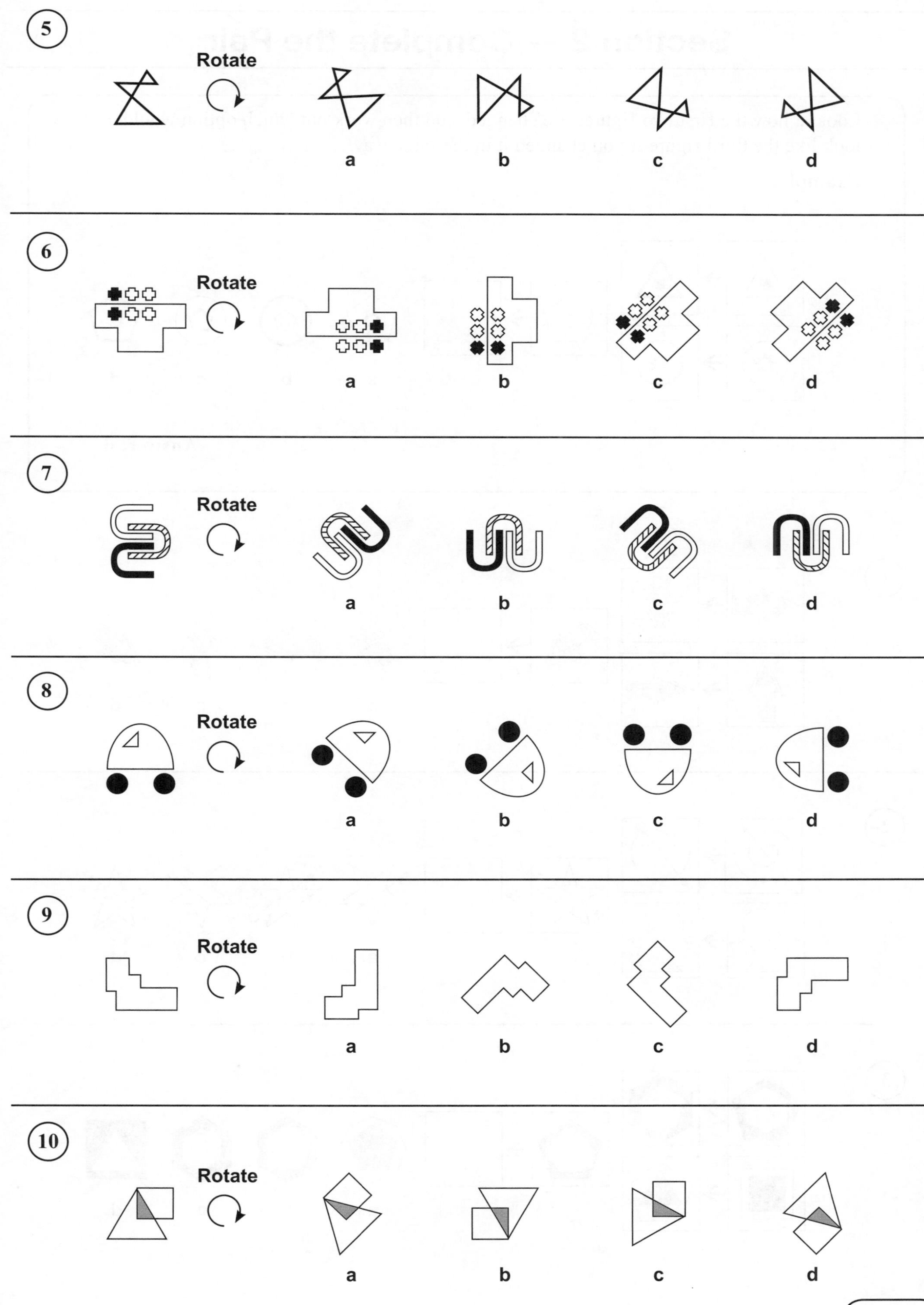
5
Rotate
a
b
c
d
6
Rotate
a
b
c
d
7
Rotate
a
b
c
d
8
Rotate
a
b
c
d
9
Rotate
a
b
c
d
10
Rotate
a
b
c
d

/ 10

Section 2 — Complete the Pair

Look at how the first two figures are changed, and then work out which option would look like the third figure if you changed it in the same way.

Example:

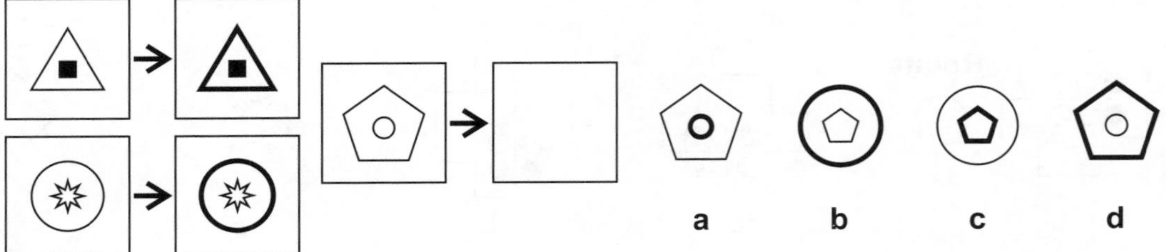

Answer: d

(1)

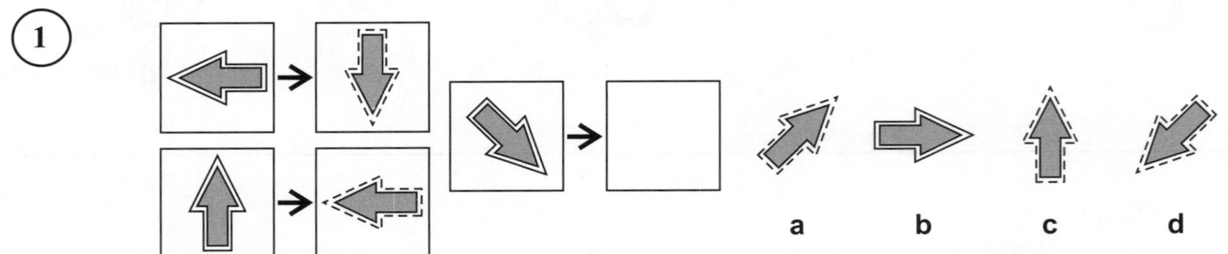

(2)

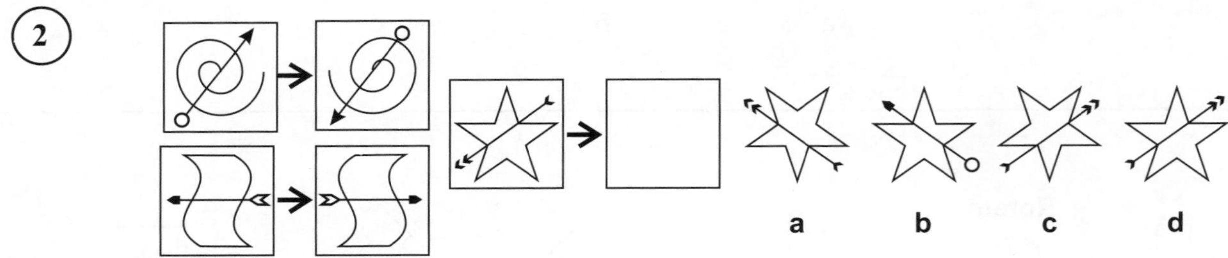

(3)

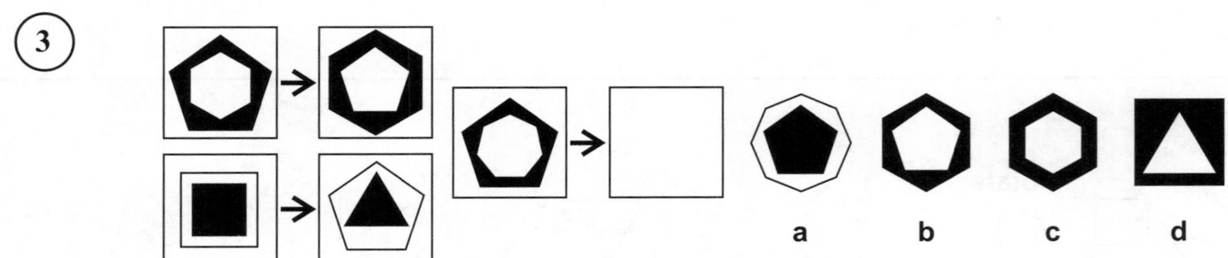

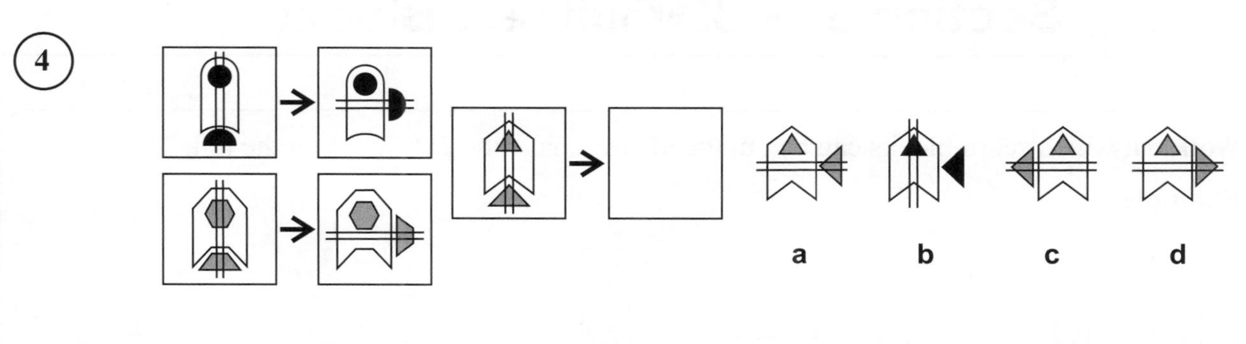

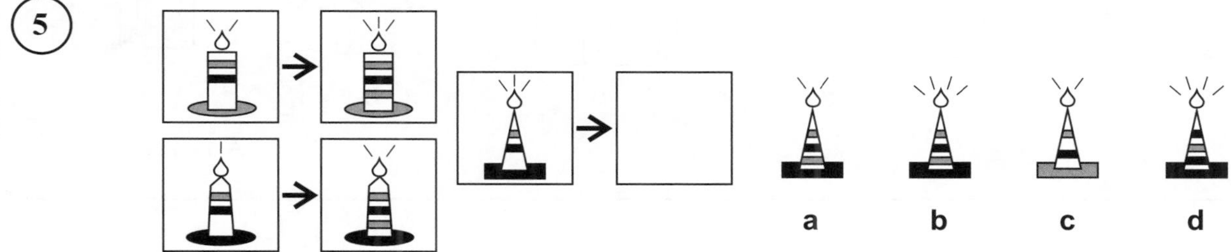

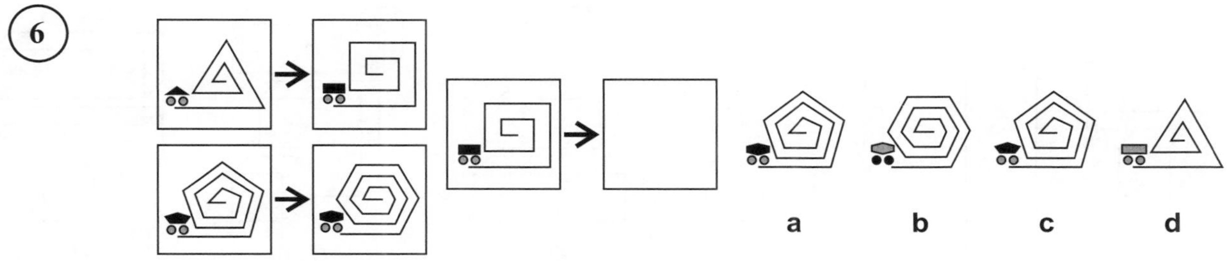

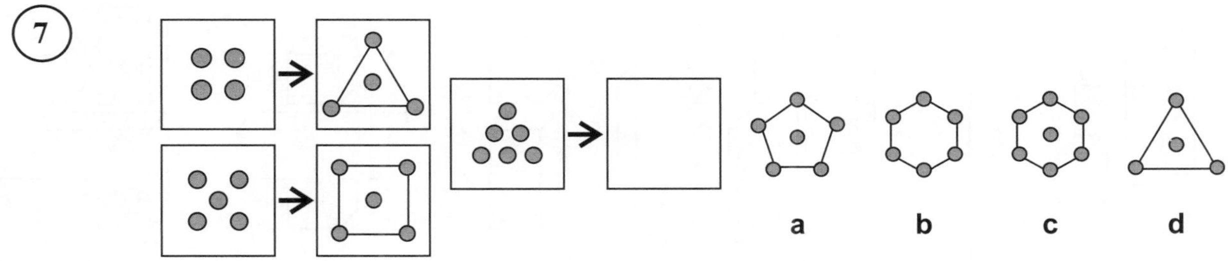

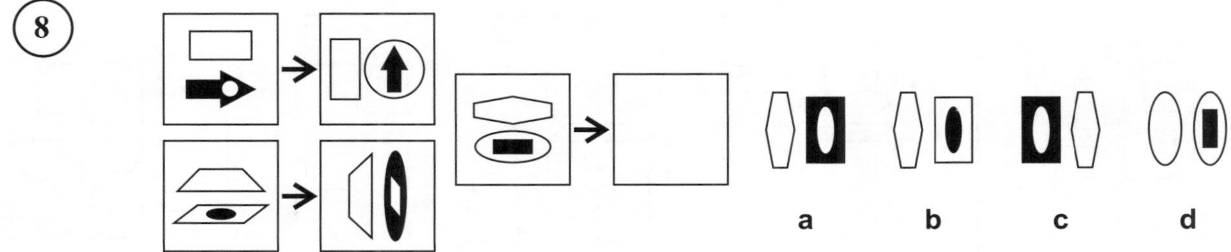

/ 8

Section 3 — 3D Building Blocks

Work out which set of blocks can be put together to make the 3D figure on the left.

Example:

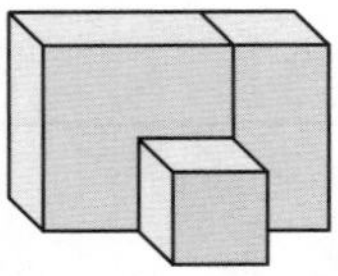

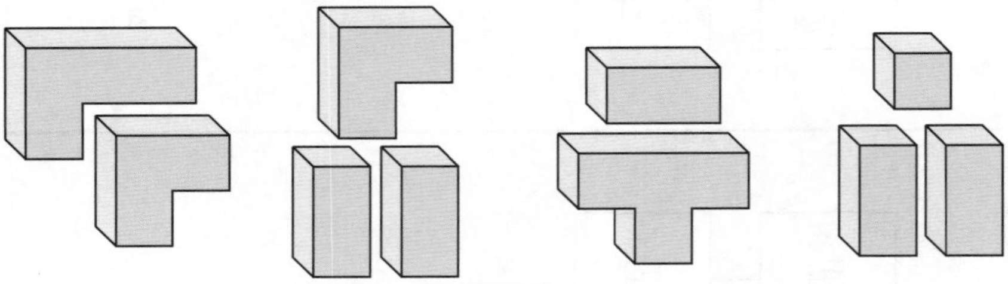

a b c d

Answer: b

1

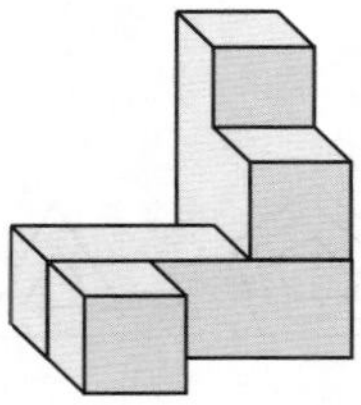

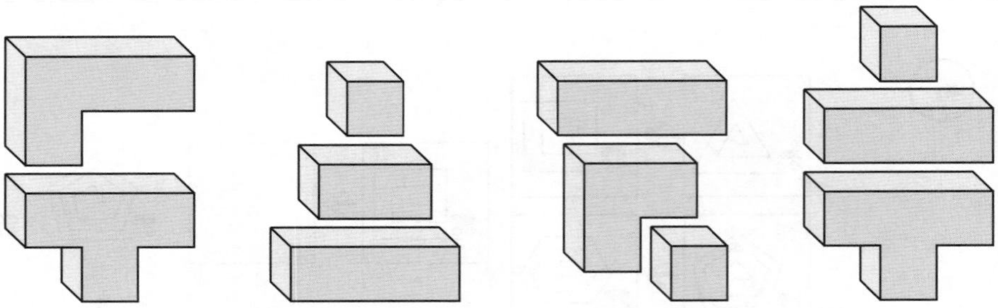

a b c d

2

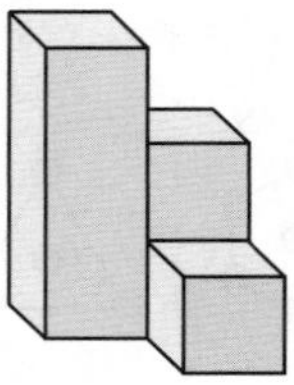

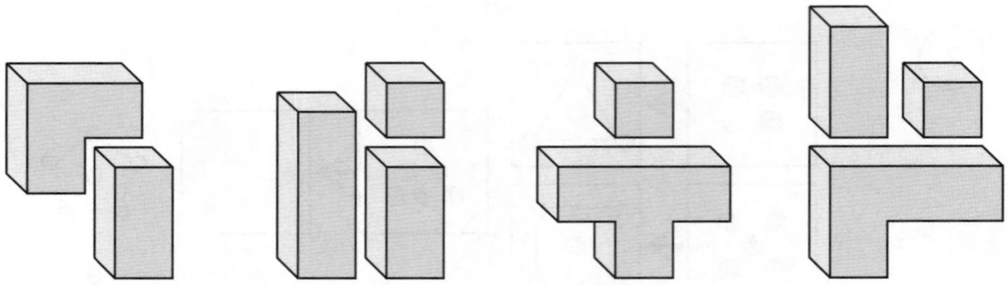

a b c d

3

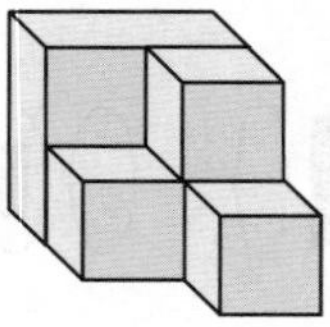

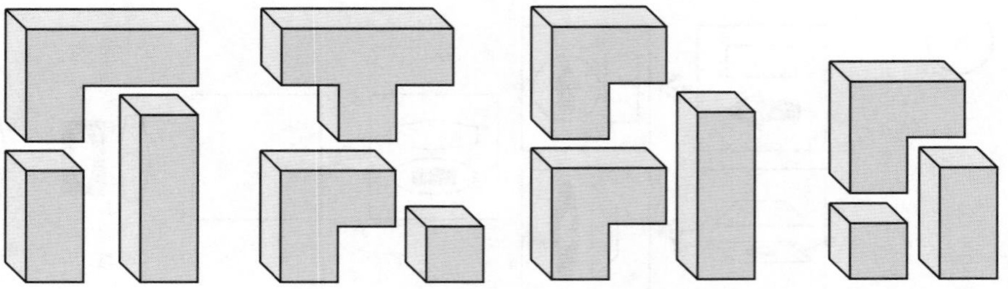

a b c d

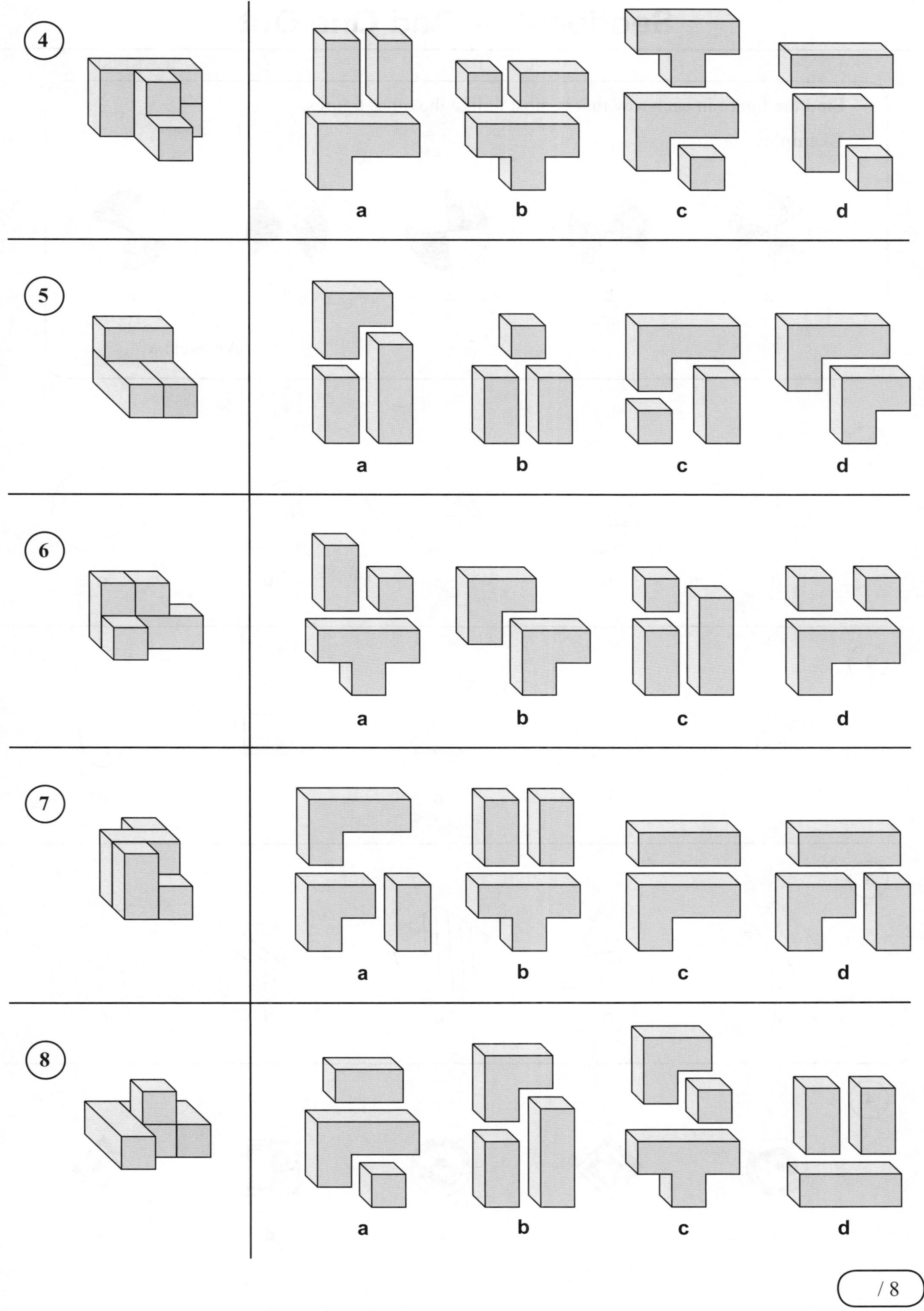

/ 8

Section 4 — Odd One Out

Find the figure in each row that is most unlike the other figures.

Example:

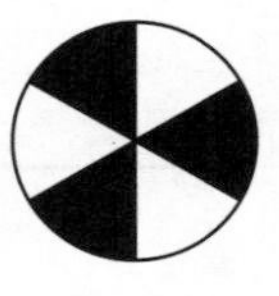
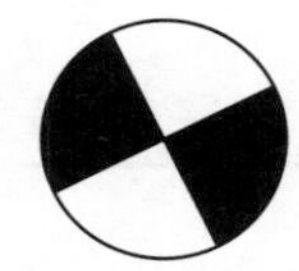
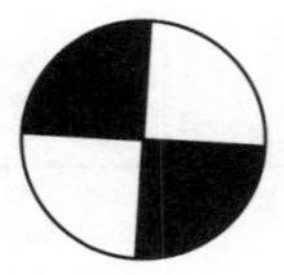

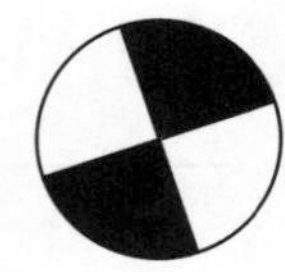

a b c d e

Answer: a

(1)

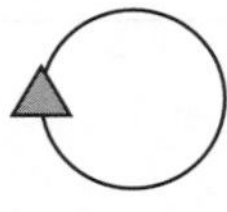
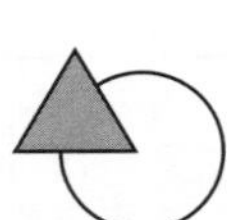

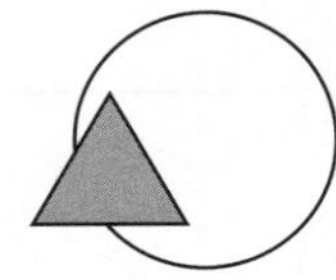

a b c d e

(2)

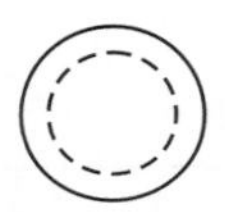
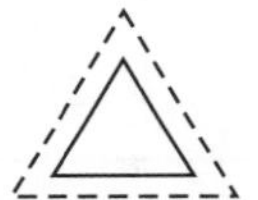
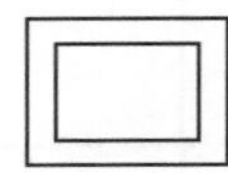

a b c d e

(3)

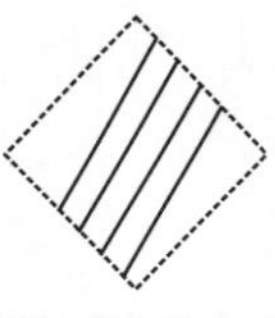
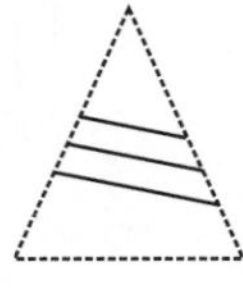
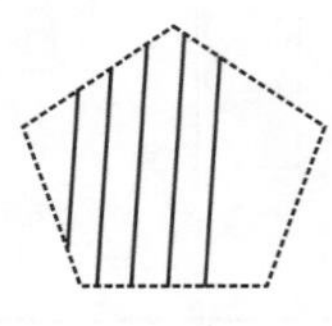
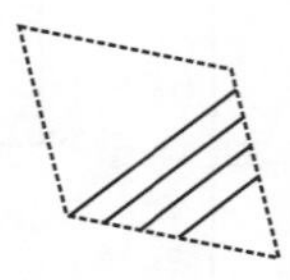
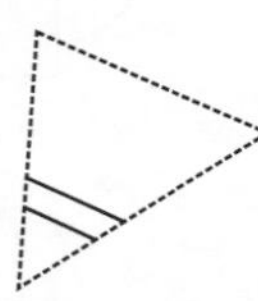

a b c d e

(4)

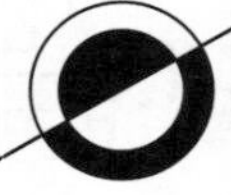

a b c d e

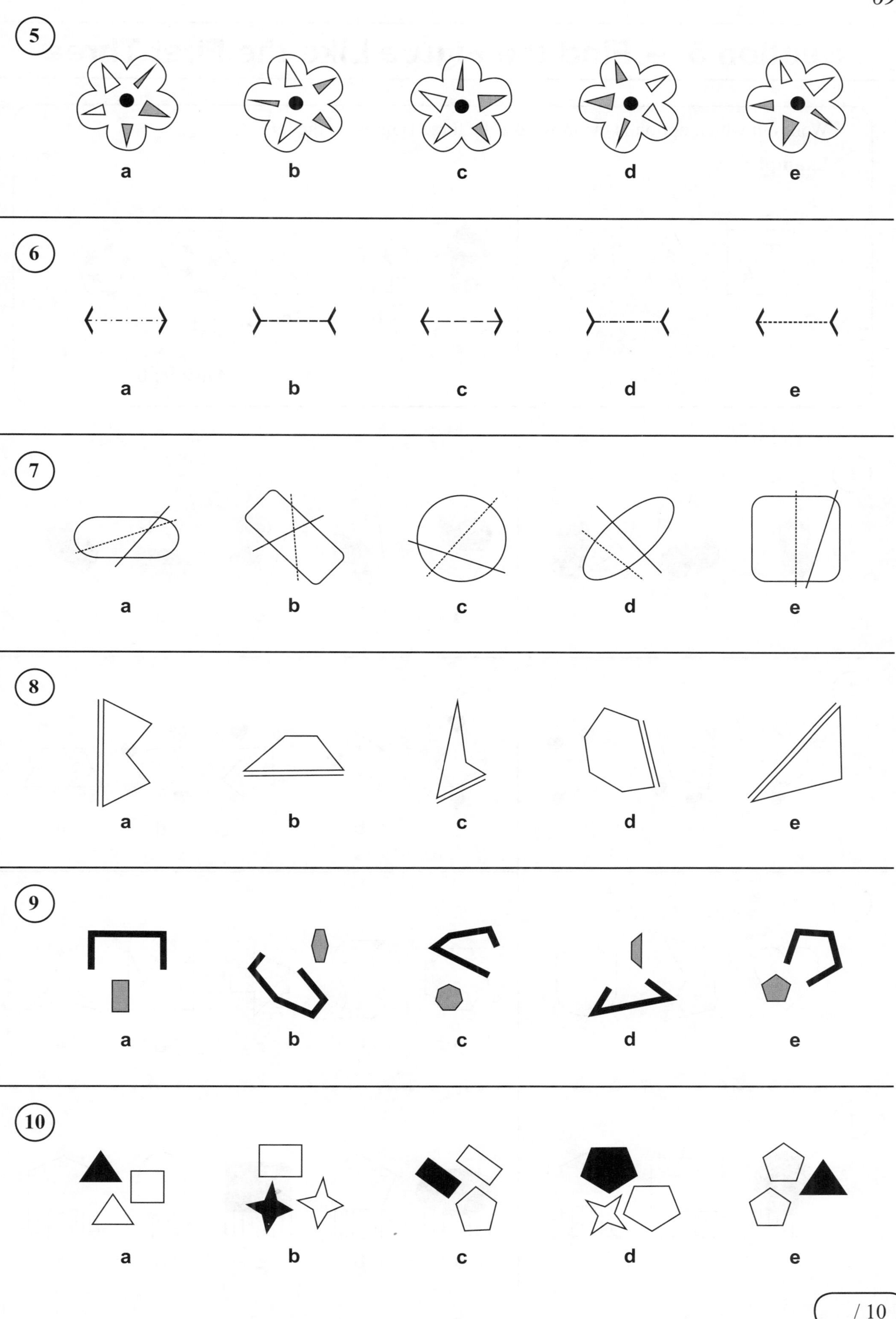

/ 10

Section 5 — Find the Figure Like the First Three

Work out which option is the most like the three figures on the left.

Example:

a b c d e

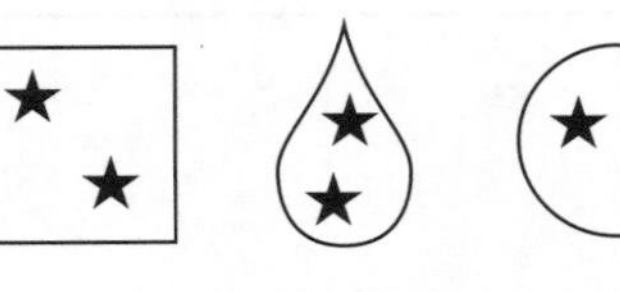

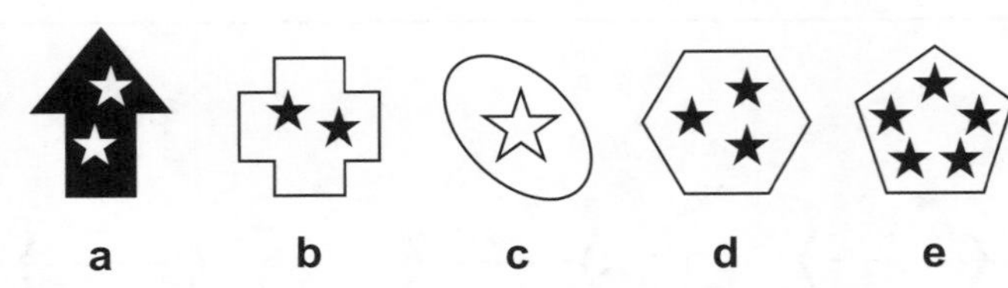

Answer: b

1

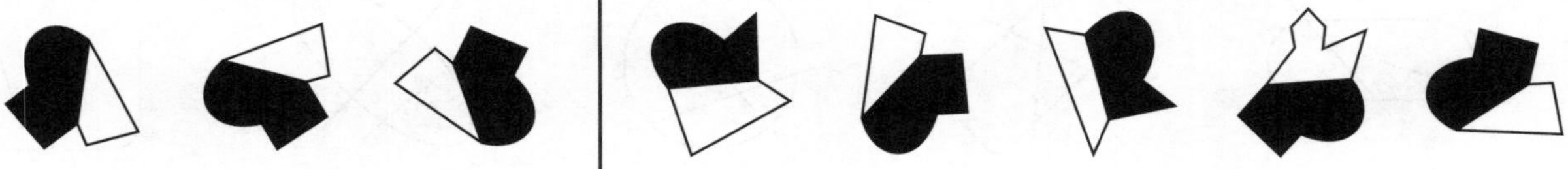

a b c d e

2

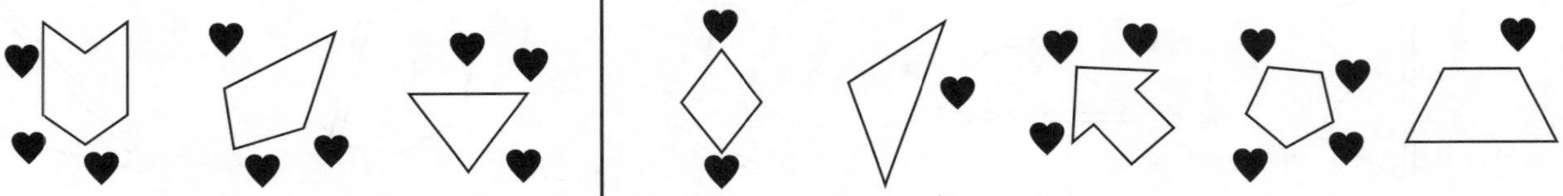

a b c d e

3

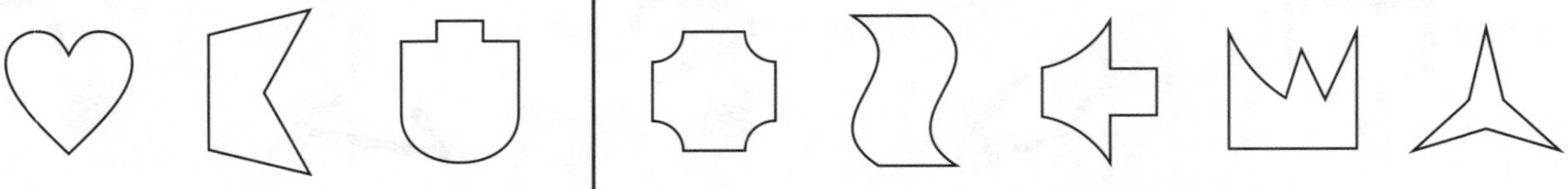

a b c d e

4

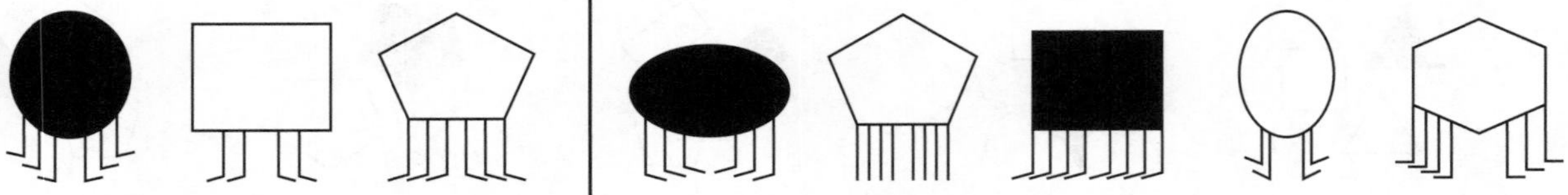

a b c d e

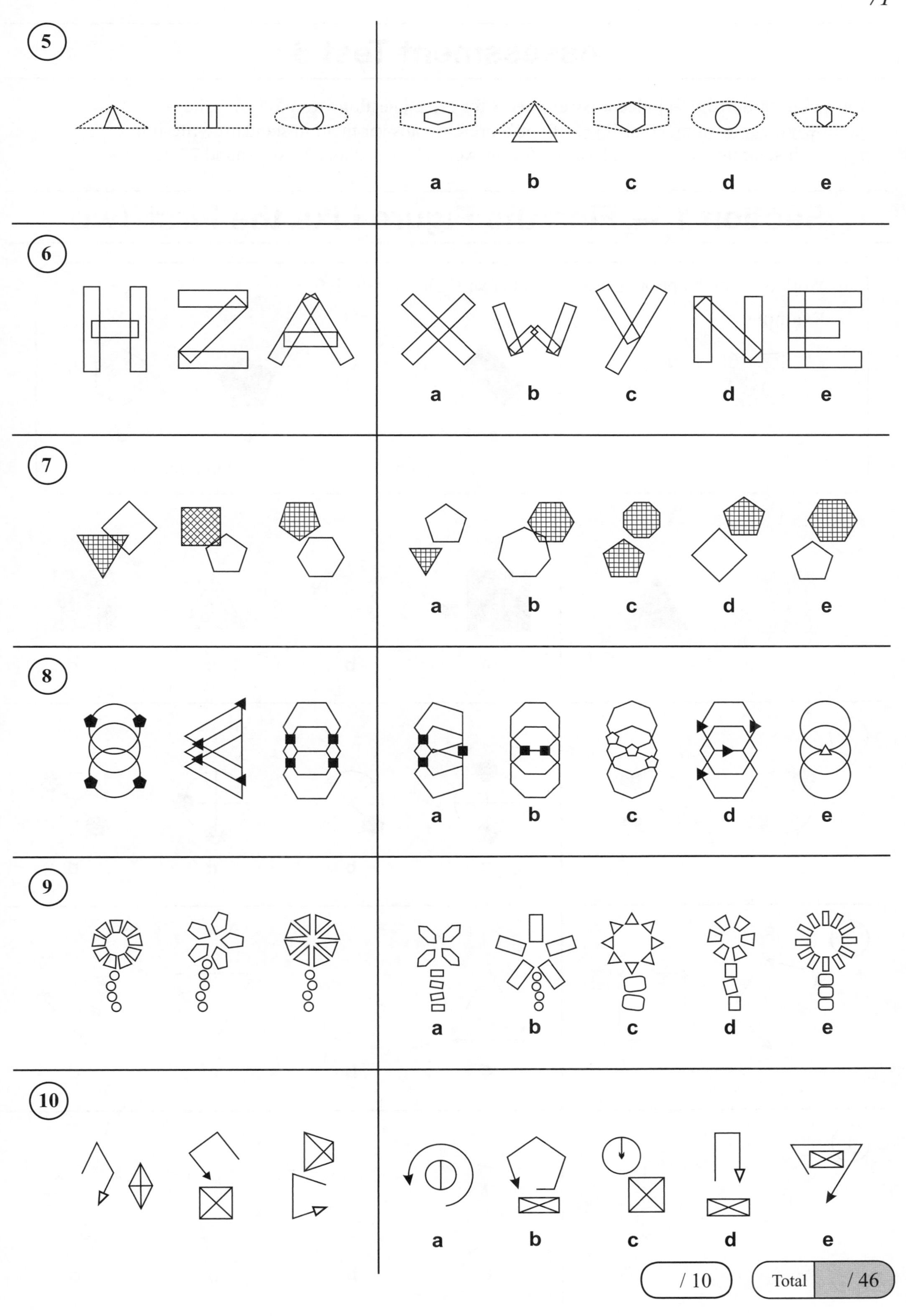

END OF TEST

Assessment Test 6

You can print **multiple-choice answer sheets** for these questions from our website — go to www.cgplearning.co.uk/11+. If you'd prefer to answer them in standard write-in format, just circle the letter underneath the answer. The test should take around 20 minutes.

Section 1 — Find the Figure Like the First Two

Work out which option is most like the two figures on the left.

Example:

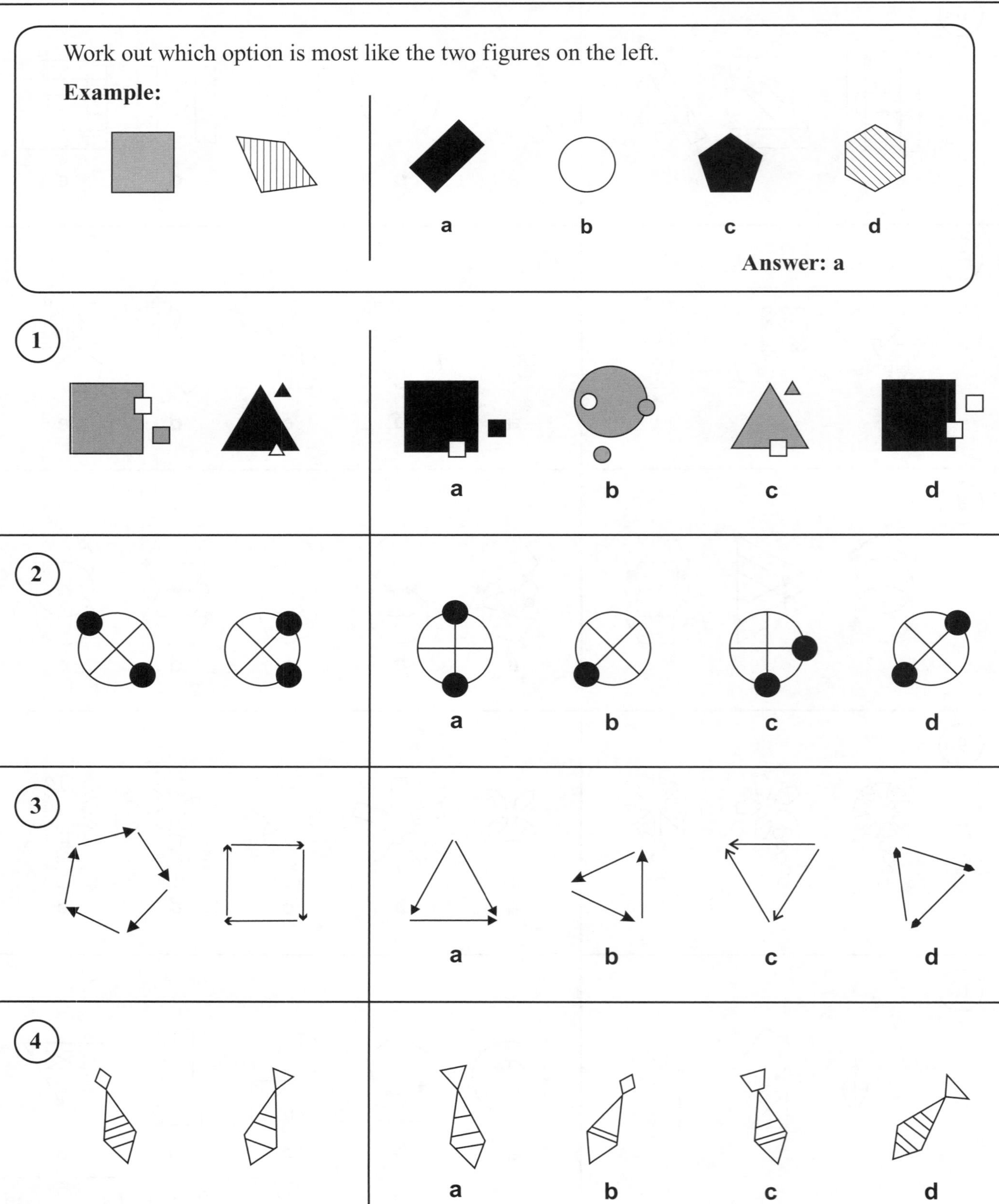

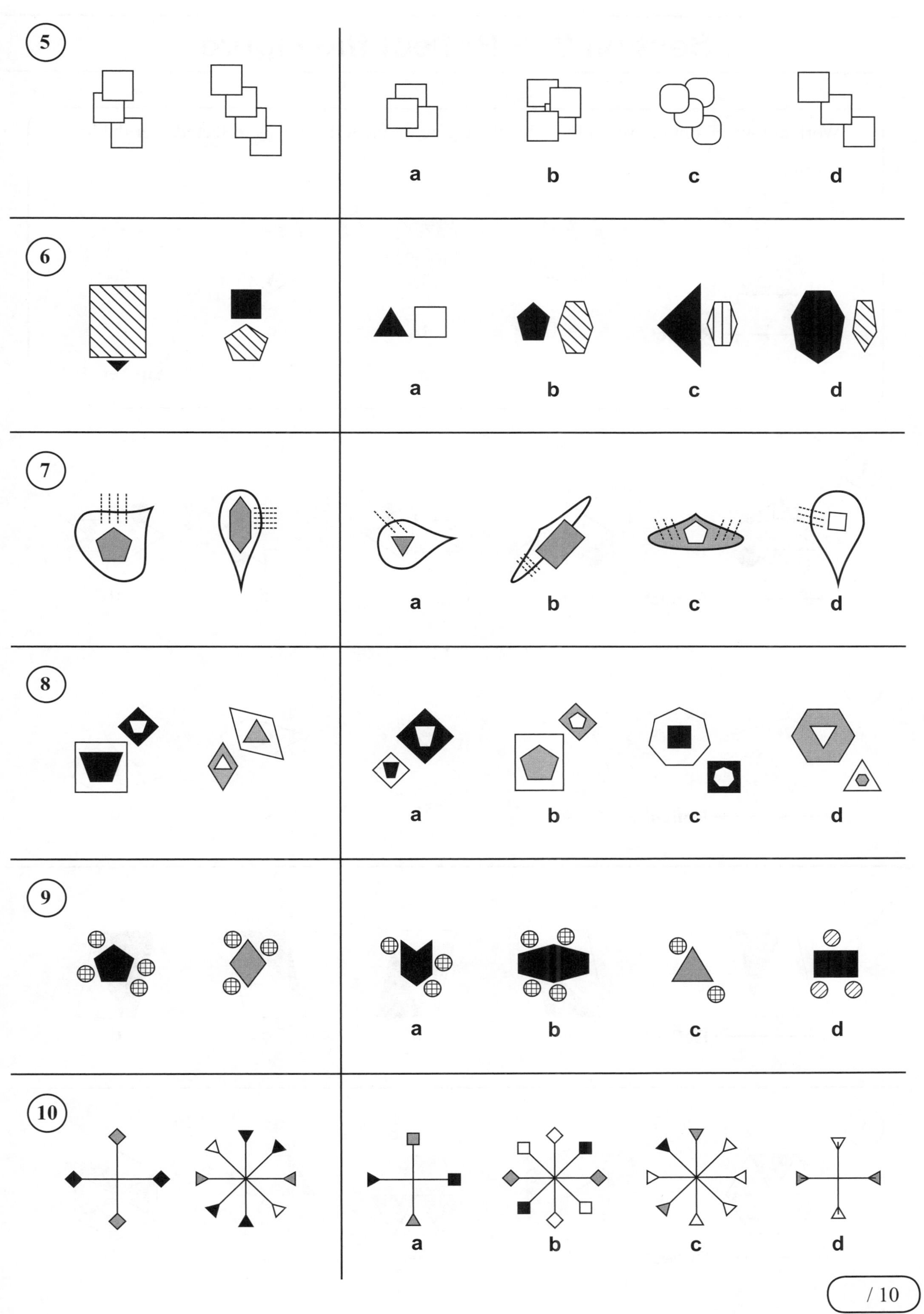

/ 10

Section 2 — Reflect the Figure

Work out which option would look like the figure on the left if it was reflected over the line.

Example:

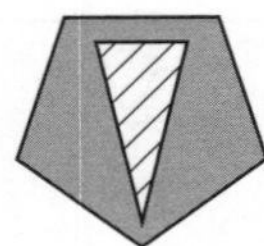
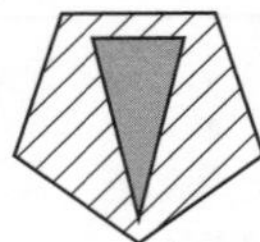
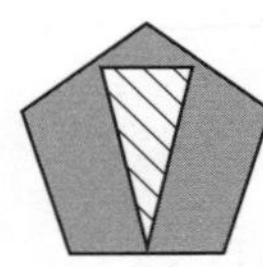

Reflect a b c d

Answer: b

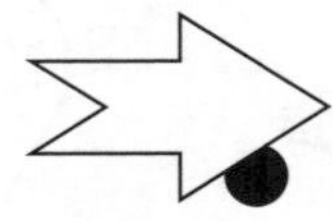
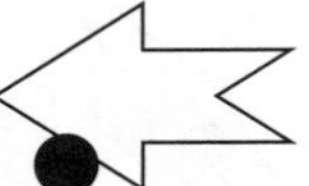

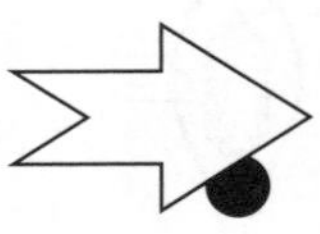
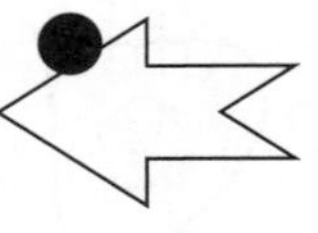

Reflect a b c d

2

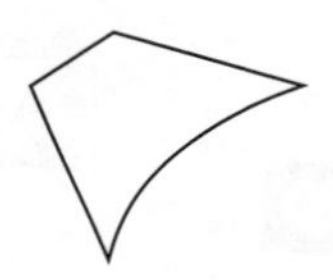
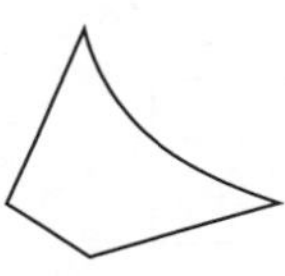
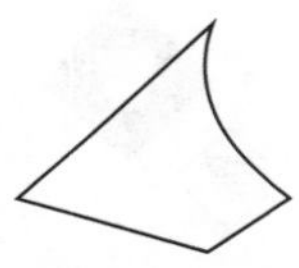
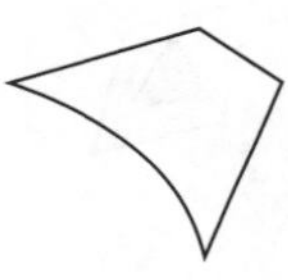
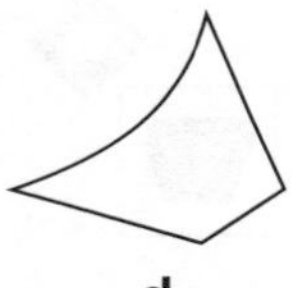

Reflect a b c d

3

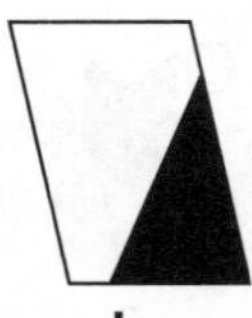

Reflect a b c d

4

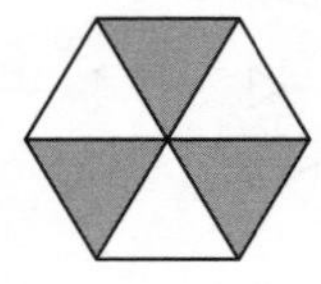
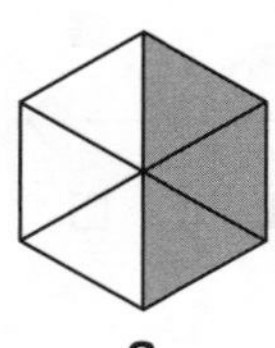
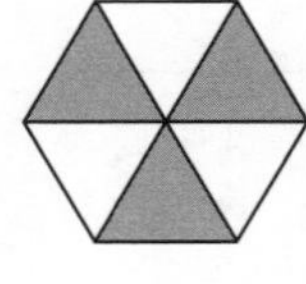
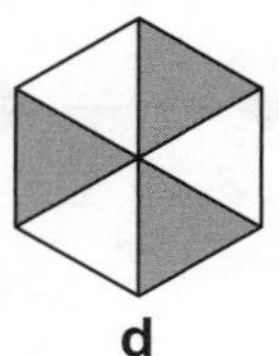

Reflect a b c d

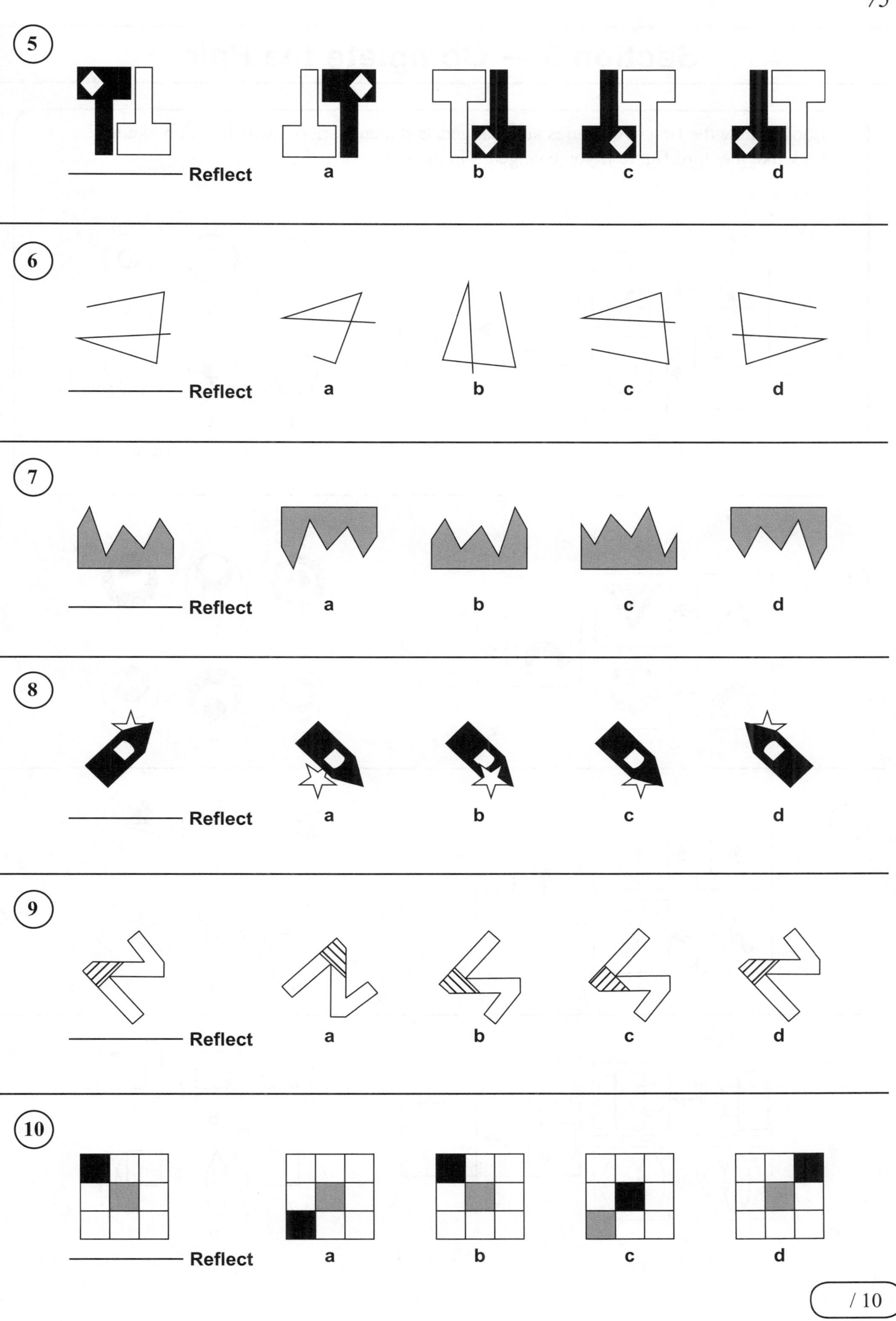
5
Reflect
a
b
c
d
6
Reflect
a
b
c
d
7
Reflect
a
b
c
d
8
Reflect
a
b
c
d
9
Reflect
a
b
c
d
10
Reflect
a
b
c
d

/ 10

Section 3 — Complete the Pair

Look at how the first two figures are changed, and then work out which option would look like the third figure if you changed it in the same way.

Example:

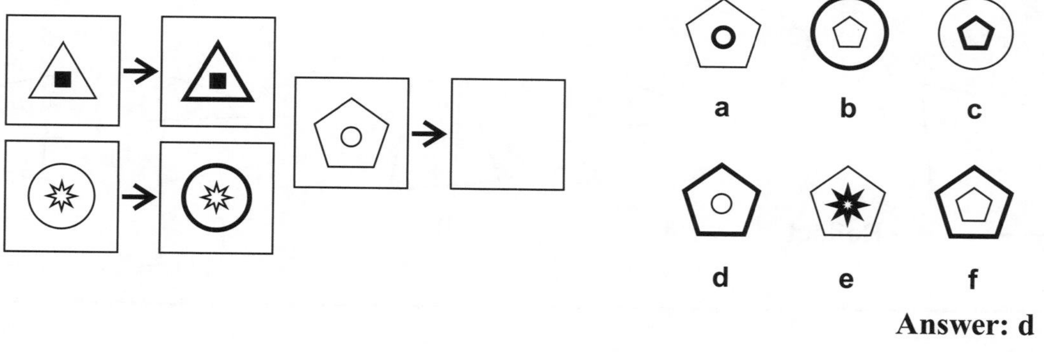

Answer: d

1

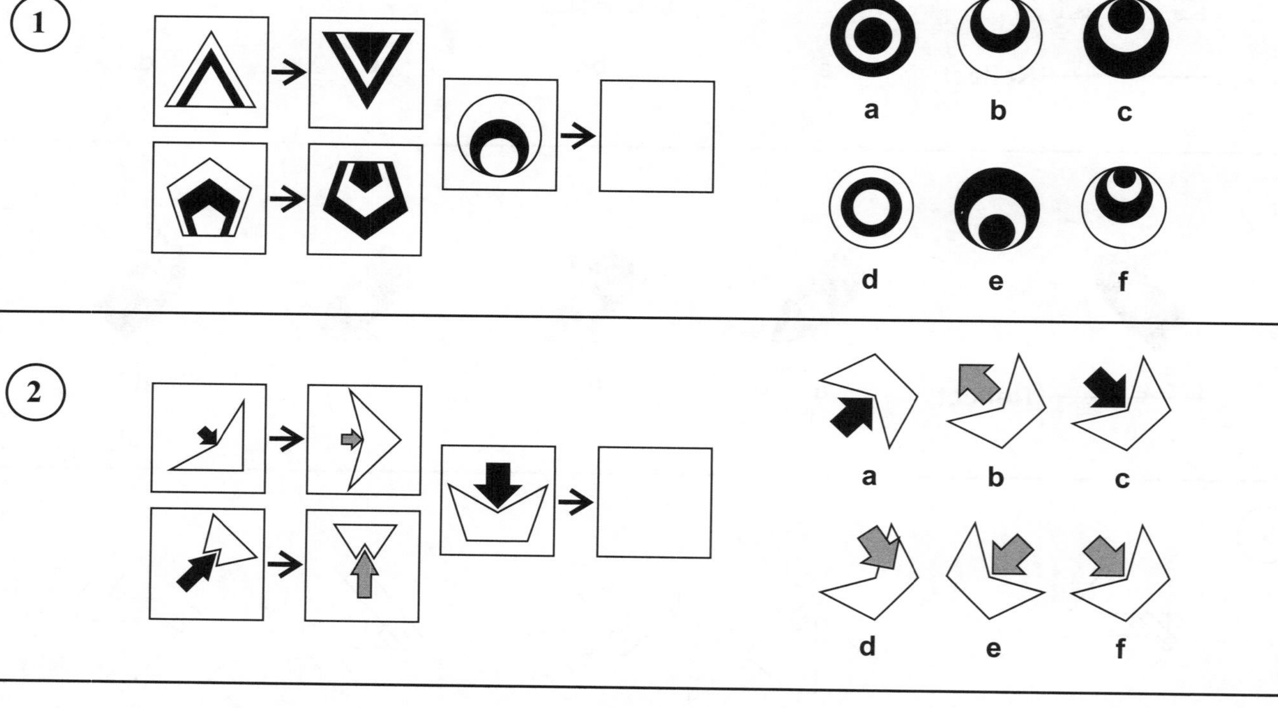

2

3

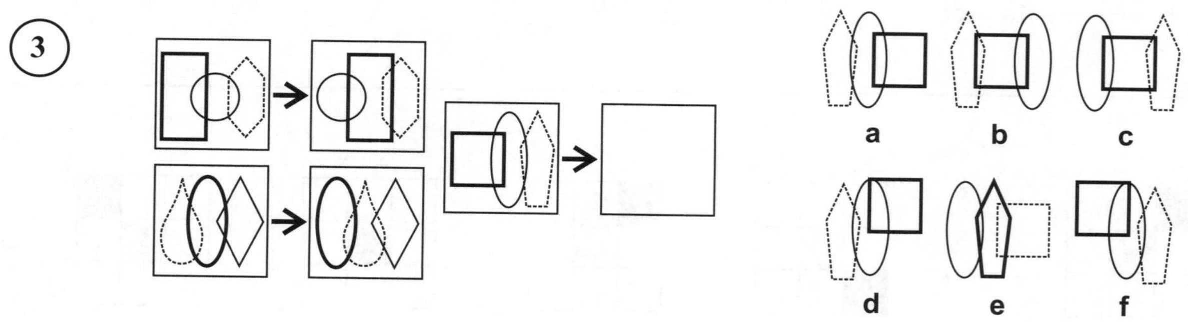

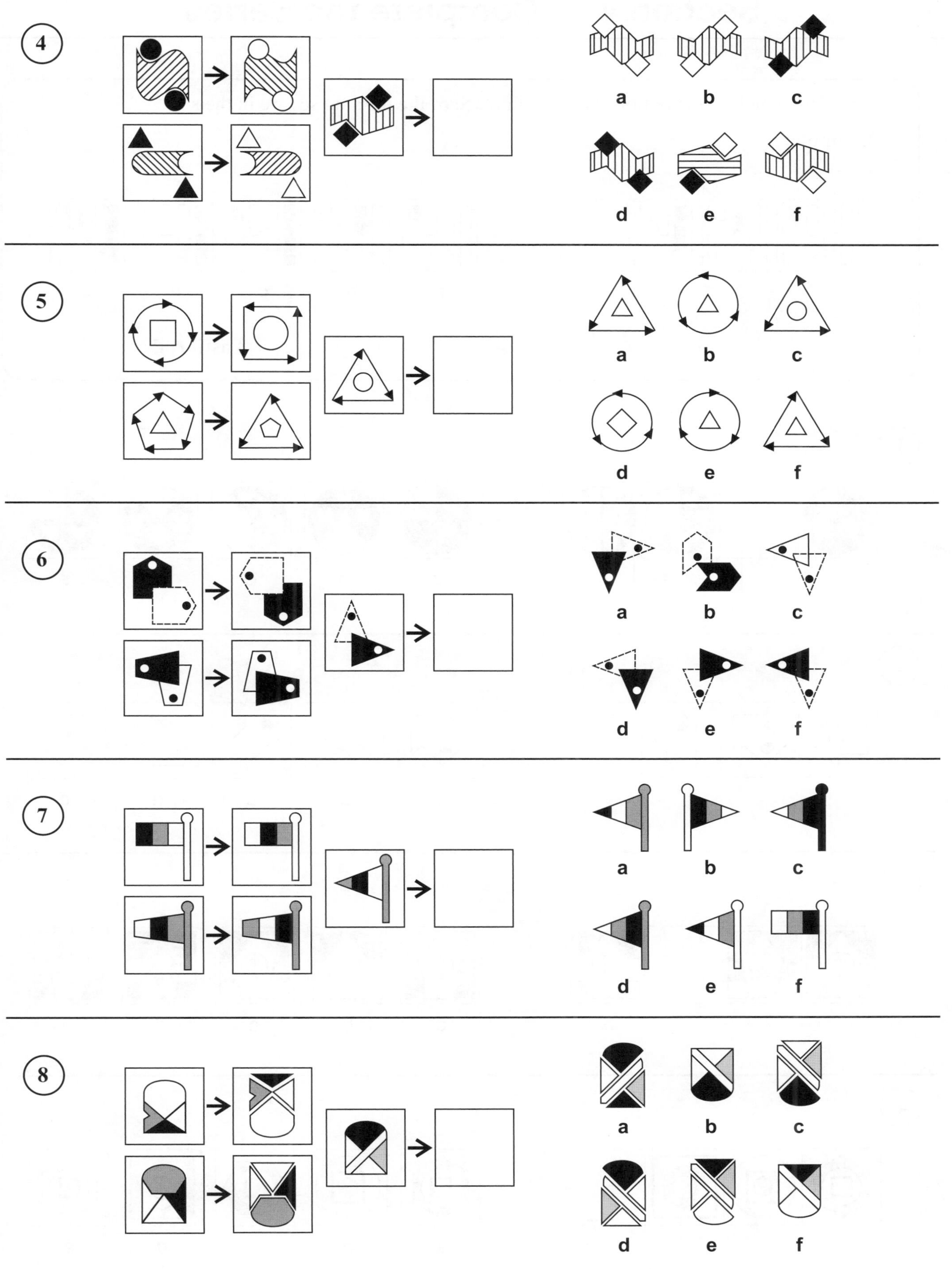

/ 8

Section 4 — Complete the Series

Work out which of the options best fits in place of the missing square in the series.

Example:

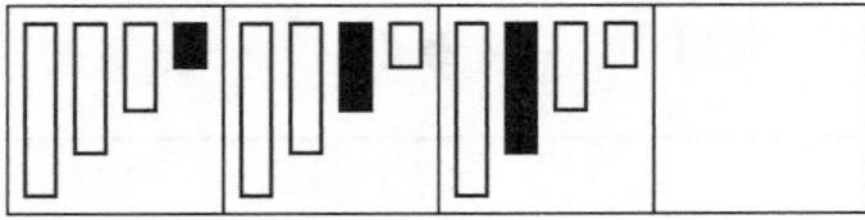

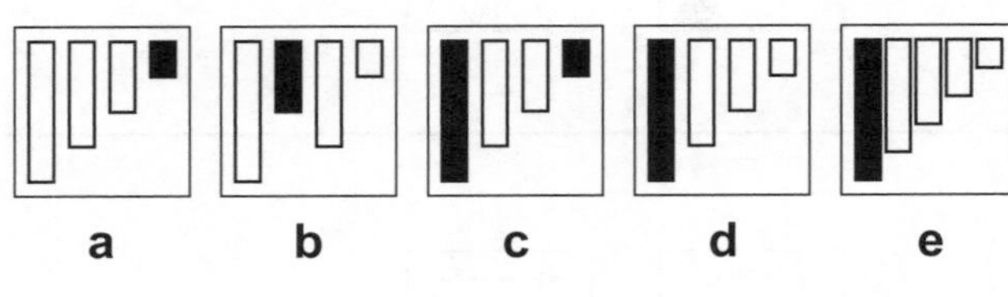

Answer: d

1

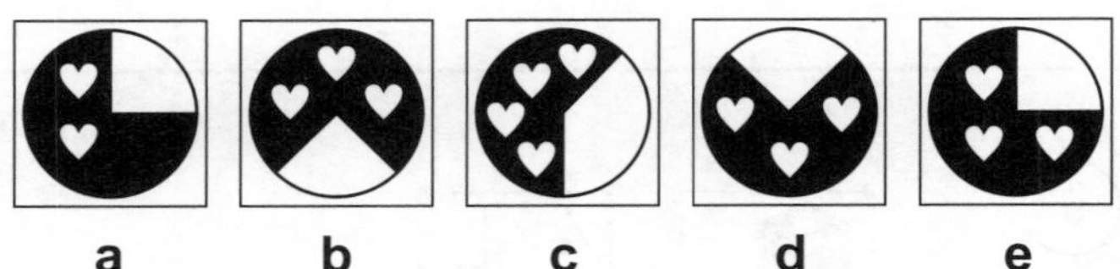

2

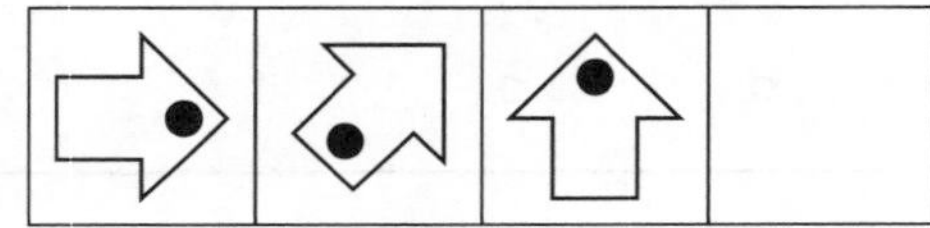

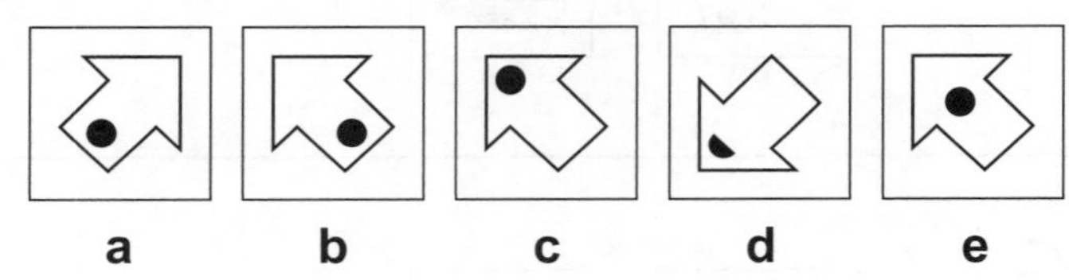

3

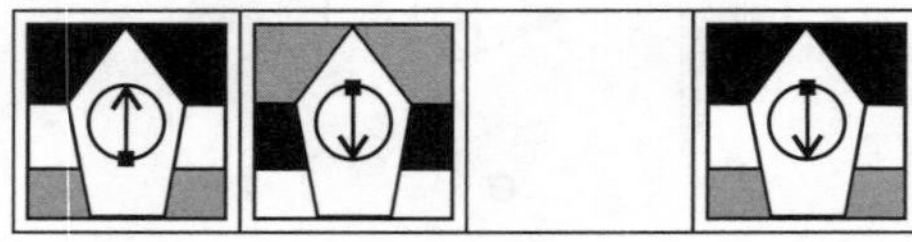

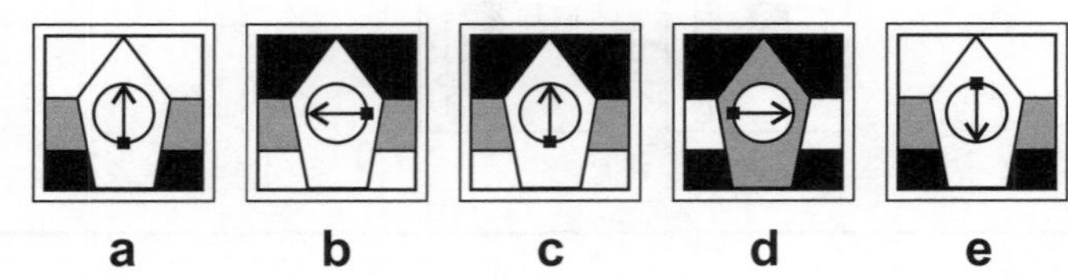

4

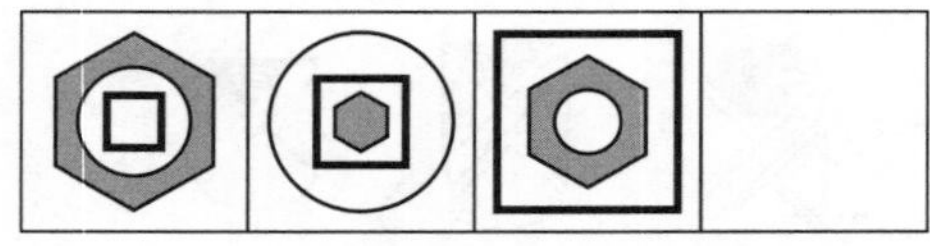

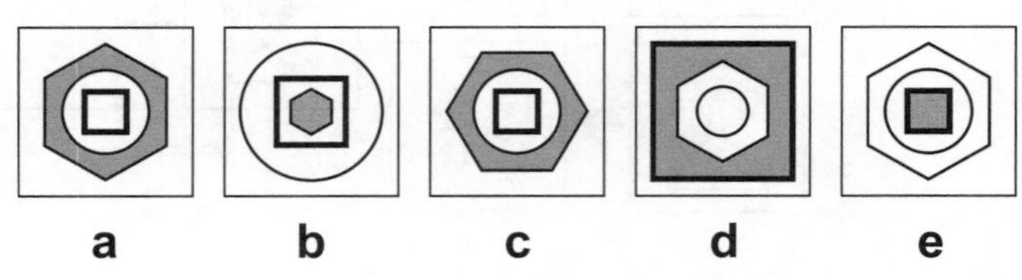

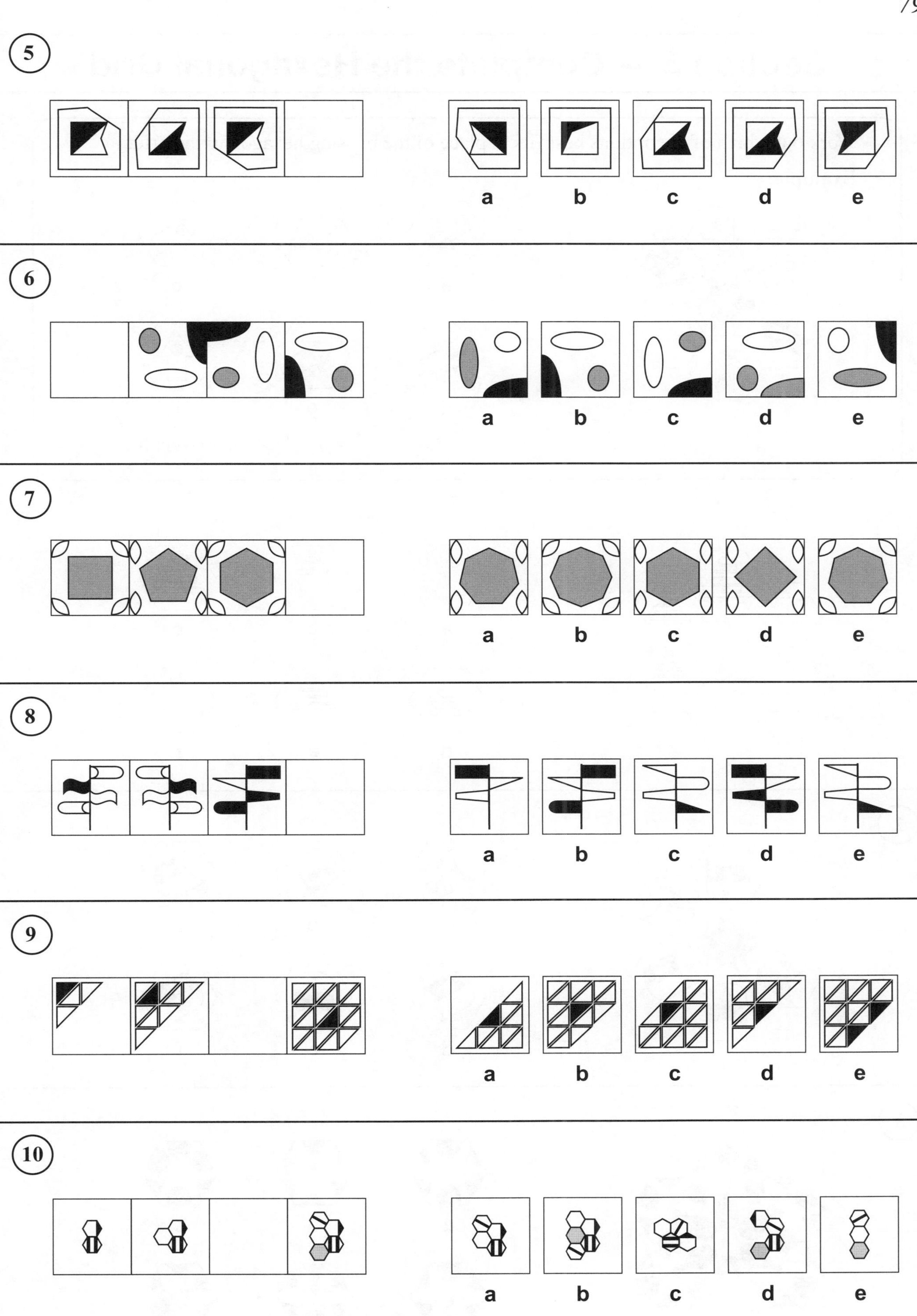

/ 10

Section 5 — Complete the Hexagonal Grid

Work out which of the options best fits in place of the missing hexagon in the grid.

Example:

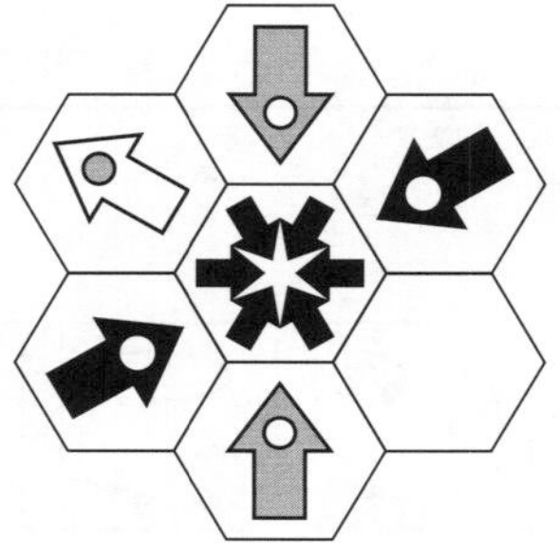

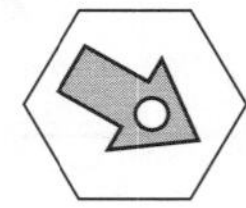
a

b

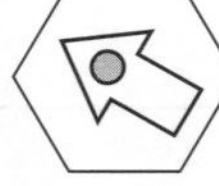
c

d

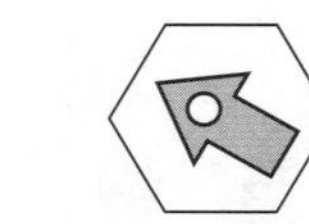

e

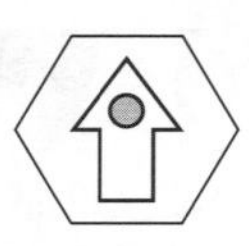
f

Answer: b

(1)

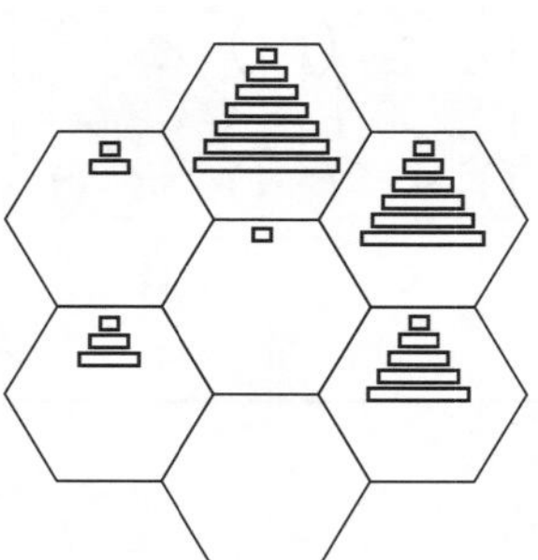

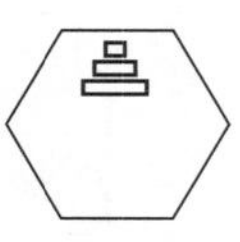
a

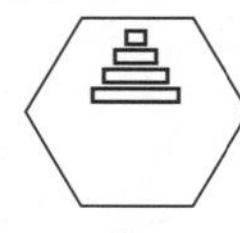
b

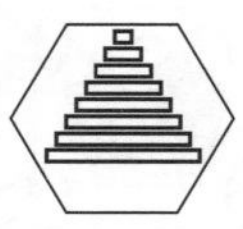
c

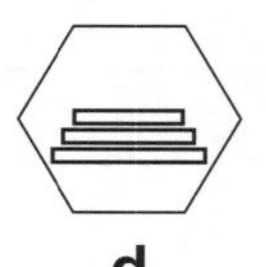
d

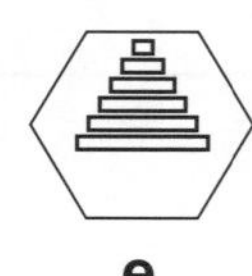
e

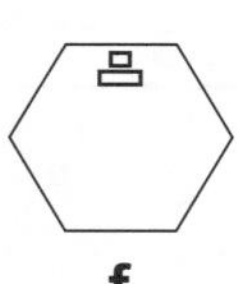
f

(2)

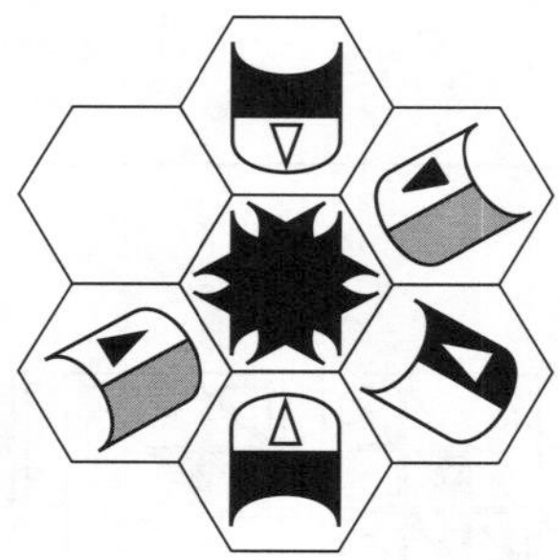

a

b

c

d

e

f

(3)

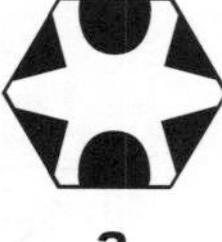
a

b

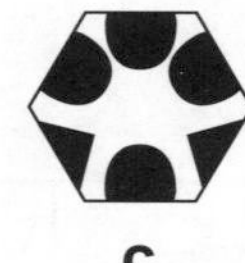
c

d

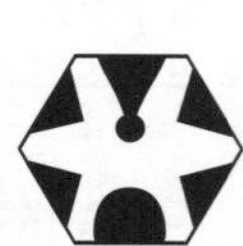
e

f

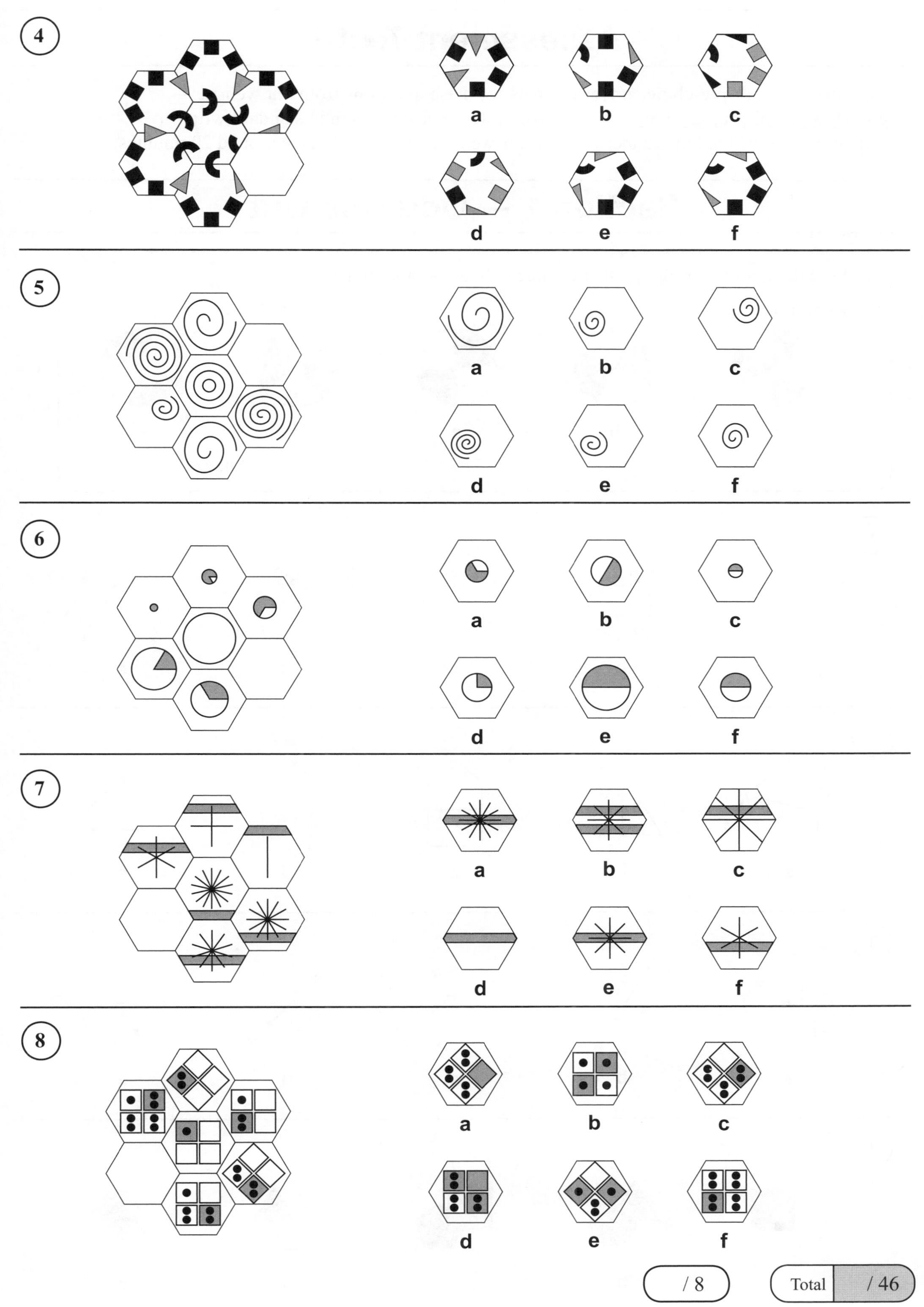

/ 8

Total / 46

END OF TEST

Assessment Test 7

You can print **multiple-choice answer sheets** for these questions from our website — go to www.cgplearning.co.uk/11+. If you'd prefer to answer them in standard write-in format, just circle the letter underneath the answer. The test should take around 20 minutes.

Section 1 — Odd One Out

Find the figure in each row that is most unlike the other figures.

Example:

a b c d e

Answer: a

1

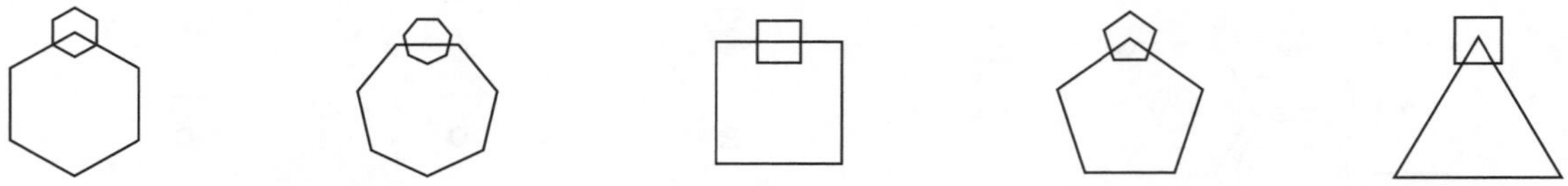

a b c d e

2

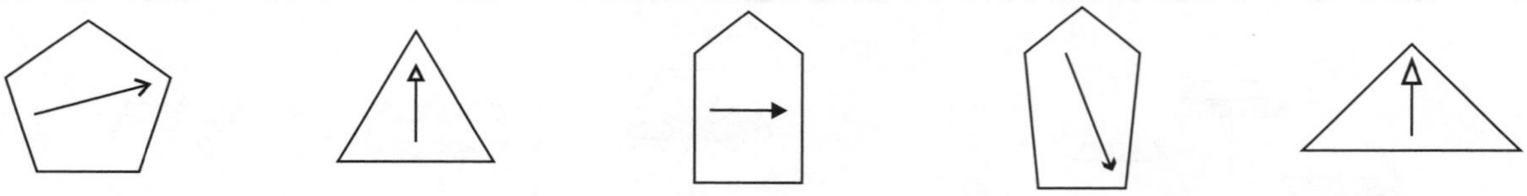

a b c d e

3

a b c d e

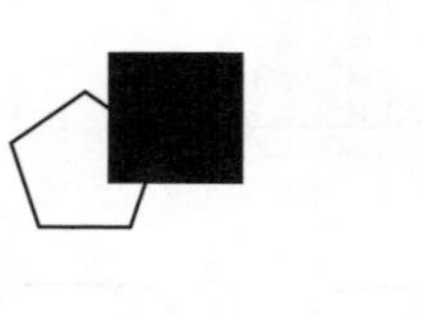

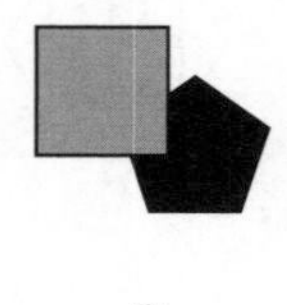

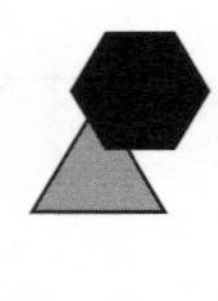

a b c d e

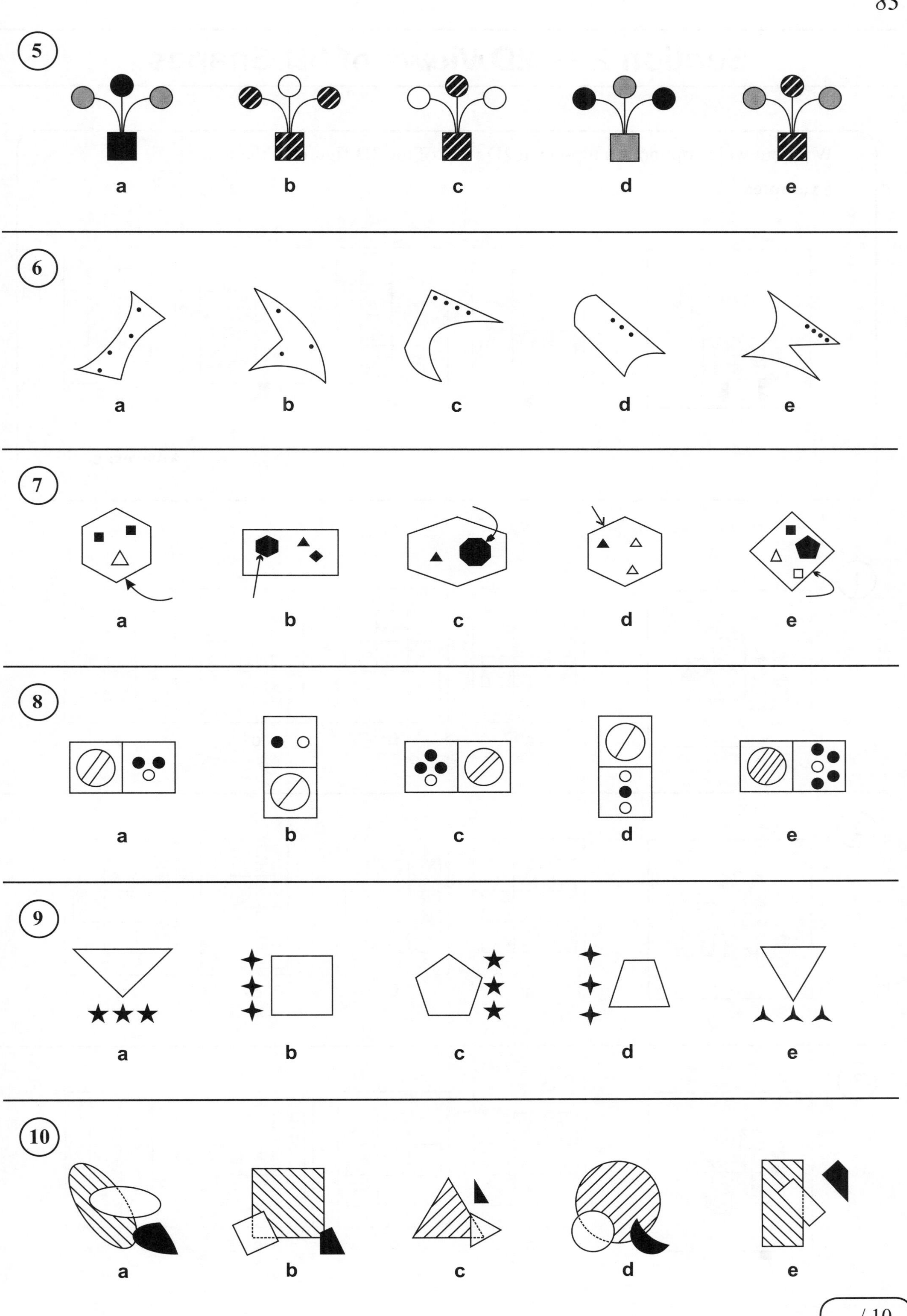

/ 10

Section 2 — 2D Views of 3D Shapes

Work out which option is a top-down 2D view of the 3D figure on the left.

Example:

a b c d

Answer: c

1

a b c d

2

a b c d

3

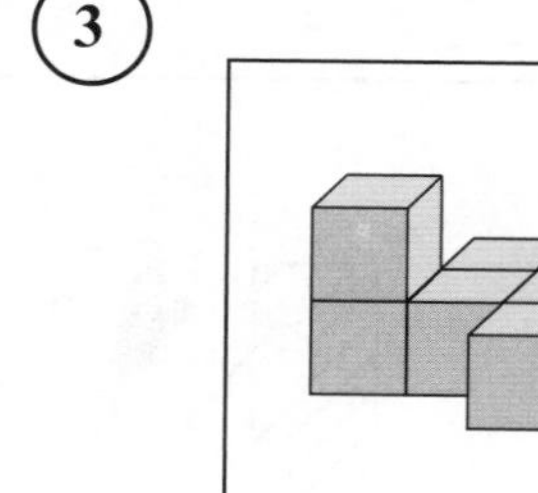

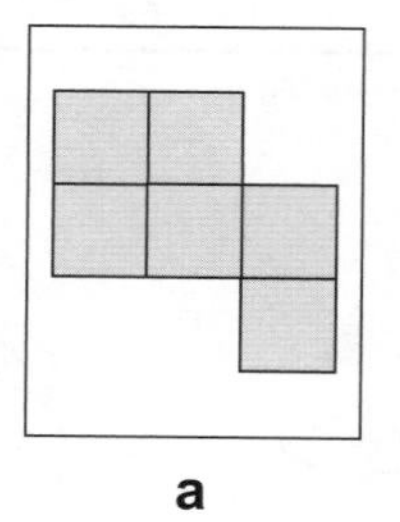

a

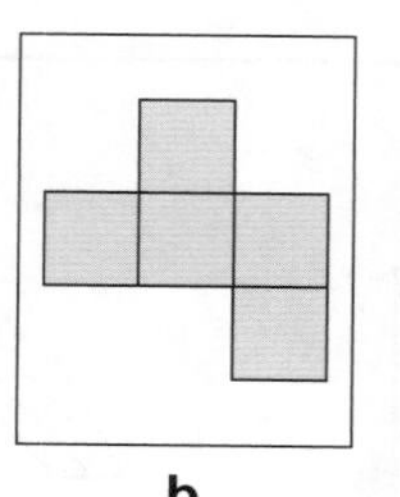

b

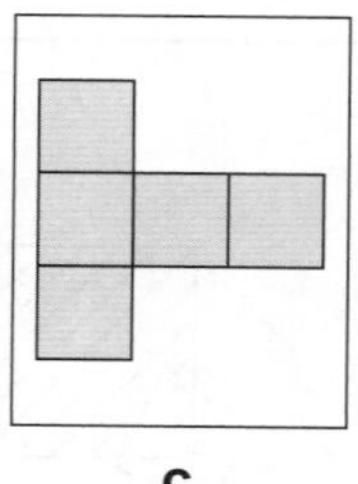

c

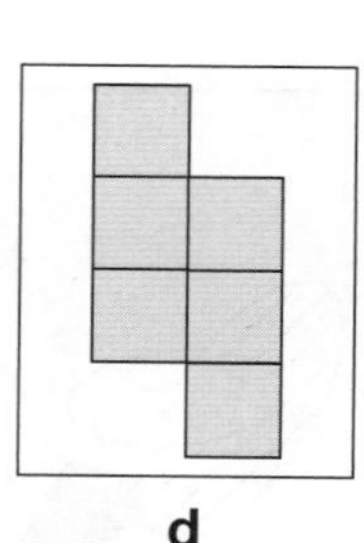

d

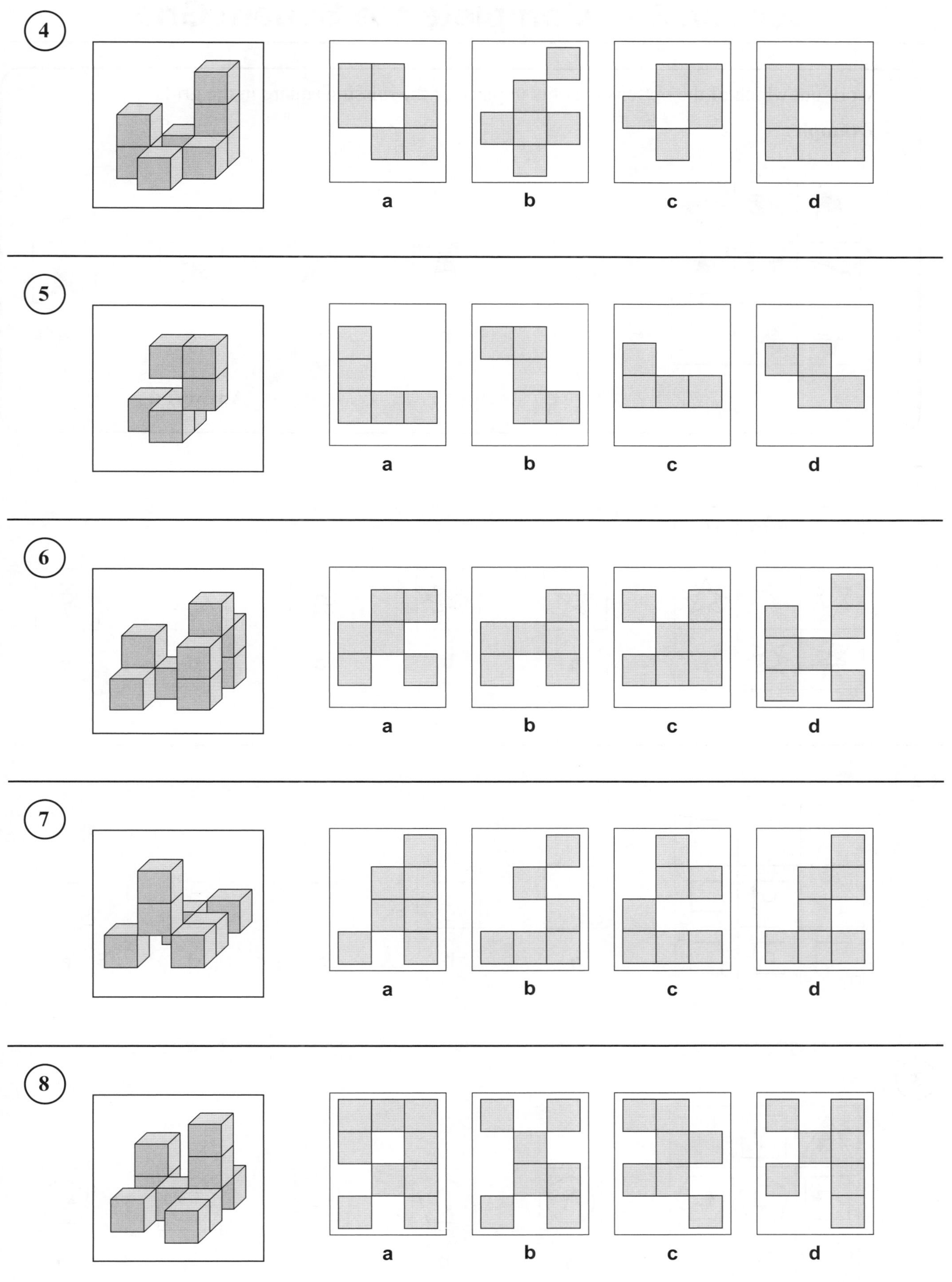

/ 8

Section 3 — Complete the Square Grid

Work out which of the options best fits in place of the missing square in the grid.

Example:

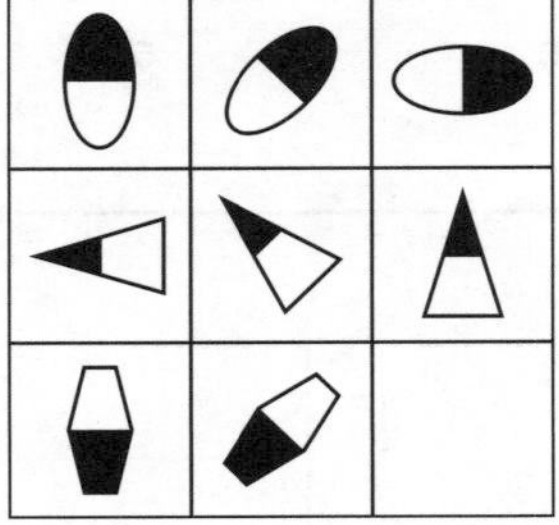

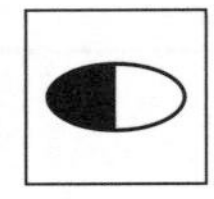
a

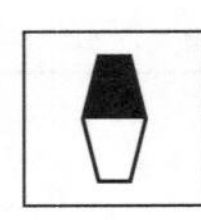
b

c

d

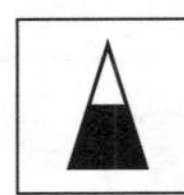
e

Answer: d

1

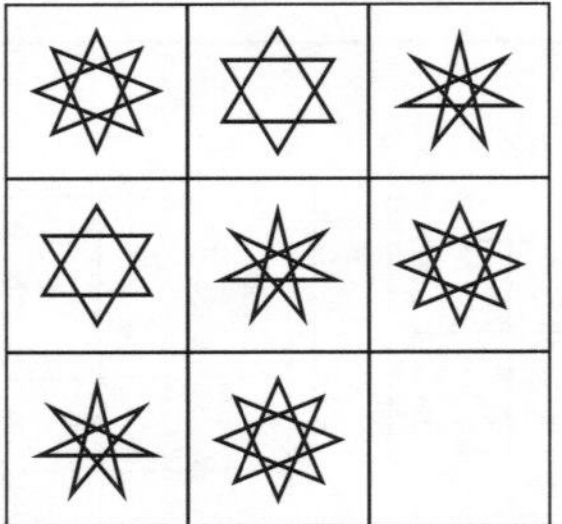

a

b

c

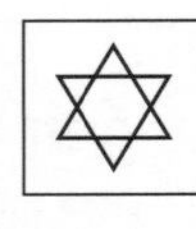
d

e

2

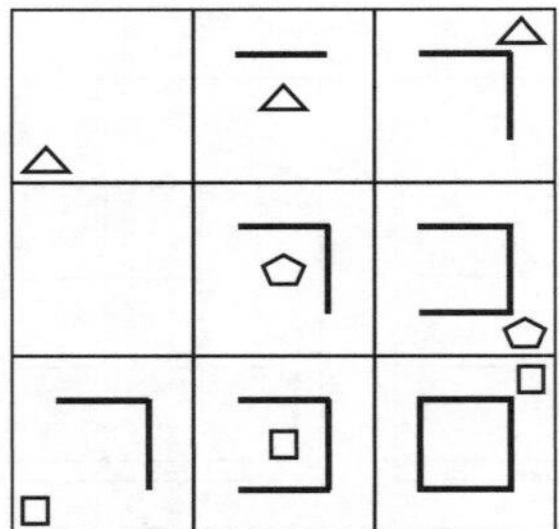

a b c d e

3

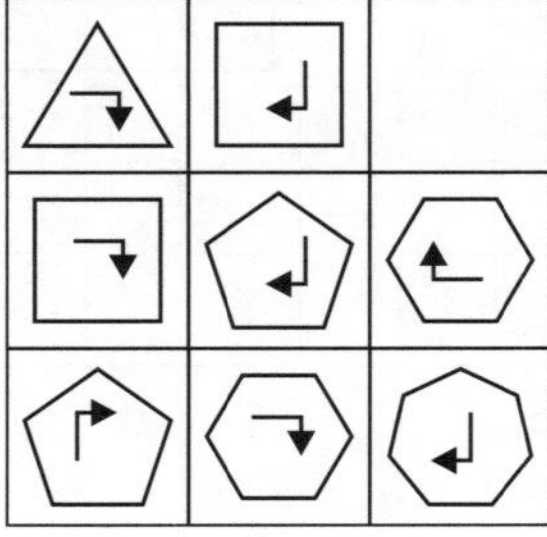

a b c d e

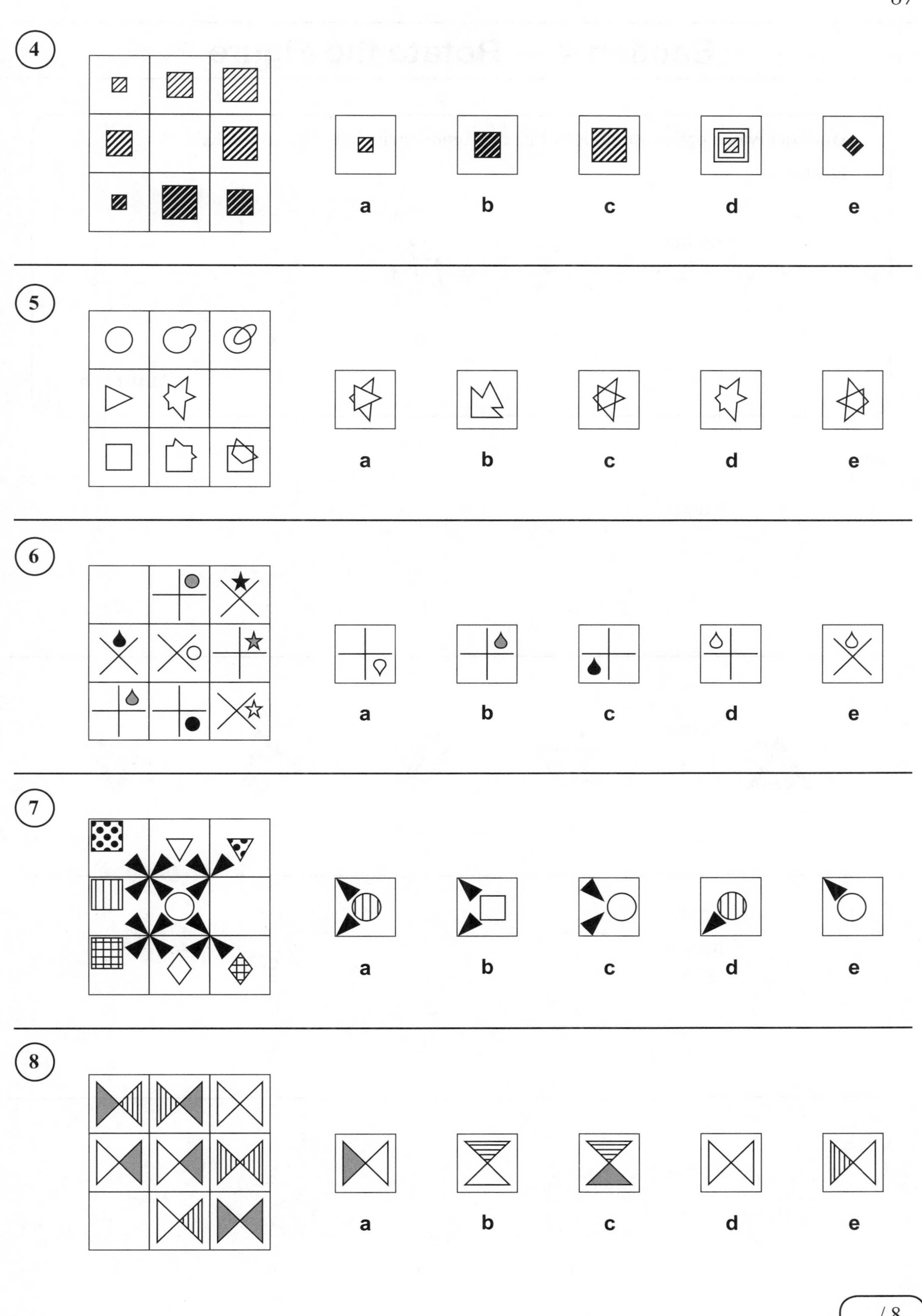

/ 8

Section 4 — Rotate the Figure

Work out which option would look like the figure on the left if it was rotated.

Example:

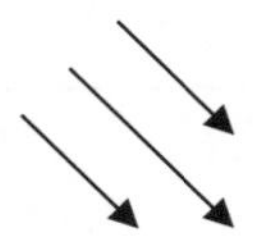

Rotate

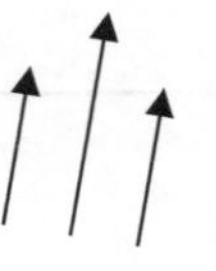

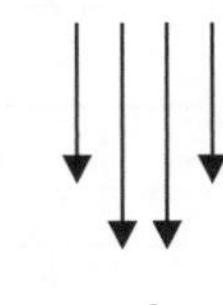

a b c d

Answer: b

(1)

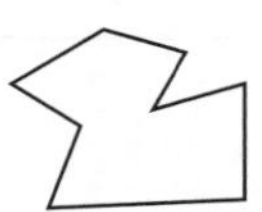

Rotate

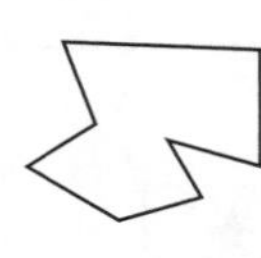

a b c d

(2)

Rotate

a b c d

(3)

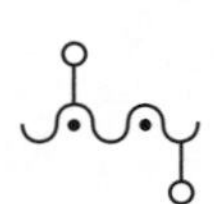

Rotate

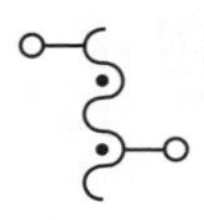

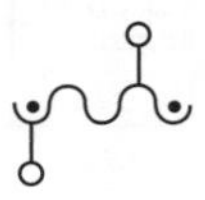

a b c d

(4)

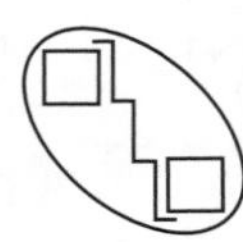

Rotate

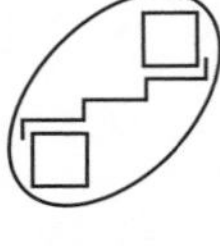

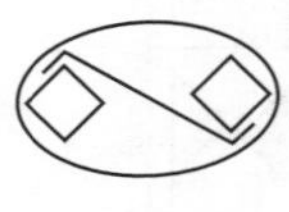

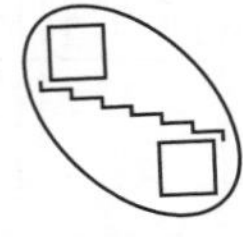

a b c d

(5)

Rotate

a b c d

(6)

Rotate

a b c d

(7)

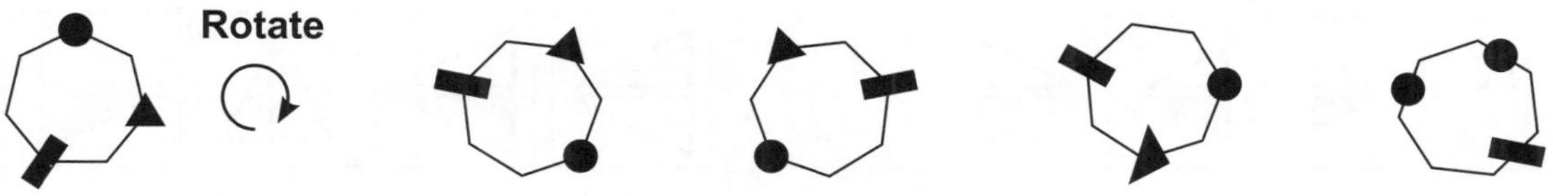

Rotate

a b c d

(8)

Rotate

a b c d

(9)

Rotate

a b c d

(10)

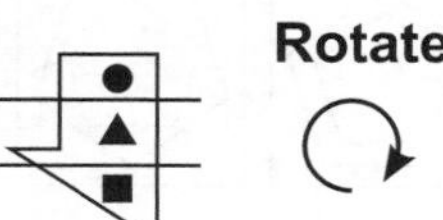

Rotate

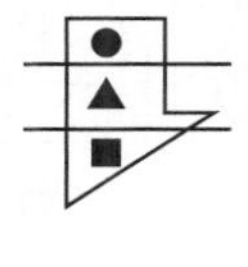

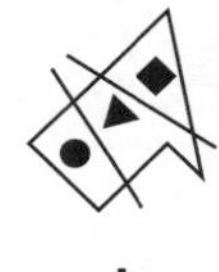

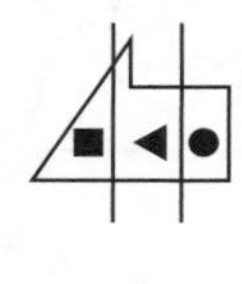

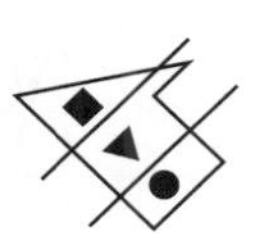

a b c d

/ 10

Section 5 — Complete the Series

Work out which of the options best fits in place of the missing square in the series.

Example:

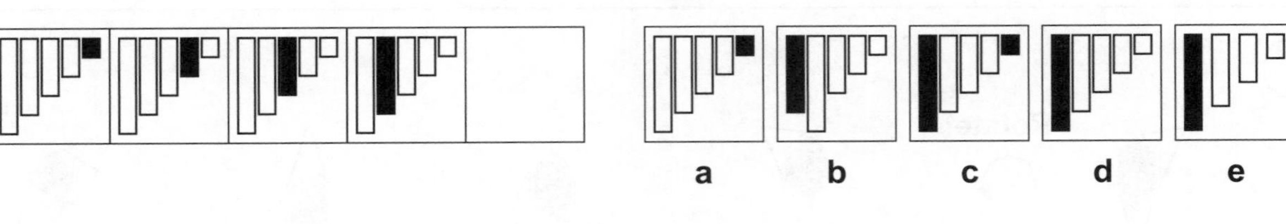

Answer: d

(1)

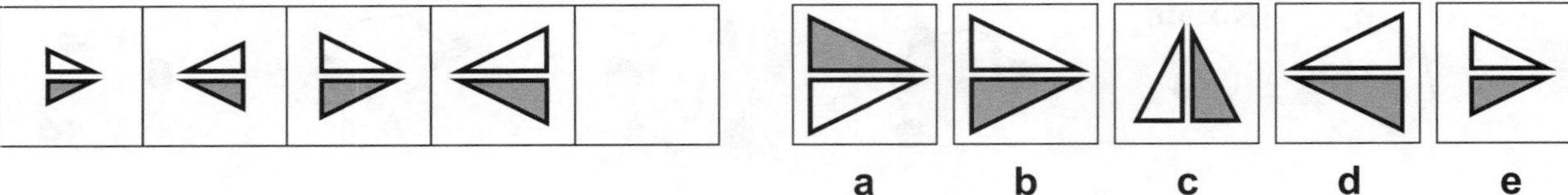

(2)

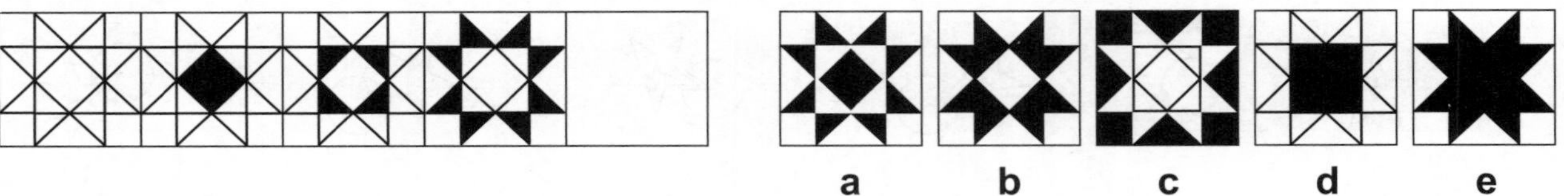

(3)

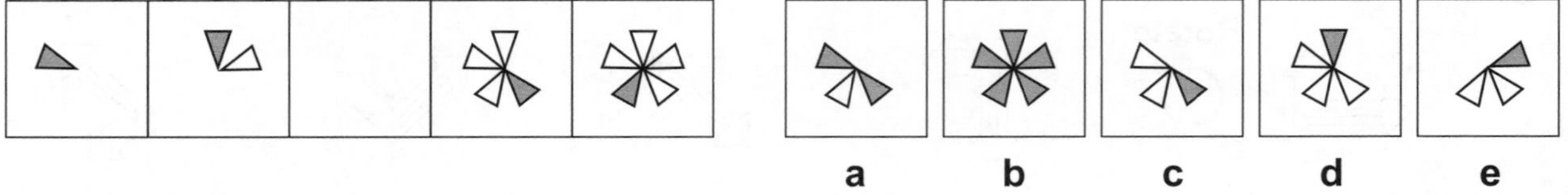

(4)

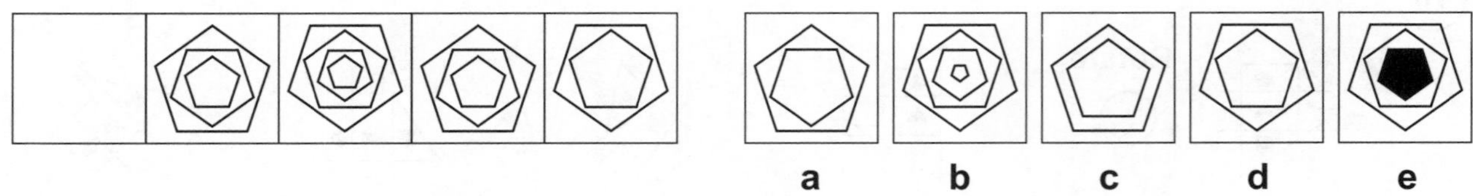

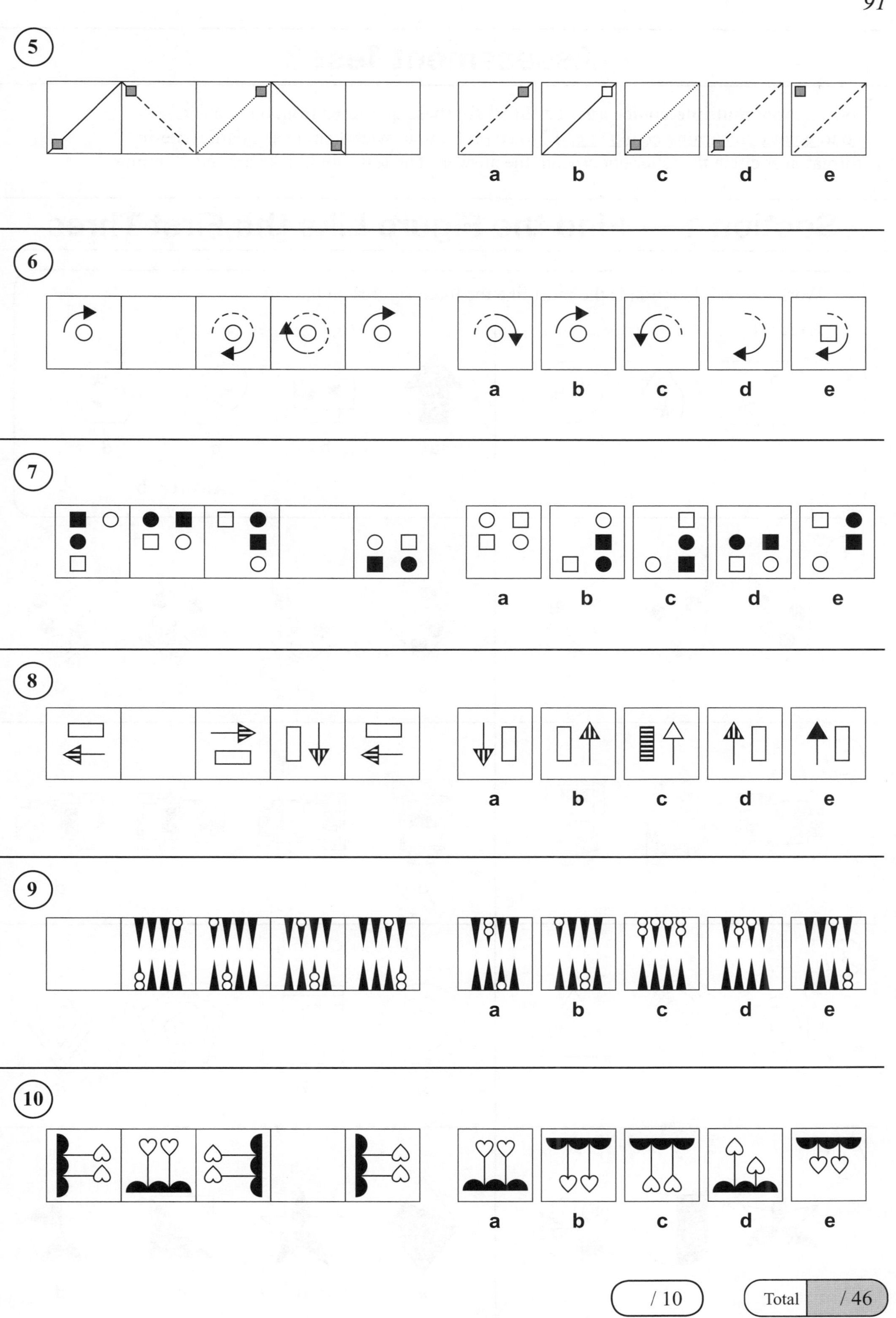

/ 10

Total / 46

END OF TEST

Assessment Test 8

You can print **multiple-choice answer sheets** for these questions from our website — go to www.cgplearning.co.uk/11+. If you'd prefer to answer them in standard write-in format, just circle the letter underneath the answer. The test should take around 20 minutes.

Section 1 — Find the Figure Like the First Three

Work out which option is the most like the three figures on the left.

Example:

a b c d

Answer: b

1

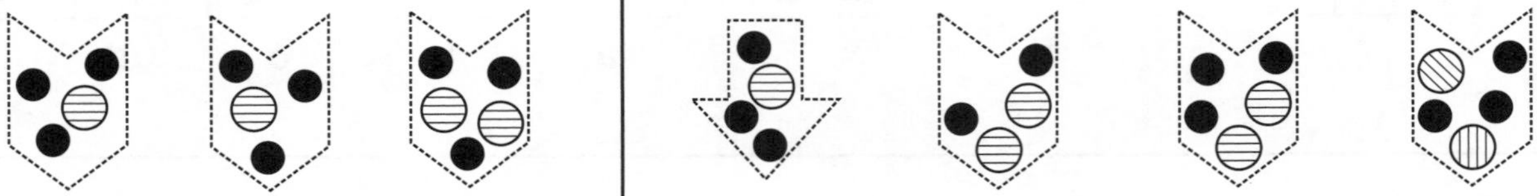

a b c d

2

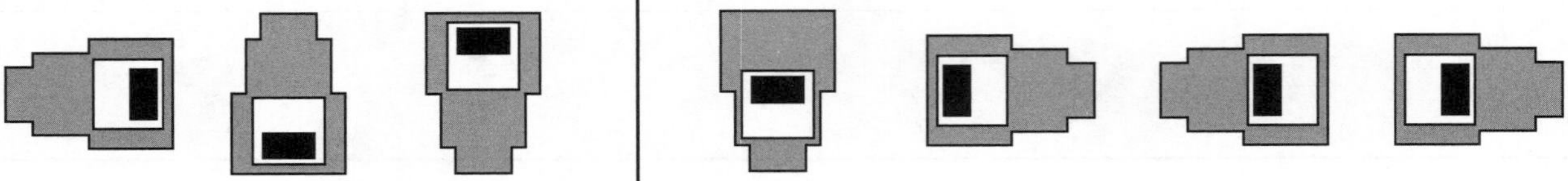

a b c d

3

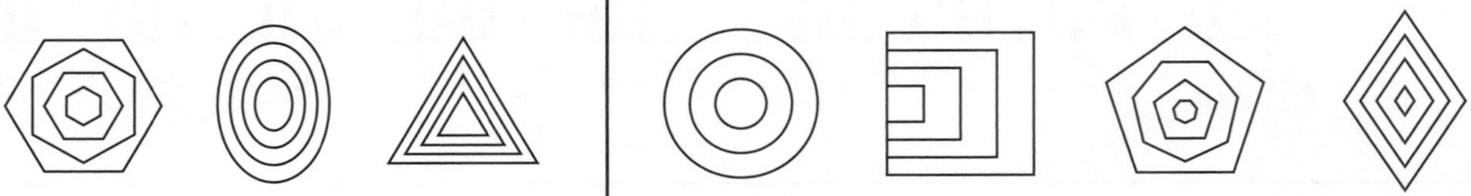

a b c d

4

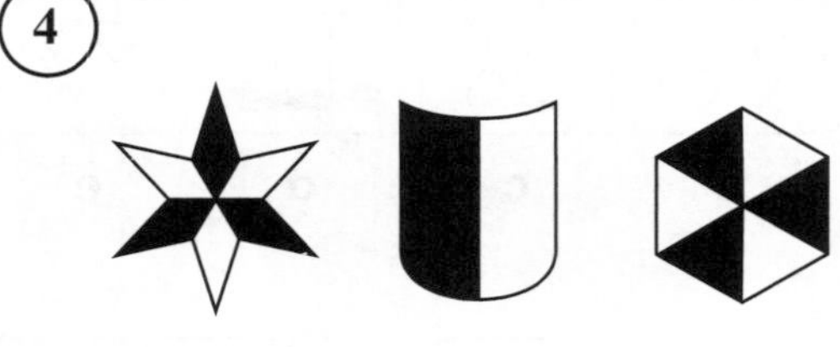

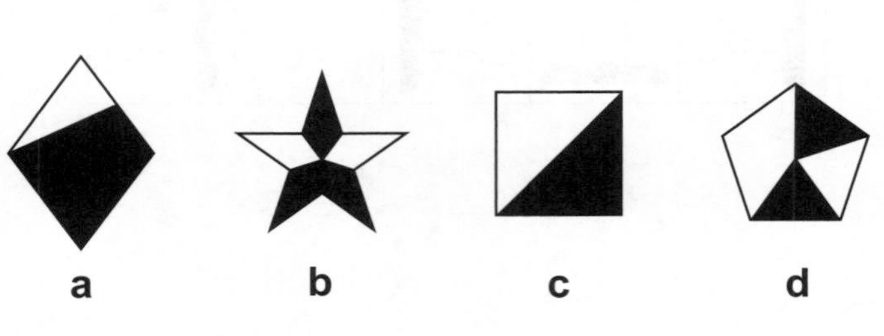

a b c d

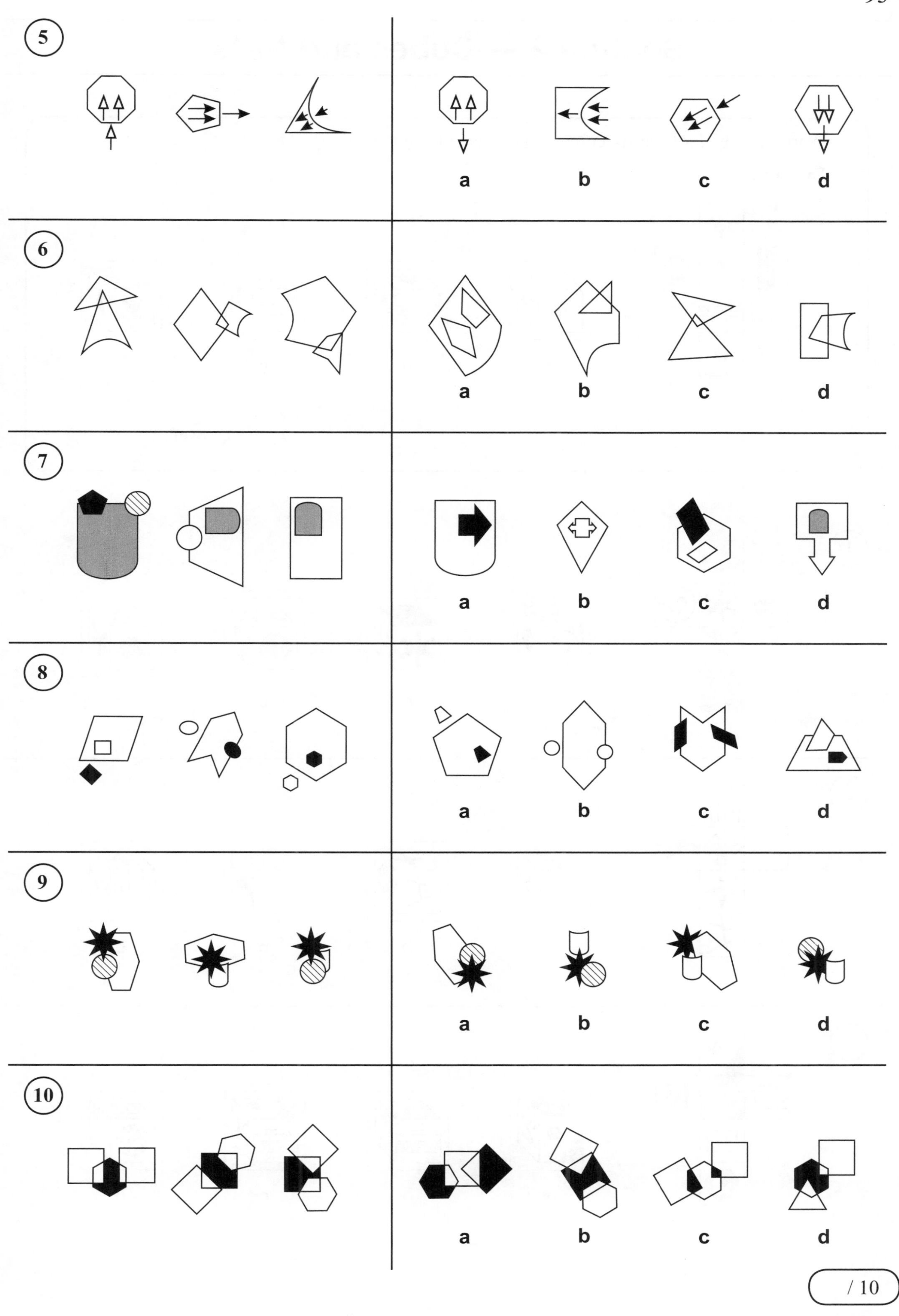

/ 10

Section 2 — Cubes and Nets

Work out which of the six cubes can be made from the net.

Example:

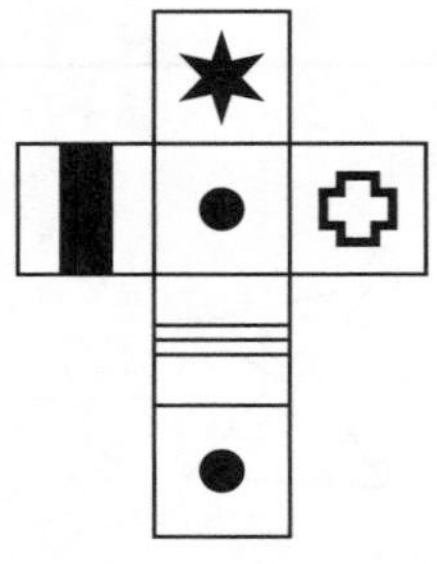

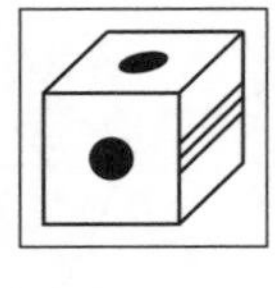

a

b

c

d

Answer: c

1

a

b

c

d

2

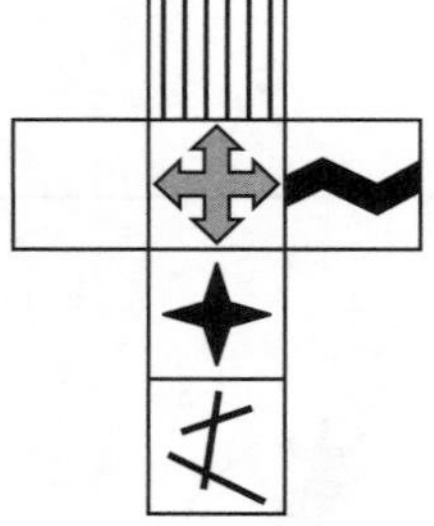

a

b

c

d

3

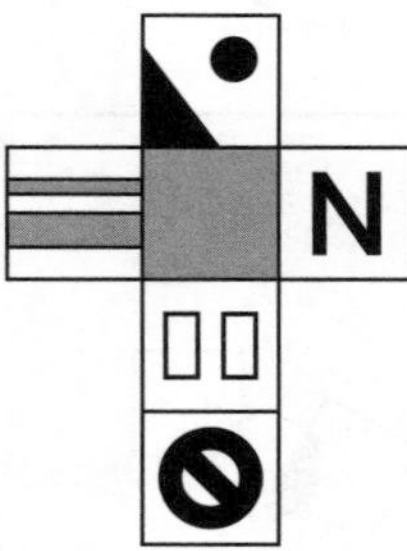

a

b

c

d

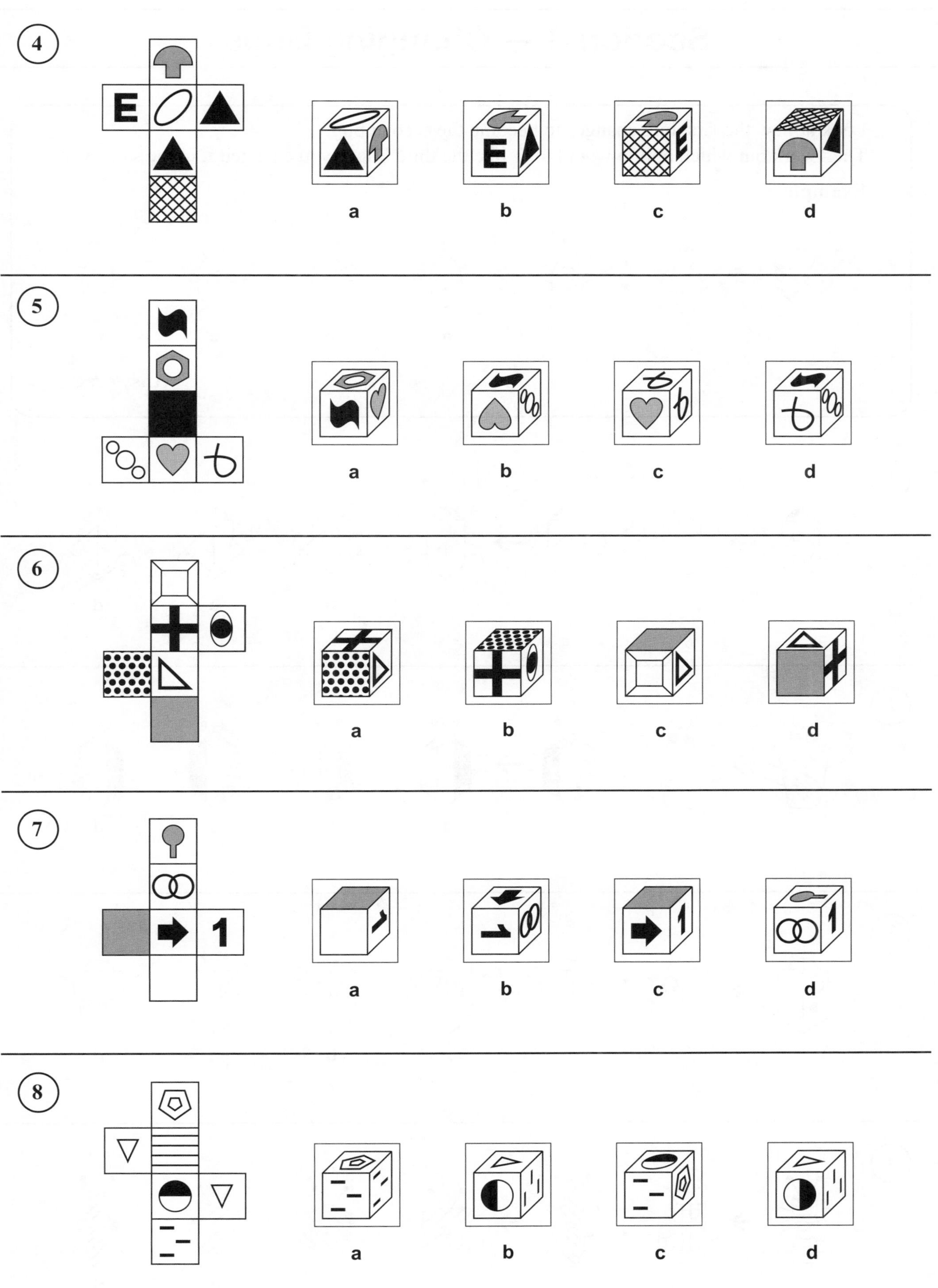

/ 8

Section 3 — Changing Bugs

Look at how the first bug changes to become the second bug.
Then work out which option would look like the third bug if you changed it in the same way.

Example:

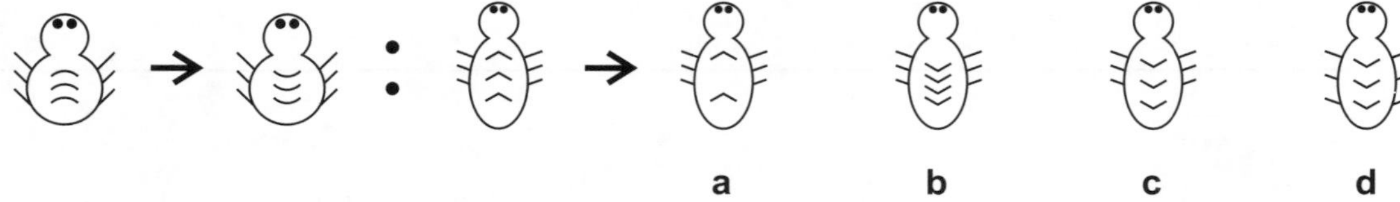

a b c d

Answer: c

1

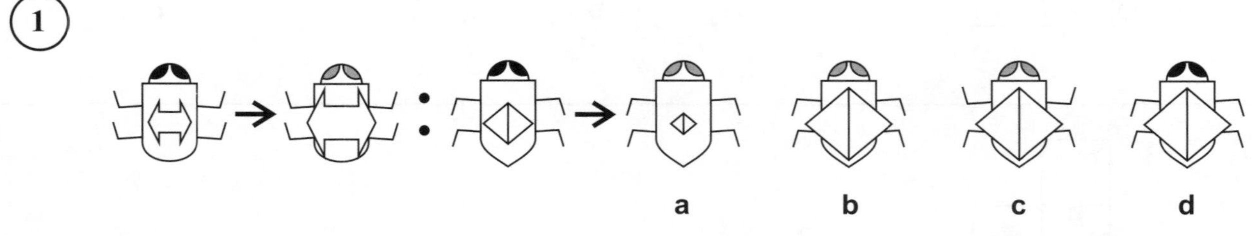

a b c d

2

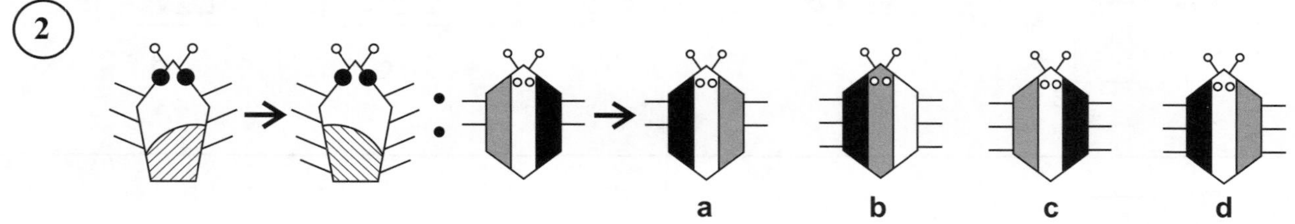

a b c d

3

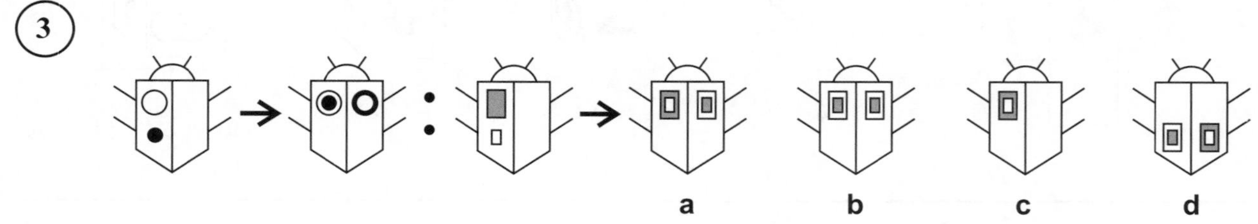

a b c d

4

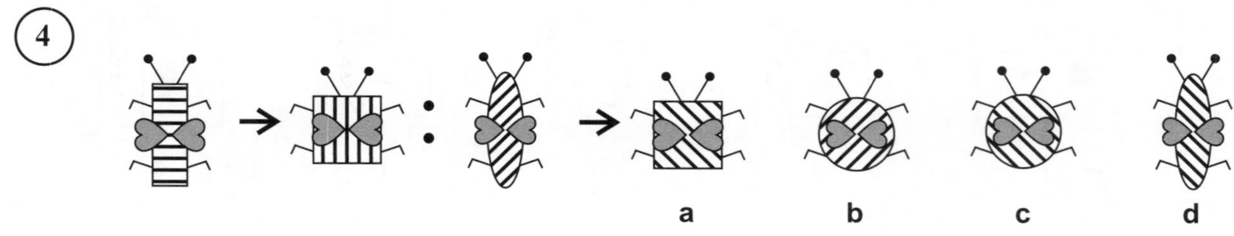

a b c d

5

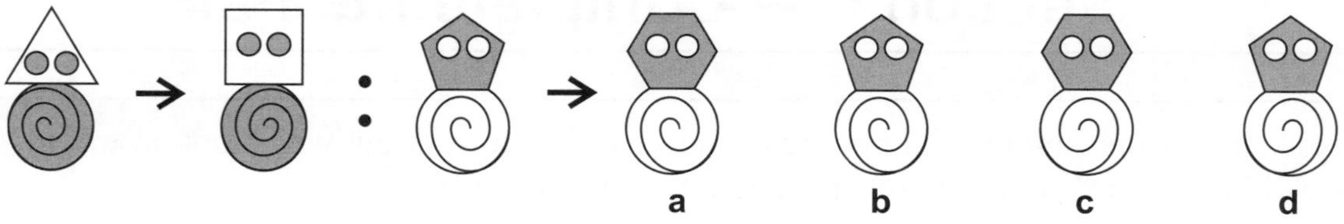

a b c d

6

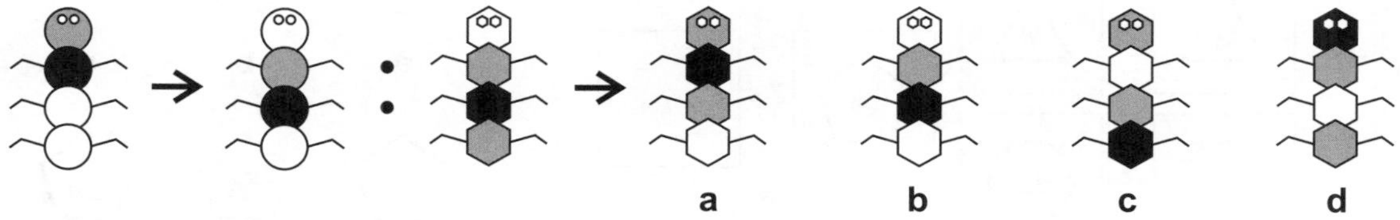

a b c d

7

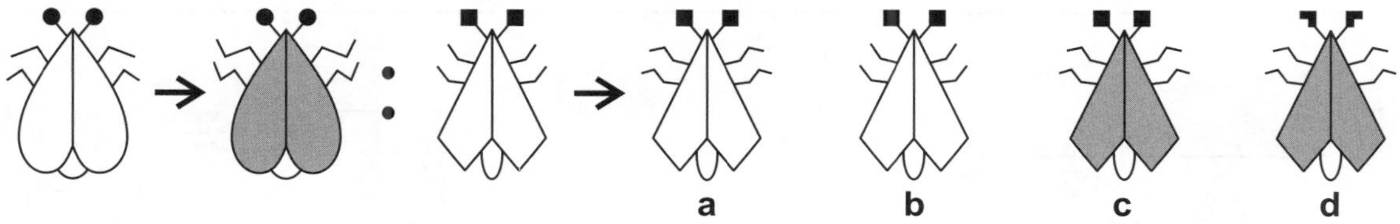

a b c d

8

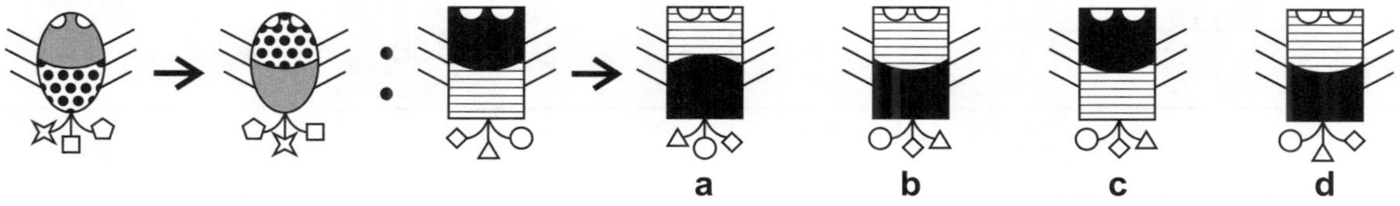

a b c d

9

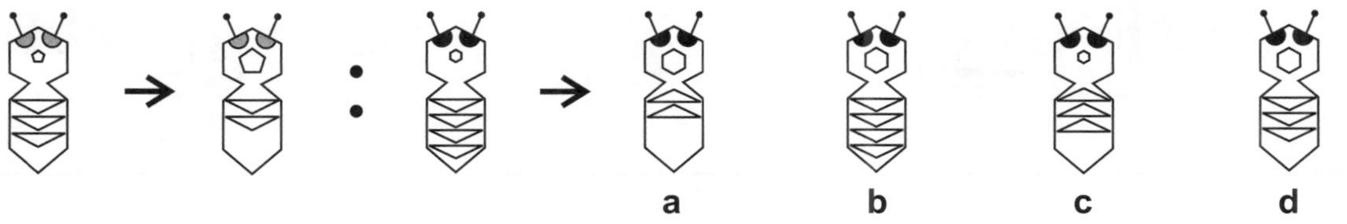

a b c d

10

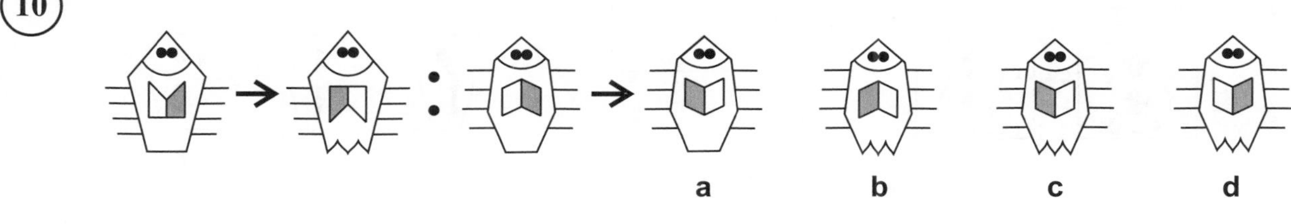

a b c d

/ 10

Section 4 — Complete the Pair

Look at how the first two figures are changed, and then work out which option would look like the third figure if you changed it in the same way.

Example:

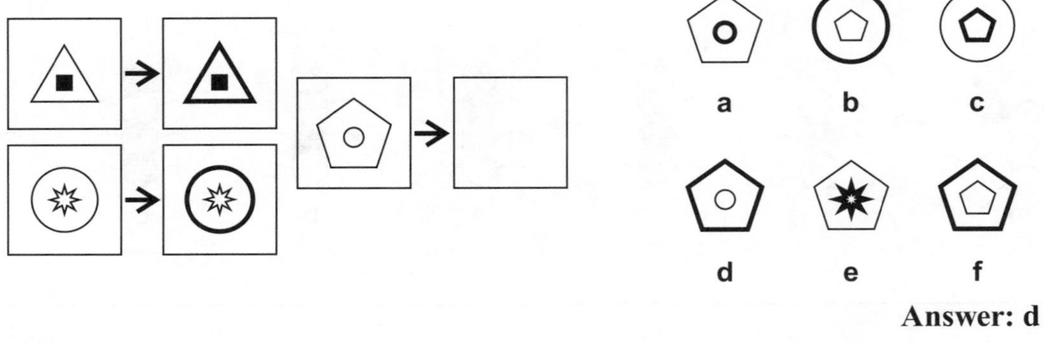

Answer: d

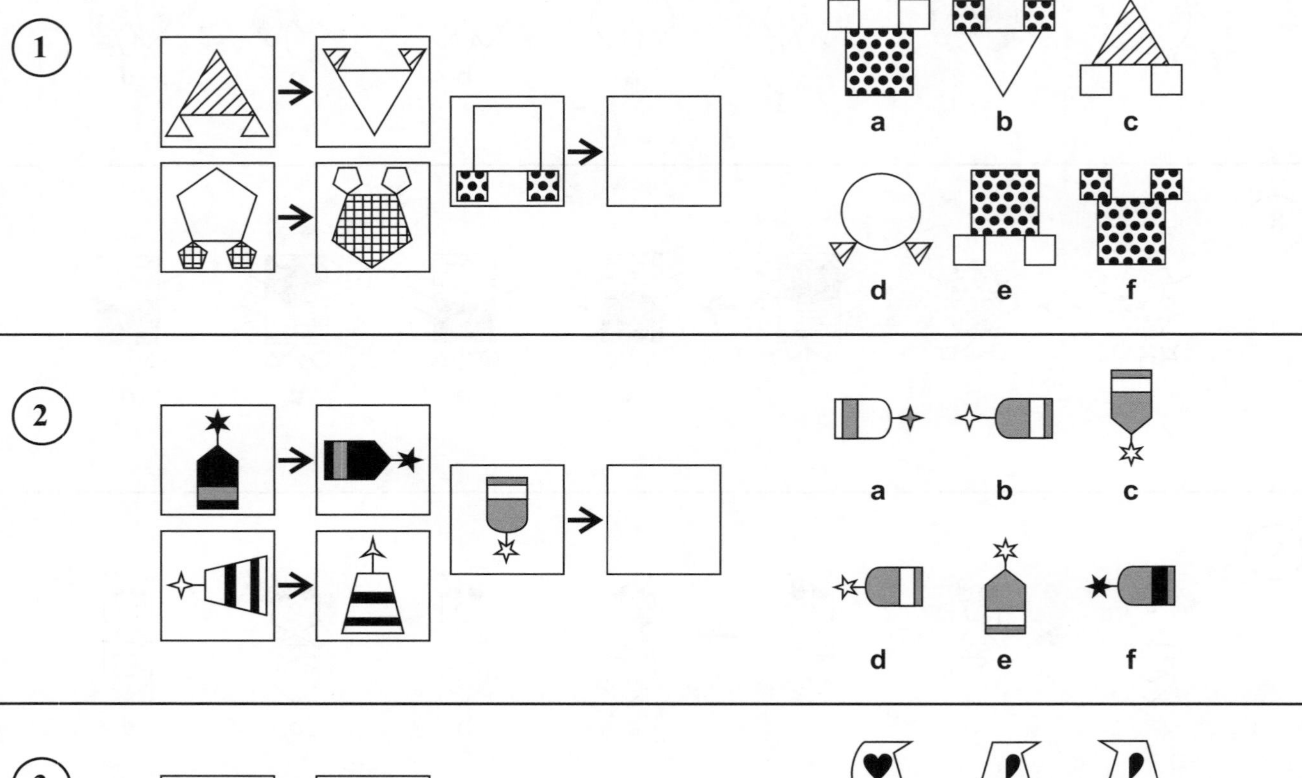

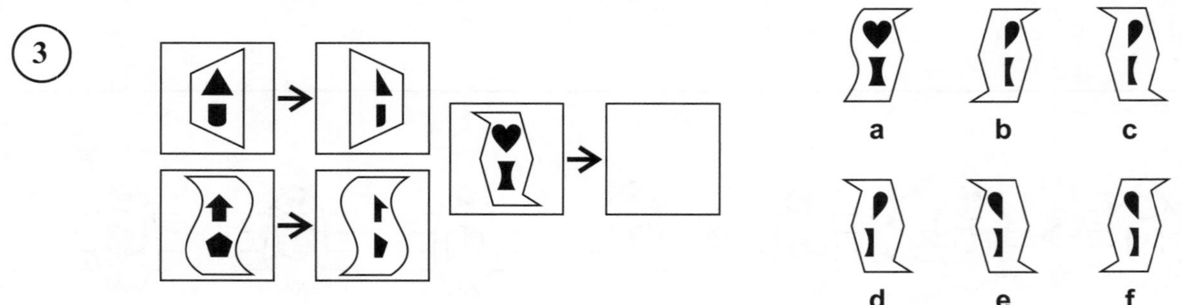

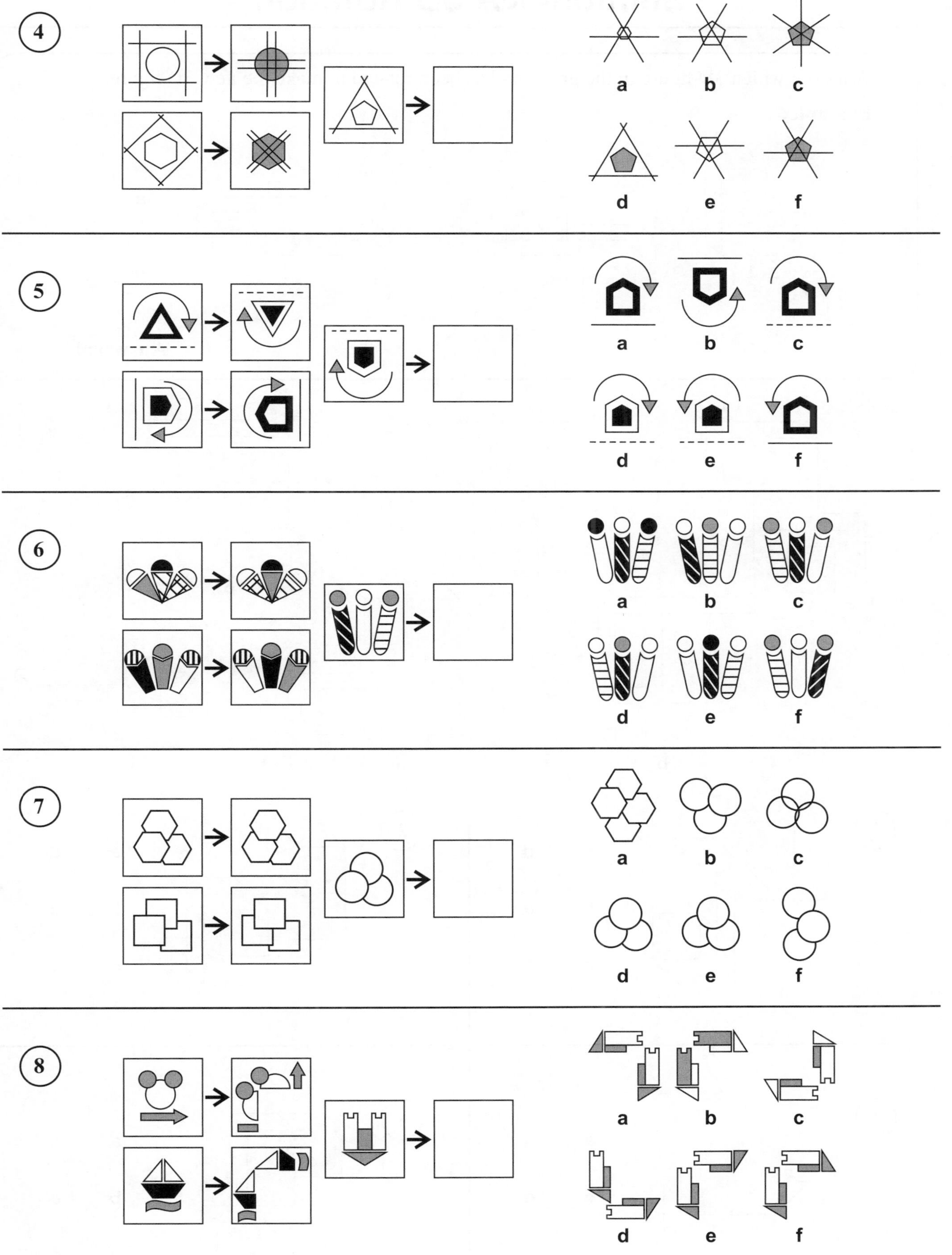

/ 8

Section 5 — 3D Rotation

Work out which 3D figure in the grey box has been rotated to make the new 3D figure.

Example:

a b

a

b

Answer: b

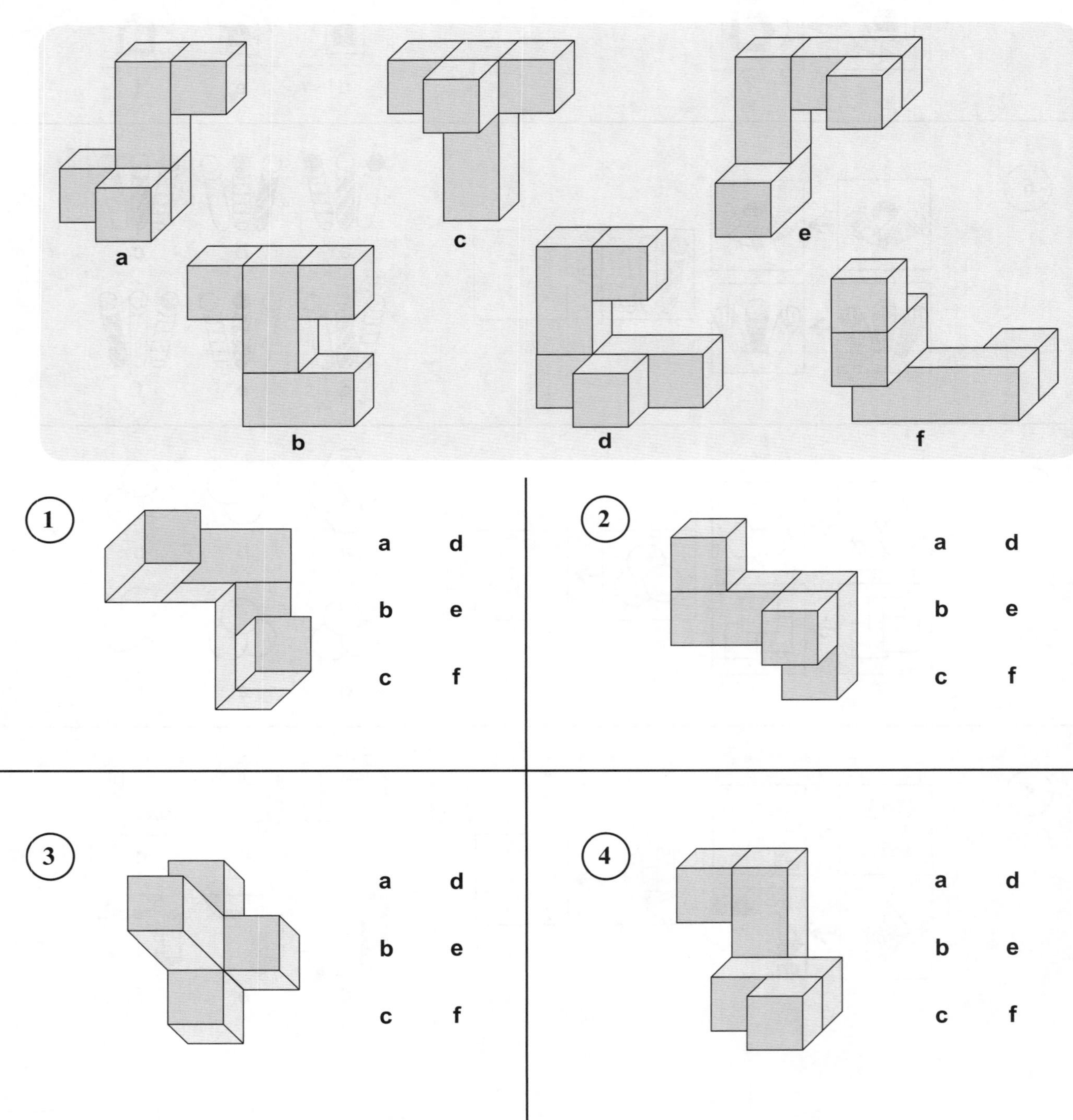

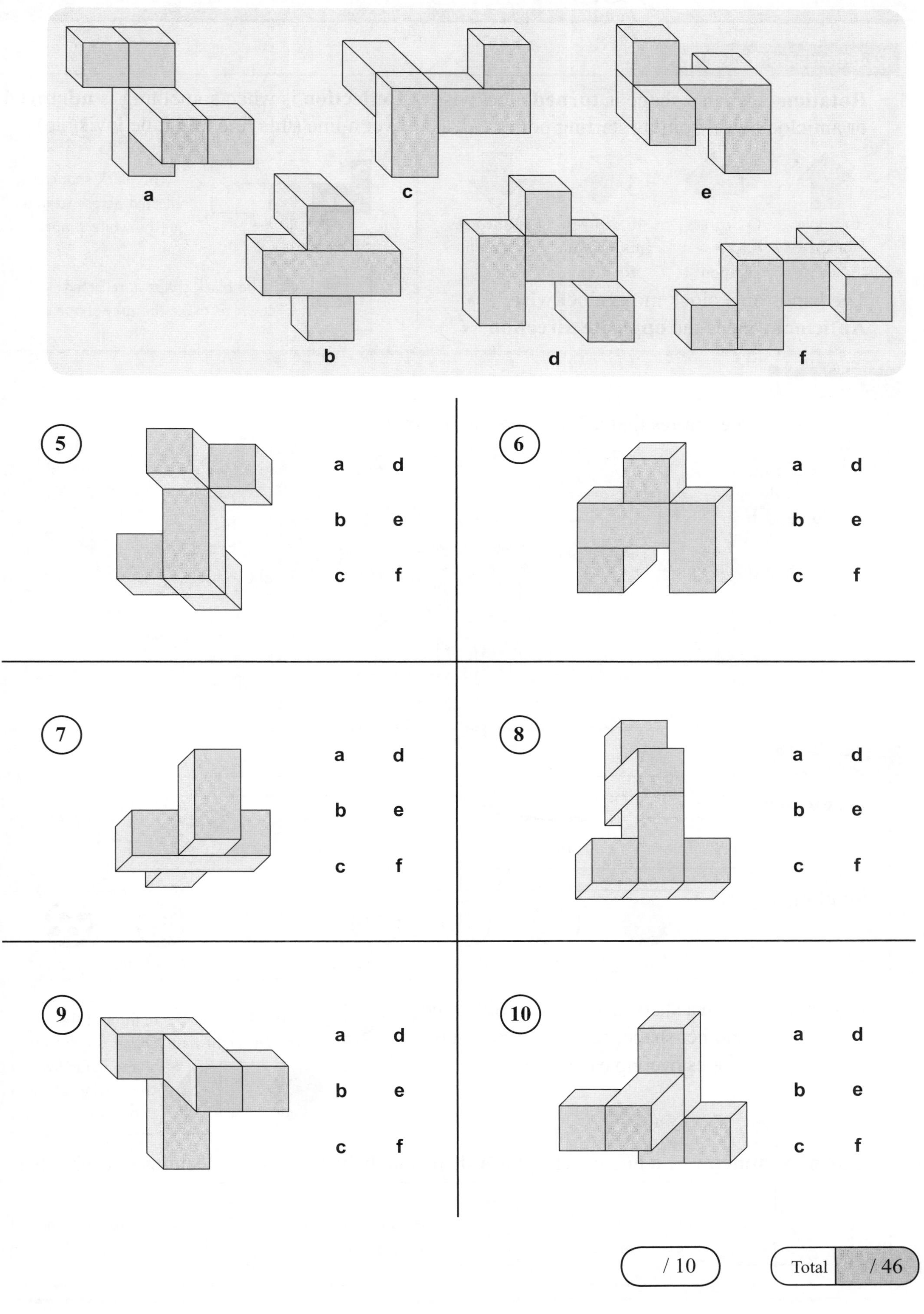

/ 10

Total / 46

END OF TEST

Glossary

Rotation and Reflection

Rotation is when a shape is **turned** clockwise or anticlockwise from its starting point.

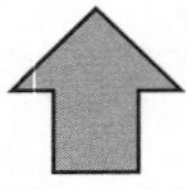

Example shape

90 degrees clockwise rotation

45 degrees anticlockwise rotation

180 degrees rotation

The hands on a clock move **clockwise**: ↻
Anticlockwise is the **opposite direction**: ↺

Reflection is when something is **mirrored** over a line (this line might be invisible).

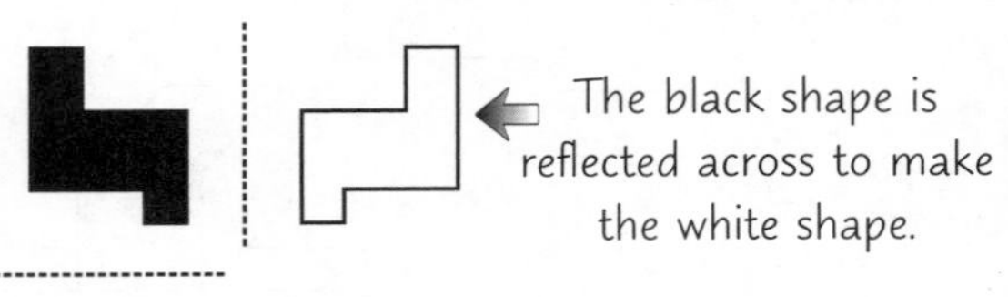

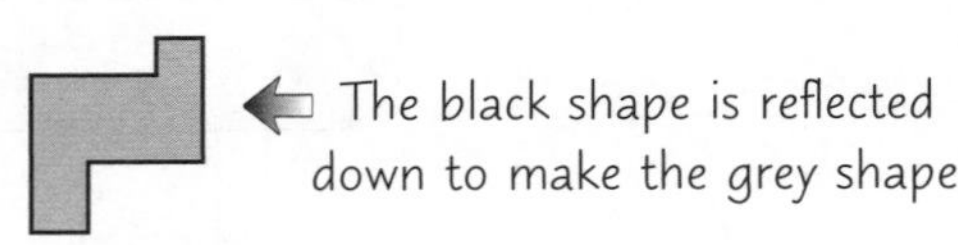

3D Rotation

There are **three planes** that a 3D shape can be rotated in.

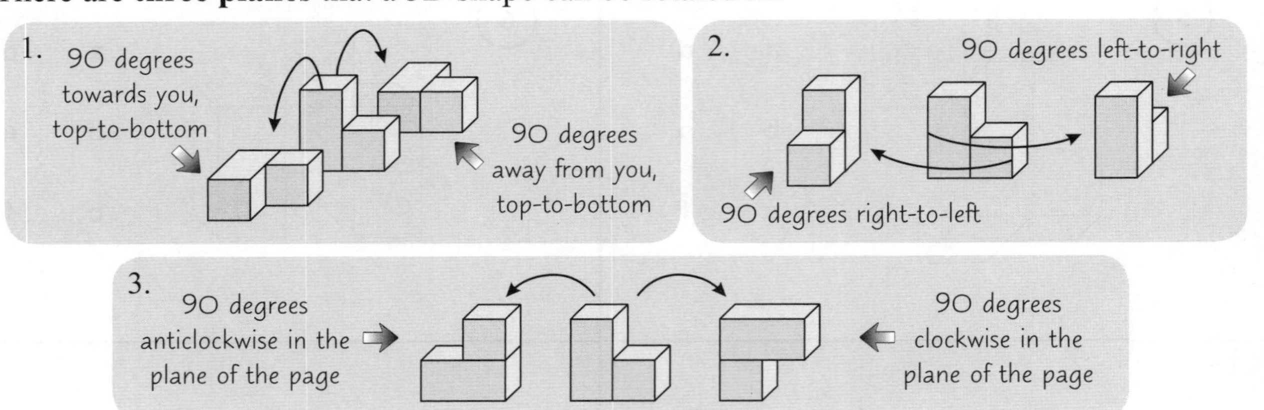

Other terms

Line Types:

Shading Types:

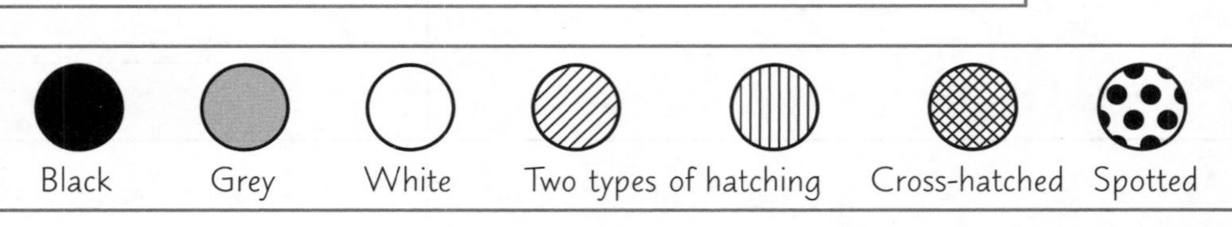

Layering — when a shape is in front of or behind another shape, or where two or more shapes overlap each other.

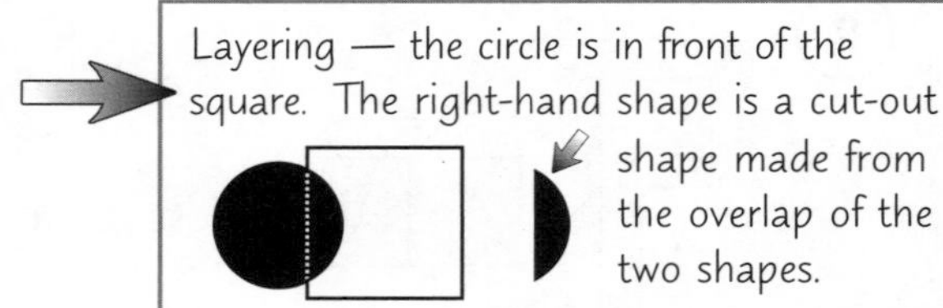

Line of Symmetry — a line which splits a shape into halves that are reflections of each other.

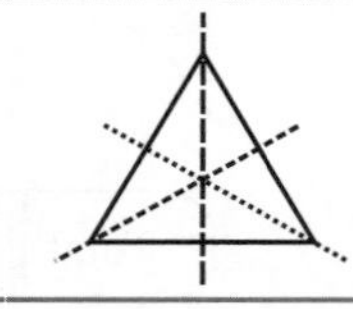

This triangle has three lines of symmetry.

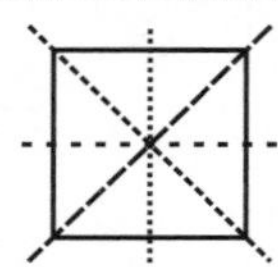

A square has four lines of symmetry.

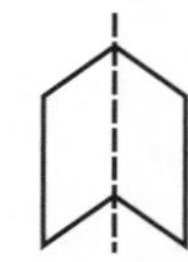

This shape has one line of symmetry.

11+

Non-Verbal Reasoning

Ages
10-11

The
Answer Book

Non-Verbal Reasoning

The 11+ Practice Book

with Assessment Tests

For the CEM (Durham University) test

11+

Practise • Prepare • Pass
Everything your child needs for 11+ success

N6QDE1

SPOTTING PATTERNS

Shapes — p.2-3

Warm Up

1. *a) 6 b) 7 c) 8 d) 8 e) 12 f) 7*

2. *a) 1 b) 0 c) 1 d) 1 e) 3 f) 2 g) 4*

3. *Number of five-sided shapes: 4*

Complete the Series

4. C
In each series square the shape gets narrower.

5. A
The shape gains an extra side in each series square. It alternates between white with a solid outline and grey with a dashed outline.

6. B
Each shape has an extra line of symmetry in each series square.

7. C
In each series square, the black circle gets bigger and the white circle gets smaller.

Complete the Square Grid

8. B
Working from left to right, the shape in each grid square gets bigger.

9. D
Each shape (pentagon, triangle and parallelogram) only appears once in each row and column. Each type of shading (grey, white and spotted) also only appears once in each row and column.

10. B
In each row, the shape in the first grid square gets bigger and moves to the back of the third grid square. The shape in the second grid square gets smaller and moves to the front of the third grid square.

Counting — p.4-5

Warm Up

1. *a) 9 b) 7 c) 9 d) 8 e) 5 f) 8 g) 6*

2. *a) 2 b) 3 c) 5 d) 2 e) 2 f) 4 g) 1*

3. *Number of shapes with three dots: 4*
Number of shapes with five objects: 3

Changing Bugs

4. C
The bug loses two legs and they curve up instead of down.

5. B
The bug gains an extra spike in its tail.

6. B
The bug loses two antennae and gains two legs.

7. D
The bug loses two legs and also loses a bend in each leg.

Complete the Hexagonal Grid

8. B
The rectangles reflect across the middle of the hexagonal grid.

9. A
Going in a clockwise direction from the top left hexagon, the number of points on the star increases by one. The grey point rotates 60 degrees clockwise.

10. A
Going in an anticlockwise direction from the bottom hexagon, the total number of objects (lines and circles) increases by one in each hexagon.

Pointing — p.6-7

Warm Up

1. *a) 2 b) 3 c) 4 d) 3 e) 2 f) 4 g) 2*

2. *a) yes b) no c) no d) no e) no f) yes g) yes*

3. *Most common direction: right*
Type of shape: circle

Odd One Out

4. E
In all other figures, the arrow points at the white shape.

5. C
In all other figures, the arrow points clockwise.

6. D
In all other figures, the arrow points to a corner.

7. B
In all other figures, the arrow points away from the grey shape.

Find the Figure Like the First Two

8. D
All figures must have two arrows pointing down and one arrow pointing up.

9. B
In all figures, all inner lines must point exactly in the direction of the small black shape.

10. C
All figures must have two arrows pointing clockwise, and one arrow pointing anticlockwise.

Shading and Line Types — p.8-9

Warm Up

1. *Number of arrows hatched the same, ignoring rotation: 3*
Number of arrows hatched the same, correcting for rotation: 3

2. *Number of shapes with the same outline: 4 (second, fourth, sixth and ninth figures).*

3. *Most common shading: grey*

Find the Figure Like the First Three

4. D
In all figures, there must be exactly one black dot and one grey dot.

5. C
All figures must be hatched in the same direction — diagonally down to the left.

6. A
The hatching of the innermost shape must be made from the hatchings of both the outer shapes added together.

7. E
In all figures, the shape with the fewest sides must have a dashed outline, and the shape with the most sides must have a solid outline.

Complete the Hexagonal Grid

8. C
The shapes reflect across the middle of the hexagonal grid, keeping the same line type.

9. B
Going in a clockwise direction, the shading of the circle becomes the shading of the square in the next hexagon.

10. B
The outline of the outer circle alternates between solid and dashed. The shading of the inner circle is the same in hexagons on opposite sides of the middle hexagon.

Order and Position — p.10-11

Warm Up

1. *a) grey b) white c) black d) white e) black*

When the rightmost shading moves a place to the right, it then appears as the leftmost shading.

2. i) *a) circle b) triangle c) star d) circle e) square f) star*

   ii) *a) grey b) grey c) black d) grey e) white f) grey*

3. *a) circle b) star c) arrow d) pentagon e) square*

Odd One Out

4. D
In all other figures, the black shape is at the top.

5. B
In all other figures, from left to right, the shapes are in the order: six-sided shape, five-sided shape, four-sided shape.

6. B
In all other figures, there is a four-sided shape at the bottom.

7. A
In all other figures, the three shapes go in the order: circle, square, triangle, going clockwise round the large shape.

Complete the Series

8. A
In each series square, the black circle moves one place to the right. The cross moves anticlockwise around the four corners of the series square.

9. A
In each series square, the square moves clockwise around the four corners of the series square. The black line inside the square moves one place to the right.

10. B
In each series square, the row of three shapes moves down. The black triangle moves one place to the left.

Rotation — p.12-13

Warm Up

1. *a) 45 b) 90 c) 45 d) 90 e) 45 f) 90*
2. *Number of identical shapes: 4 (second, third, fifth and seventh figures).*
3. *Number of clockwise rotations: 3 (third, fourth and sixth figures).*

Complete the Square Grid

4. B
Working from top to bottom, the pentagon rotates 90 degrees clockwise.

5. B
Working from left to right, the whole grid square rotates 90 degrees anticlockwise. The black shading moves from the large circle to the middle-sized circle and then to the small circle.

6. C
Working from left to right, the shape rotates 45 degrees clockwise in each grid square.

7. C
Working from left to right, the arrow rotates 90 degrees anticlockwise and moves one position clockwise round the four sides of each grid square.

Rotate the Figure

8. B
The figure is rotated 45 degrees clockwise. Options A and C are rotated reflections. Option D is a different shape.

9. A
The figure is rotated 90 degrees anticlockwise. Option B is a rotated reflection. In option C, the dashed square overlaps the grey rectangle. Option D has the wrong shading.

10. C
The figure is rotated 180 degrees. In option A, the arrowheads are at the wrong ends of the lines. Option B has too many arrowheads. In option D, the arrowhead is at the wrong end of the dashed line.

Reflection — p.14-15

Warm Up

1. *a) reflection b) reflection c) rotation d) reflection e) rotation f) rotation*

2. *a) no b) no c) yes d) yes e) no f) yes*

3. *Number of reflections: 4 (second, fourth, sixth and seventh figures).*

Reflect the Figure

4. B
Option A is a downwards reflection. Option C is a reflection across and downwards. In option D, the small black shape has not been reflected correctly.

5. C
Option A is a 180 degree rotation. Option B has too many grey sections. Option D is identical to the original figure.

6. B
In option A, the black and grey shapes have swapped shadings. In option C, the black wave has not reflected and the white circle is in front of the lightning bolt. In option D, the white circle is positioned incorrectly and the black shape has changed.

7. D
Options A and B are rotations. In option C, the figure has not been reflected.

Complete the Pair

8. A
The figure reflects downwards.

9. D
The shape reflects diagonally over the dashed line.

10. C
The large shape does not change. The small shape reflects across the centre of the large shape.

Layering — p.16-17

Warm Up

1. *a) 4 b) 5 c) 6 d) 3 e) 6 f) 4 g) 4*

2. *a) 3 b) 2 c) 4 d) 2 e) 1 f) 3*

3. *a) S b) D c) S d) D e) S f) D*

Odd One Out

4. B
In all other figures, the white shape at the bottom is in front of the heart shape.

5. C
In all other figures, the grey shape is layered in between the other two shapes.

6. C
In all other figures, the circle with the cross is at the back.

7. C
In all other figures, the small shape made by the overlap of the two large shapes has four sides.

Complete the Pair

8. D
The shapes become solid white and the shape at the top of the figure goes to the front. The shape at the bottom of the figure goes to the back.

9. C
The inner shape made by the overlap between the top and middle shapes takes the shading of the top shape. The inner shape made by the overlap between the bottom and middle shapes takes the shading of the bottom shape. The top and bottom shapes disappear.

10. A
The shape made by the overlap of the two shapes separates from the top and bottom shapes. The bottom shape disappears and the top shape turns black.

3D SHAPES

Rotating 3D Shapes — p.18-19

Warm Up

1. *a) 3 b) 2 c) 2 d) 3 e) 3 f) 1*

2. *Number of figures that are the same: 2 (the fourth and sixth figures)*

3D Building Blocks

3. D
The right-hand block of set D rotates 90 degrees top-to-bottom and becomes the right-hand block of the figure on the left. The block on the left of set D moves to become the left hand block of the figure.

4. A
The block at the top of set A rotates 90 degrees right-to-left and becomes the block in the middle of the figure on the left. The bottom block of the set rotates 90 degrees left-to-right and moves to the left of the figure. The middle block of the set becomes the back block of the figure.

5. D
The bottom right block of set D rotates 180 degrees in the plane of the page and becomes the back left block of the figure on the left. The block at the top of the set moves to become the middle right block at the back of the figure. The bottom left block of the set rotates 90 degrees in the plane of the page and moves to become the front middle block of the figure.

3D Rotation

6. B
Shape B rotates 180 degrees left-to-right.

7. C
Shape C rotates 90 degrees clockwise in the plane of the page. It then rotates 90 degrees left-to-right.

8. **D**

Shape D rotates 90 degrees anticlockwise in the plane of the page. It then rotates 90 degrees left-to-right.

9. **A**

Shape A rotates 90 degrees towards you, top-to-bottom. It then rotates 180 degrees left-to-right.

2D and 3D Shapes — p.20-21

Warm Up

1. *a) yes b) no c) no d) yes e) yes f) no*

2. *The number of cubes that can be made: 3 (the second, third and fifth cubes)*

2D Views of 3D Shapes

3. **A**

On the left-hand side of the figure there is a gap between the top and bottom blocks. This rules out option B. There are five blocks visible from above, which rules out options C and D.

4. **C**

There are two blocks visible at the bottom of the figure, which rules out option A. There are four blocks visible from above, which rules out options B and D.

5. **B**

The block on the left-hand side of the figure is next to the middle block in the line of three blocks, which rules out option A. There is only one block visible on the left-hand side of the figure, which rules out options C and D.

Cubes and Nets

6. **D**

Option A is ruled out because the 8-pointed star and the white circle must be on opposite sides. Option B is ruled out because if the circle was on the top and the triangle was at the front, the face on the right would be the grey star. Option C is ruled out because the grey star and the black square must be on opposite sides.

7. **B**

Option A is ruled out because if the triangle was on the top and the black square was at the front, the face on the right would be the circle. Option C is ruled out because the arrow could not be pointing at the circle. Option D is ruled out because there is no black arrow on the net.

8. **C**

Option A is ruled out because the two black arrows must be on opposite sides. Option B is ruled out because on the net there are no white and black arrows that point directly at each other. Option D is ruled out because the two grey arrows must be on opposite sides.

ASSESSMENT TEST 1

Section 1 — Complete the Series

1. **C**

The square rotates 90 degrees clockwise in each series square.

2. **C**

The whole series square reflects across each time.

3. **C**

All of the circles move up one row in each series square. When they reach the top, they go back to the bottom in the next series square.

4. **A**

The cube turns one face to the left in each series square. The front cube face becomes the left hand cube face, and a new cube face appears at the front.

5. **A**

In each series square, the grey square in the previous series square becomes white, and one of the black squares becomes grey.

6. **C**

The squares in this series are in two pairs. In each pair the whole figure rotates 90 degrees and the rectangle and the arrow swap shadings.

7. **B**

The circle gets bigger and its colour alternates between black and white. The star gets an extra point in each series square.

8. **B**

The hatching rotates 45 degrees anticlockwise in each series square. The raindrop rotates 90 degrees anticlockwise.

9. **C**

The two-headed arrow rotates 90 degrees in each series square. The line with the circles rotates 45 degrees clockwise in each square.

10. **A**

The top white dot moves one place to the right in each series square. The bottom white dot moves one place to the left in each series square.

Section 2 — 3D Building Blocks

1. **D**

The block on the left of set D rotates 90 degrees in the plane of the page to become the back shape of the figure on the left. The block on the right of set D moves to the middle and front of the figure.

2. **B**

The block on the left of set B becomes the back block in the figure on the left. The block on the bottom right of set B rotates 180 degrees in the plane of the page to become the middle block of the figure on the left. The block on the top right of set B moves to the front of the figure on the left.

3. B

The block at the top of set B rotates 90 degrees clockwise in the plane of the page to become the block on the right of the figure on the left. The block at the bottom of set B rotates 90 degrees, right-to-left and moves to the front left of the figure.

4. A

One of the blocks at the top of set A moves to become the block on the right of the figure on the left. The other block at the top of set A rotates towards you 90 degrees top-to-bottom, and moves to the bottom left of the figure. The block at the bottom of set A rotates 90 degrees, left-to-right and moves to become the top left-hand part of the figure.

5. D

The block at the bottom of set D rotates towards you 90 degrees, top-to-bottom. It then rotates 90 degrees, right-to-left and moves to become the front bottom block in the figure on the left. The block in the middle of set D rotates 90 degrees, left-to-right and moves to the top left of the figure. The small block at the top of set D moves to become the back right-hand part of the figure.

6. D

The block on the bottom left of set D rotates 90 degrees clockwise in the plane of the page to become the block at the back right of the figure on the left. The block at the top of set D rotates 90 degrees, right-to-left and moves to the left side of the figure at the front. The small block on the bottom right of set D moves to become the front right block in the figure.

7. C

The block at the bottom of set C rotates away from you by 90 degrees, top-to-bottom and moves to become the bottom block in the figure on the left. The block at the top of set C moves on top of the first block. The block in the middle of set C rotates 90 degrees in the plane of the page and moves to the back right of the figure.

8. B

The block at the top of set B rotates away from you by 90 degrees, top-to-bottom. It then rotates 90 degrees clockwise in the plane of the page and moves to the middle of the figure on the left at the back. The block on the bottom left of set B rotates away from you by 90 degrees, top-to-bottom and moves to the right of the figure. The block on the bottom right of set B rotates 180 degrees in the plane of the page and moves to become the front left block in the figure.

Section 3 — Find the Figure Like the First Two

1. B

All figures must be triangles with a flat side at the bottom.

2. C

All figures must have the same number of dots as inner lines.

3. C

All figures must have a black shape at the front.

4. B

All figures must have two shapes and an arrow pointing up.

5. B

All figures must have a dot next to the middle of the flat side of the large white shape.

6. B

All figures must have a large shape with the same small shape overlapping it on the left-hand side.

7. D

All figures must have a large shape with five sides. There must be the same number of raindrops as the number of dashed circles inside the five-sided shape.

8. C

All the vase shapes must be shaded black up to the same level. All figures must have a smaller version of this black shading next to the vase shape.

9. B

All figures must have one less inner line than the number of sides of the shape.

10. D

In all figures, the shaded parts of the two inner shapes must equal one whole inner shape.

Section 4 — Rotate the Figure

1. B

The figure is rotated 90 degrees anticlockwise. In options A, C and D, the arrow is positioned incorrectly.

2. B

The figure is rotated 90 degrees anticlockwise. In options A and C, the small black drop and inner line are positioned incorrectly. Option D is a rotated reflection.

3. D

The figure is rotated 90 degrees anticlockwise. In option A, the thick black line has become white and the small white shape has become black. Option B is a rotated reflection. In option C, there is no small white shape.

4. A

The figure is rotated 180 degrees. Option B is a rotated reflection. In option C, the circle and triangle have swapped places. In option D, the triangle has been shaded grey and the arrow is positioned incorrectly.

5. C

The figure is rotated 135 degrees clockwise. Option A is a reflection. In option B, the black circles are too far apart. In option D, one of the black circles has become white.

6. C

The figure is rotated 45 degrees anticlockwise. Option A is a rotated reflection. In option B, the squares have swapped colours. In option D, the dots are positioned incorrectly.

7. C

The figure is rotated 45 degrees anticlockwise. Option A is a rotated reflection. In option B, the raindrops are positioned incorrectly. In option D, the raindrops are rotated incorrectly.

8. A

The figure is rotated 135 degrees clockwise. Options B and C are the wrong shape. Option D is a rotated reflection.

9. D

The figure is rotated 135 degrees anticlockwise. In option A, the semicircle is reflected across. In option B, the semicircle is reflected down. In option C, the stars have swapped places.

10. A

The figure is rotated 90 degrees anticlockwise. In options B and C, the tree shapes are positioned incorrectly. Option D is a rotated reflection.

Section 5 — Complete the Hexagonal Grid

1. D

Going in a clockwise direction, each arrow shape rotates 60 degrees clockwise and the small circle alternates between black and grey.

2. C

Each outer hexagon has three half-stars and two triangles. The half-stars must face inwards and the triangles must face outwards.

3. A

The star shapes reflect across the middle of the hexagonal grid.

4. B

Going in a clockwise direction from the top middle hexagon, each hexagon gains an extra shape.

5. A

Going in a clockwise direction from the top middle hexagon, the grey shading in each cross shape increases. Each cross shape rotates 60 degrees clockwise.

6. C

The shapes reflect across the middle of the hexagonal grid.

7. D

Going in a clockwise direction from the top middle hexagon, the single-headed arrow rotates 30 degrees clockwise and the double-headed arrow rotates 60 degrees clockwise.

8. B

Each outer hexagon has a black circle segment on its two inner corners. The shapes in the outer hexagons alternate between a grey circle with a white ellipse and white circle with a grey ellipse. Going in a clockwise direction, these shapes rotate 30 degrees clockwise.

ASSESSMENT TEST 2

Section 1 — Odd One Out

1. C

All other figures have a black circle.

2. B

In all other figures, the hatching in the small shape goes diagonally down to the left.

3. B

All other figures are made of two identical shapes.

4. B

In all other figures, the two shapes are overlapping.

5. C

All other figures have an arrow pointing towards the grey semicircle.

6. A

All other figures have only one arrowhead which touches the outline of a shape.

7. D

In all other figures, the two shapes cut out from the large shape are reflections of each other.

8. D

All other figures have one less shape in each row than in the row below.

9. C

All other figures have a small triangle inside the right-hand side of the hourglass shape.

10. A

All other figures have one less dot than the number of points on each star.

Section 2 — Complete the Pair

1. D

The dashed lines become solid and the solid lines become dashed.

2. B

All the black sections become white and all the white sections become black. (Or the shapes, including their shadings, are reflected across.)

3. B

The two shapes swap places. The big shape gains an extra side.

4. D

The big and small shapes swap shadings. The small shape rotates 180 degrees.

5. A

A reflection of the figure is added behind the original figure, above it and to the right.

6. A

The top shape gets smaller and becomes the bottom shape. The bottom shape gets bigger and becomes the top shape. The 'x' shapes rotate 45 degrees.

7. B

The short arrow rotates 45 degrees anticlockwise. The long arrow rotates 90 degrees anticlockwise.

8. C

The two black triangles move up behind the large shape until they are half-way up it. The three dots rotate 90 degrees around the middle dot.

Section 3 — 3D Rotation

1. B

Shape B has been rotated 90 degrees anticlockwise in the plane of the page. It has then been rotated 90 degrees left-to-right.

2. F

Shape F has been rotated 90 degrees anticlockwise in the plane of the page.

3. **A**
Shape A has been rotated 90 degrees right-to-left.

4. **E**
Shape E has been rotated 90 degrees towards you, top-to-bottom.

5. **E**
Shape E has been rotated 90 degrees anticlockwise in the plane of the page. It has then been rotated 90 degrees away from you, top-to-bottom.

6. **A**
Shape A has been rotated 90 degrees right-to-left.

7. **B**
Shape B has been rotated 90 degrees, left-to-right.

8. **F**
Shape F has been rotated 90 degrees anticlockwise in the plane of the page.

9. **D**
Shape D has been rotated 90 degrees towards you, top-to-bottom.

10. **C**
Shape C has been rotated 90 degrees clockwise in the plane of the page.

Section 4 — Find the Figure Like the First Three

1. **A**
All figures must have a line going through them which shows a line of symmetry.

2. **C**
All figures must be made of two straight lines and two curved lines.

3. **A**
All figures must be identical apart from rotation.

4. **B**
All figures must be grey with one white quarter.

5. **D**
All figures must have a line which crosses both shapes.

6. **C**
In all figures, the number of sides of both shapes must add up to eight.

7. **A**
In all figures, the shape with the smallest number of sides must have a dashed outline.

8. **D**
All figures must have the same number of crosses as the number of curved lines.

9. **B**
All figures must have a four-sided shape inside the large arrow shape. The two arrows must point at each other.

10. **D**
In all figures, it must be possible to arrange all the shapes into a square.

Section 5 — Complete the Square Grid

1. **A**
Working from top to bottom, the outer shape in the first row gets smaller in each grid square. The star shape is the same in each column.

2. **C**
Working from top to bottom, each shape moves one grid square left. The shape in the left-hand grid square disappears, and a new shape appears in the right-hand grid square.

3. **B**
The third grid square in each row contains the shapes from the first two grid squares in the row.

4. **B**
Working from top to bottom, the figure rotates 45 degrees anticlockwise in each grid square.

5. **A**
Working from top to bottom, the number of small inner shapes increases by one. The large outer shape reflects across in each grid square.

6. **D**
Working from top to bottom, the number of corners in the arrow line increases by one in each grid square. The type of arrow head is the same in each column.

7. **A**
Each group of shapes (squares, circles and triangles) only appears once in each row and column. Each different arrangement of black and white shading only appears once in each row and column.

8. **D**
Working from left to right, the third grid square in each row is made up of the figure in the middle grid square on top of a 90 degree anticlockwise rotation of the figure in the first grid square.

ASSESSMENT TEST 3

Section 1 — Complete the Hexagonal Grid

1. **D**
The hexagons on opposite sides of the hexagonal grid are identical.

2. **B**
Each outer hexagon has three circles positioned along two of its inner sides (but not the innermost side). The hexagons alternate between having four grey circles and two white circles, and having four white circles and two grey circles.

3. **C**
Going in an anticlockwise direction from the bottom left hexagon, a black triangle is added at the bottom of the hexagon and all the triangles move one side anticlockwise.

4. D

Each figure reflects across the middle of the hexagonal grid.

5. A

Going in a clockwise direction, each outer hexagon rotates 60 degrees clockwise.

6. C

Each figure reflects across the middle of the hexagonal grid.

7. D

Going in an anticlockwise direction from the top left hexagon, each outer hexagon gains one extra circle. The small cross moves one corner anticlockwise in each hexagon.

8. B

Going in a clockwise direction from the top right hexagon, the hatched section gets bigger in each outer hexagon. The hatching rotates 90 degrees in each hexagon.

Section 2 — Reflect the Figure

1. B

In options A and D, the white trapezium has become a parallelogram. Option C is a downwards reflection.

2. B

Option A is the wrong shape. Option C is a 180 degree rotation. Option D is a downwards reflection.

3. B

In option A, the grey shape has not been reflected. In option C, the raindrop has not been reflected. Option D is a downwards reflection.

4. A

Option B is a downwards reflection. Option C is not reflected and the triangles have swapped shadings. In option D, the black triangle has moved behind the grey shape and the hatched triangle has moved in front of it.

5. D

In option A, the cube has reflected across, but the arrow has rotated 180 degrees. In options B and C, the cube has not been reflected.

6. B

In option A, the spiral has not been reflected and the triangle has rotated. Option C is a downwards reflection. Option D is a 180 degree rotation.

7. A

In option B, the grey shading has moved position but the shape has not been reflected. Option C is the wrong shape. Option D is a 90 degree anticlockwise rotation.

8. C

In option A, the grey shading has moved. Option B is a downwards reflection. In option D, the large shape has not been reflected.

9. B

In option A, the hatched rectangle has not been reflected. In option C, the hatched rectangle and the grey rectangle are in the wrong positions. In option D, the grey rectangle has moved in front of the white rectangle.

10. D

Option A is a downwards reflection. In option B, the hatching has not been reflected. Option C is a 90 degree anticlockwise rotation.

Section 3 — Complete the Square Grid

1. D

Working from left to right, the figures in the first and second squares of each row are added together to make the figure in the third square.

2. B

Working from left to right, the figure in the first square of each row are identical to the figure in the third square.

3. D

Working from left to right, one dot is added in each grid square and the whole figure rotates 90 degrees clockwise.

4. B

The three different directions the arrows point in (diagonally down to the left, diagonally down to the right and up) only appear once in each row and column.

5. C

Working from left to right, the two arrows rotate 90 degrees clockwise in each grid square. The large shapes stay the same (including their shading).

6. C

Working from top to bottom, each grid square rotates 90 degrees clockwise and the arrowheads change. The shading of the small square alternates between black and white.

7. D

The large shape stays the same across each row. The white triangle stays in the same position in each column.

8. D

Working from left to right, the whole grid square rotates 90 degrees clockwise. The circles change shading from black to grey to white.

Section 4 — Find the Figure Like the First Two

1. B

All figures must have two white shapes that are identical apart from size.

2. C

All figures must have a large black outer shape, which is reflected downwards and shrunk to become the white shape in front of it.

3. B

All figures must have a star with a dotted line through one of its lines of symmetry.

4. B

Each figure must have an outer shape with one more side than the inner shape.

5. E

All figures must have the same number of short straight lines crossing the S shape as the number of black shapes.

6. E

All figures must have the same number of dots as the number of curved lines inside the circle.

7. D

All figures must have stars with five points. One star must be overlapping one side of the large shape.

8. A

All figures must have three small shapes that all have four sides. There must be one of each type of shading (white, grey and hatched diagonally down to the left) in each figure.

9. B

All figures must have a grey heart, two white ellipses and two black triangles. The two triangles must partly overlap the two ellipses.

10. C

In all figures, the inner shapes must add up to one whole circle. All figures must have two small lines crossing the outline of the large shape.

Section 5 — Complete the Series

1. A

In each series square, an extra triangle is added diagonally below the triangle(s) in the previous series square. The colour of each triangle alternates between black and white in each series square.

2. D

The two black triangles reflect across in each series square. The arrow's shading alternates between white and grey.

3. B

The large hexagon reflects across in each series square. The circle moves half a side anticlockwise round the square (alternately between the square's sides and corners).

4. C

In each series square there is an extra triangle.

5. C

In each series square, the white circle segment rotates 45 degrees anticlockwise around the black dot. The grey shape reflects along the side that is furthest clockwise around the edge of the series square.

6. C

In each series square, the solid line rotates 90 degrees anticlockwise. The dotted line rotates 90 degrees clockwise around the centre of the series square.

7. B

The shading moves to the outside of the next cylinder, going up diagonally to the right.

8. B

In each series square, the box shape alternates between two positions. The first position has the front rectangle with its long side along the bottom of the series square. The second position has the front rectangle with its short side along the bottom of the series square. A new inner line is added in each series square.

9. A

In each series square, the star shape loses one point, and one more point becomes black.

10. D

The squares in this series are in two pairs. In each pair, the bottom inner shape disappears and the arrows reverse direction. The colours of the figure swap between black and white.

ASSESSMENT TEST 4

Section 1 — Changing Bugs

1. C

The bug reflects across.

2. D

The bug gets smaller and the shading of its eyes swaps with the shading of its head.

3. A

The shape on the bug's back rotates 90 degrees clockwise. Each of the bug's antennae gains an extra line.

4. C

The shape of the bug's body swaps with the smaller shape on its back. The top and bottom pairs of legs become the same as the middle pair of legs.

5. C

All the different types of shading move up one body segment (including the shading of the bug's head). The bug's eyes move apart.

6. C

On the bug's shell, the small white circle moves to the front. The bug's body then becomes the same colour as the circle at the back.

7. A

Each of the bug's legs gains a foot. The shape of the foot is the same as the small shape inside the section of the body that the leg is attached to. The small inner shapes then disappear.

8. B

The pattern on the bug's back reflects downwards and its shading changes to match the bug's head. Its right-hand legs change to match the left-hand legs.

9. D

The spiral on the bug's body rotates 90 degrees clockwise. The bug's body loses a side.

10. A

Each antenna gains an extra loop and the three different shapes on its back each move one position clockwise.

Section 2 — Odd One Out

1. E
In all other figures, the inner and outer shapes are the same shape.

2. D
In all other figures, the shapes go clockwise in the order: circle, square, triangle, and the wavy line is between the circle and the square.

3. C
In all other figures, the two shapes are identical apart from rotation.

4. D
In all other figures, the dashed line inside the rectangle has the same shading as the shapes inside the other rectangle.

5. B
In all other figures, the arrow goes in an anticlockwise direction.

6. D
In all other figures, the small line crosses over the top corner of the triangle.

7. B
In all other figures, the shape with the fewest sides is white.

8. D
All other figures have the same number of lines as black hexagons.

9. C
In all other figures, the square is in the top half and the diamond shape is in the bottom half.

10. A
In all other figures, the grey shape has four sides.

Section 3 — Cubes and Nets

1. C
Option A is ruled out because the cube face with five dots and the grey cube face must be on opposite sides. Option B is ruled out because the net doesn't have two identical faces. Option D is ruled out because the cube face with the wavy line and the black cube face with the white stripe must be on opposite sides.

2. B
Option A is ruled out because the cube face with the circles and the cube face with the division sign must be on opposite sides. Options C and D are both ruled out because the cube face with the hatched shading and the white cube face must be on opposite sides.

3. D
Option A is ruled out because the cube face with the arrow shape and the white cube face must be on opposite sides. Option B is ruled out because the net doesn't have two identical faces. Option C is ruled out because the cube face with the wavy lines and the cube face with the grey stripe must be on opposite sides.

4. C
Option A is ruled out because the cube face with the spiral and the white cube face must be on opposite sides. Option B is ruled out because the cube face with the four black squares and the cube face with the three grey rectangles must be on opposite sides. Option D is ruled out because the net doesn't have two identical faces.

5. A
Option B is ruled out because the grey cube face and the cube face with the letter W must be on opposite sides. Option C is ruled out because the cube face with the two black lines and the black cube face must be on opposite sides. Option D is ruled out because the letter V does not appear on the net.

6. A
Option B is ruled out because the net doesn't have two identical faces. Option C is ruled out because the black cube face with the white star and the cube face with the grey wavy stripe must be on opposite sides. Option D is ruled out because the cross-hatched cube face and the cube face with the two diagonal lines must be on opposite sides.

7. A
Option B is ruled out because the net doesn't have two identical faces. Option C is ruled out because the white cube face and the cube face with the shield shape must be on opposite sides. Option D is ruled out because the cube face with the black arch and the cube face with the zig-zag line must be on opposite sides.

8. C
Option A is ruled out because the black cube face and the grey face with the white hexagon must be on opposite sides. Option B is ruled out because the cube face with the black star and the cube face with the lines must be on opposite sides. Option D is ruled out because if the cube face with the circle and the cross was on the top and the cube face with the black star was at the front, the cube face on the right would be the black face.

Section 4 — Reflect the Figure

1. C
Option A is a 90 degree anticlockwise rotation. In option B, the grey triangle has not been reflected. In option D, the arrow has not been reflected.

2. B
Option A is a 135 degree clockwise rotation. Option C is a downwards reflection. Option D is a 45 degree anticlockwise rotation.

3. D
Option A is a 180 degree rotation. Option B has been reflected but it is missing a small line. Option C has not been reflected and the lines and the black dot are positioned incorrectly.

4. C
Option A is a 90 degree anticlockwise rotation. Option B is a 180 degree rotation. Option D is a downwards reflection.

5. **D**

Option A has not been reflected and has incorrect shading. Option B is a downwards reflection and the circle and square have swapped places. Option C has not been reflected and the circle has moved behind the triangle.

6. **A**

Option B has been reflected but the horizontal rectangle has moved to the front. Option C is a downwards reflection. Option D has not been reflected and the horizontal rectangle has moved to the front.

7. **B**

Option A is a 180 degree rotation. Option C is a downwards reflection. In option D the top two triangles have been reflected across but the bottom two triangles have been reflected downwards.

8. **C**

In option A, the shield shapes are wrong. Option B is a 90 degree anticlockwise rotation. In option D, the shield shapes have not been reflected.

9. **B**

Option A is a rotated reflection. Option C is the wrong shape. Option D is a 90 degree anticlockwise rotation.

10. **D**

Option A is a downwards reflection. In option B, the black shapes have swapped places. In option C, the small shapes have swapped places but the large shape has not been reflected.

Section 5 — 2D Views of 3D Shapes

1. **C**

There should be four blocks visible from above, which rules out options B and D. The block at the front of the shape is in the middle, which rules out option A.

2. **A**

There should be four blocks visible from above, which rules out options C and D. There are two blocks at the front of the shape, which rules out option B.

3. **D**

There should be five blocks visible from above, which rules out options A and B. There is only one block at the front, which rules out option C.

4. **B**

There should be five blocks visible from above, which rules out options A and C. There is only one block at the front of the shape, which rules out option D.

5. **A**

There should be six blocks visible from above, which rules out options B and C. There are three blocks visible on the left-hand side of the shape, which rules out option D.

6. **D**

On the right-hand side of the shape there is a gap the size of two blocks between the block at the front of the shape and the block at the back of the shape. This rules out options A, B and C.

7. **A**

On the right-hand side of the shape there is a gap the size of two blocks between the block at the front of the shape and the block at the back of the shape. This rules out options B, C and D.

8. **A**

There should be seven blocks visible from above, which rules out option D. The figure is four blocks long from front to back. This rules out option C. There are three blocks at the front of the shape, which rules out option B.

ASSESSMENT TEST 5

Section 1 — Find the Figure That is Not a Rotation

1. **D**

The thick line is incorrectly positioned.

2. **A**

The black and white stars have swapped places.

3. **A**

The figure is a rotated reflection.

4. **B**

The figure is a rotated reflection.

5. **C**

The figure is a rotated reflection.

6. **B**

The small cross shapes have been rotated incorrectly.

7. **B**

The figure is a rotated reflection.

8. **C**

The triangle has been rotated incorrectly.

9. **D**

The figure is a rotated reflection.

10. **C**

The figure is a rotated reflection.

Section 2 — Complete the Pair

1. **A**

The figure rotates 90 degrees anticlockwise. The outline of the outer arrow becomes dashed.

2. **D**

The large shape reflects across and the arrow rotates 180 degrees.

3. **C**

The outer shape gains an extra side. The inner shape loses a side.

4. **D**

The pair of vertical lines rotates 90 degrees. The shape at the bottom rotates 90 degrees clockwise and moves to the middle of the right-hand side of the white shape.

5. **B**

The long white shape gains an extra grey stripe below its other two stripes. An extra line is added above the raindrop at the top.

6. **C**

The spiral shape gains a side. The small black shape gains a side (so it has the same number of sides as the new spiral shape).

7. **A**

One dot moves to the middle. The other dots move outwards and are joined up by lines to make a big shape.

8. **A**

The whole figure rotates 90 degrees anticlockwise. The inner shape on the right gets bigger and the outer shape on the right gets smaller.

Section 3 — 3D Building Blocks

1. **D**

The block at the bottom of set D rotates 90 degrees clockwise in the plane of the page. It then rotates 90 degrees left-to-right and moves to become the back right-hand part of the figure on the left. The block in the middle of set D moves to become the middle part of the figure. The small block at the top of set D moves to become the front left-hand part of the figure.

2. **B**

The block on the left of set B moves to become the left-hand part of the figure on the left. The block on the bottom right of set B moves to become the back right-hand part of the figure. The small block at the top of set B moves to become the front right-hand part of the figure.

3. **B**

The block at the top of set B rotates 90 degrees clockwise in the plane of the page. It then rotates towards you 90 degrees top-to-bottom to become the bottom of the figure on the left. The block on the bottom left of set B moves to become the back part of the figure. The small block on the bottom right of set B moves to the right of the figure, at the top.

4. **C**

The figure at the top of set C rotates 180 degrees in the plane of the page. It then rotates 90 degrees left-to-right to become the middle shape of the figure on the left. The block in the middle of set C moves to become the back part of the figure. The small block on the right of set C moves to the bottom right of the figure.

5. **A**

The block on the bottom left of set A rotates towards you 90 degrees top-to-bottom and moves to become the front right-hand part of the figure on the left. The block on the right of set A rotates towards you 90 degrees top-to-bottom and moves to become the front left-hand part of the figure. The block at the top of set A rotates 90 degrees clockwise in the plane of the page and moves to become the back part of the figure.

6. **D**

The block at the bottom of set D rotates towards you 180 degrees top-to-bottom and moves to become the bottom shape in the figure on the left. One of the blocks at the top of set D moves to the top middle of the figure. The other block from the top of set D moves to become the front left-hand part of the figure.

7. **A**

The block at the top of set A rotates 180 degrees in the plane of the page. It then rotates 90 degrees left-to-right and moves to become the right-hand part of the figure on the left. The block on the bottom left of set A moves to become the middle part of the figure. The block on the right of set A moves to become the front left-hand part of the figure.

8. **C**

The block at the bottom of set C rotates 90 degrees anticlockwise in the plane of the page. It then rotates towards you 90 degrees top-to-bottom and moves to become the left-hand part of the figure on the left. The block on the top left of set C rotates 90 degrees clockwise in the plane of the page. It then rotates 90 degrees away from you top-to-bottom and moves to become the back right-hand part of the figure. The small block on the right of set C moves to the top middle of the figure.

Section 4 — Odd One Out

1. **D**

All other figures have white circles instead of a white ellipse.

2. **D**

In all other figures, there is one shape with a solid outline and one shape with a dashed outline.

3. **E**

In all other figures, the number of inner lines is the same as the number of sides of the shape.

4. **A**

All other figures are made up of the outline of three shapes, divided in half. (The two halves of each of the shapes are shaded differently from each other.)

5. **B**

All other figures are identical apart from rotation.

6. **E**

In all other figures, the two arrows at the end of the line point in different directions.

7. **D**

In all other figures, the line that divides the shape in half is dashed.

8. **C**

In all other figures, the outer line is next to the longest side of the shape.

9. **C**

In all other figures, the thick black line is a larger version of the outline of the grey shape, with a single side missing.

10. **E**

In all other figures, the black shape is identical to one of the white shapes.

Section 5 — Find the Figure Like the First Three

1. B
All figures must be identical apart from rotation.

2. C
All figures must have three black hearts.

3. C
All figures must have exactly one line of symmetry.

4. D
All figures must have the same number of legs on both sides, and all feet must point outwards.

5. C
In all figures, the large dashed shape must be a horizontally stretched version of the inner shape. The small shape must be the same height as the large shape.

6. D
All figures must have three overlapping rectangles.

7. B
All figures must have a hatched shape with one less side than the number of sides of the white shape.

8. D
All figures must have four black shapes.

9. B
In all figures, the stalk must be made up of circles.

10. D
All figures must have an arrow and a four-sided shape with a cross in it. The arrow must be the shape made by three sides of the shape with the cross.

ASSESSMENT TEST 6

Section 1 — Find the Figure Like the First Two

1. A
All figures must have two small shapes that are the same type of shape as the large shape. One of the small shapes must be shaded in the same colour as the large shape, and the other one must be white.

2. D
All figures must have an X shape in the circle rather than a cross (diagonal not horizontal lines). The figure must have two black circles.

3. D
In all figures, the arrows must go in a clockwise direction.

4. A
All figures must have the same number of inner lines as the number of sides of the small shape at the top.

5. D
All figures must have the top square at the very front.

6. B
All figures must have one hatched shape and one black shape. The hatched shape must have one more side than the black shape.

7. A
All figures must have a grey shape inside a white raindrop shape. The dashed lines must only cross over the raindrop's outline once.

8. B
All figures must have two sets of the same two shapes but in different sizes. The outer shape in the top set of shapes must be a 45 degree rotation of the outer shape in the bottom set of shapes.

9. C
In all figures, the big shape must have one more side than the number of circles. All circles must be cross-hatched.

10. B
In all figures, the shapes at opposite ends of each line must be identical.

Section 2 — Reflect the Figure

1. B
Option A is a reflection across, and the black circle is in front of the arrow. Option C is the same as the original figure. Option D has been rotated 180 degrees and the black circle is in front of the arrow.

2. A
Option B is a different shape. Option C is a reflection across. Option D is a 180 degree rotation.

3. B
In option A, only the shading has been reflected. In option C, only the shading has reflected across. Option D has the wrong shading.

4. C
Option A has the wrong shading. Option B is the same as the original figure. Option D is a 30 degree clockwise rotation.

5. D
Option A is a reflection across. In option B, the T-shapes have not been reflected. In option C, the T-shapes have reflected downwards but the diamond is positioned incorrectly.

6. C
Option A is a different shape. Option B is a 90 degree clockwise rotation. Option D is a reflection across.

7. A
Option B is a reflection across. Option C is a different shape (it has four peaks). Option D is a 180 degree rotation.

8. C
Option A is a downwards reflection, but the star is positioned incorrectly. Option B is a downwards reflection, but the star has moved in front of the rocket shape. Option D is a reflection across.

9. B
Option A is a 90 degree clockwise rotation. In option C, the shape is reflected downwards but the hatching has not reflected. Option D is the same as the original figure.

10. A

Option B is the same as the original figure. Option C is a downwards reflection but the black square and grey square have swapped positions. Option D is a reflection across.

Section 3 — Complete the Pair

1. C

The entire figure is reflected downwards. Black shading becomes white and white shading becomes black.

2. F

The entire figure rotates 45 degrees anticlockwise, and the arrow changes from black to grey.

3. C

The left-hand shape and the middle shape swap places.

4. B

The hatched shape reflects across. The black shapes turn white.

5. B

The shape that the arrows make changes to become the inner shape. The old inner shape changes to become the outer shape made by the arrows. The arrows go from pointing clockwise to anticlockwise.

6. F

The entire figure rotates 180 degrees.

7. D

Each shading on the flag moves one place to the right.

8. C

The entire figure is reflected downwards. The different parts of the shield shape all separate.

Section 4 — Complete the Series

1. E

Each series square gains an extra heart shape. The white section of the circle gets bigger in a clockwise direction.

2. B

In each series square, the arrow rotates 45 degrees anticlockwise. The position of the dot alternates between the point and the base of the arrow.

3. A

In each series square, the three different types of background shading (black, white and grey) move down one rectangle. The arrow alternates between pointing up and pointing down.

4. A

In each series square, the outermost shape shrinks and becomes the new inner shape and the two other shapes get bigger.

5. D

In each series square, the outer shape rotates 90 degrees anticlockwise. The shading in the inner shape alternates between the two halves.

6. C

Each series square rotates 90 degrees anticlockwise.

7. A

In each series square, an extra side is added to the central grey shape. The leaf shape in each corner alternates between being vertical and diagonal.

8. D

The squares in this series are in two pairs. In each pair, the first figure reflects across to make the second figure in the pair.

9. B

Each series square gains an extra row of triangles. The black triangle moves one row diagonally towards the new row.

10. A

In each series square, a new hexagon is added.

Section 5 — Complete the Hexagonal Grid

1. B

Going in an anticlockwise direction from the top left hexagon, the figure gains an extra rectangle at the bottom.

2. D

The shield shapes reflect across the middle of the hexagonal grid.

3. E

Each outer hexagon has four triangles, one half-ellipse, and one triangle with a small circle on its innermost corner. The half-ellipse must be on the outer side of the hexagon when it is placed in the grid.

4. F

Each outer hexagon must have a black square on each of its outer edges. The inner edge must have half a black arch. The other two of the hexagon's sides must each have half an isosceles triangle. The isosceles triangles must both point towards the centre of the hexagonal grid.

5. B

The spirals reflect across the middle of the hexagonal grid.

6. F

Going in a clockwise direction from the top left hexagon, the circle gets bigger and the white sector becomes bigger.

7. E

Going in an anticlockwise direction from the top right hexagon, a straight line is added and the grey bar moves down the hexagon.

8. C

Going in a clockwise direction from the top hexagon, the grid of squares rotates 45 degrees anticlockwise. One extra circle is added.

ASSESSMENT TEST 7

Section 1 — Odd One Out

1. E

In all other figures, the small shape is a smaller version of the big shape.

2. C
In all other figures, the arrow is pointing at a corner.

3. C
In all other figures, there is a black circle at both ends of the line.

4. E
In all other figures, the shape with the fewest sides is at the front.

5. B
In all other figures, the square has the same shading as the top middle circle.

6. E
All other figures have a large shape made up of four lines.

7. E
In all other figures, the arrow points to the shape with the most sides.

8. C
In all other figures, the number of black dots is the same as the number of lines going through the circle.

9. A
In all other figures, the number of points on a single star is the same as the number of sides of the large shape.

10. D
In all other figures, the black shape is the shape made by the overlap of the white and the hatched shapes.

Section 2 — 2D Views of 3D Shapes

1. C
There is only one block at the front of the figure, which rules out options A and D. There are three blocks on the left-hand side, which rules out option B.

2. D
There are only five blocks visible from above, which rules out options A and B. The block on the right does not have any blocks next to its sides, which rules out option C.

3. B
There are only five blocks visible from above, which rules out options A and D. There is only one block visible on the left-hand side, which rules out option C.

4. C
There are only five blocks visible from above, which rules out options A, B and D.

5. D
There are only four blocks visible from above, which rules out options A and B. There are only two blocks visible at the front, which rules out option C.

6. B
There are only six blocks visible from above, which rules out options C and D. There are three blocks visible on the right-hand side, which rules out option A.

7. B
There are only six blocks visible from above, which rules out options A, C and D.

8. D
There are only seven blocks visible from above, which rules out option A. There are four blocks visible on the right-hand side, which rules out options B and C.

Section 3 — Complete the Square Grid

1. D
Each different type of star (six-pointed, seven-pointed and eight-pointed) only appears once in each row and column.

2. B
Working from left to right, a thick line is added in the middle of each grid square. The small shape moves diagonally within each row.

3. E
Working from left to right, the large shape gains a side in each grid square. The arrow rotates 90 degrees clockwise.

4. A
The squares in the same row all have the same shading. Each size of square only appears once in each row.

5. C
In each row, a new shape is added to the shape in the left-hand grid square to make the right-hand grid square — with all overlapping lines between the two shapes showing. In the middle grid square, the overlapping shapes lose their overlapping lines.

6. D
Working from top to bottom, the cross rotates 45 degrees clockwise in each series square. The small shape stays in the same corner of the cross as it rotates, but the shape itself doesn't rotate. The different colours of the small shape (black, grey and white) only appear once in each row and column.

7. A
There are black triangles in every corner of the central grid square, and in every corner that touches it. In each row, the shape in the right-hand grid square is made up of the shading of the square from the left-hand grid square, added to the outline of the shape from the middle grid square.

8. E
Each different shading (white, grey and hatched) appears twice in each row and column. The rotation of the triangles is the same in each grid square.

Section 4 — Rotate the Figure

1. B
The figure is rotated 90 degrees clockwise. Option A is the wrong shape. Options C and D are rotated reflections.

2. C
The figure is rotated 135 degrees clockwise. In option A, the black dot is positioned incorrectly. Option B has incorrect shading. Option D is a reflected rotation.

3. A
The figure is rotated 135 degrees anticlockwise. Options B and D are the wrong shape. Option C is a rotated reflection.

4. **B**
The figure is rotated 90 degrees clockwise. Option A is a rotated reflection. Option C has too few zig-zags in the line, while option D has too many.

5. **D**
The figure is rotated 180 degrees. In option A, the heart is in the wrong position. In option C, the heart has been rotated incorrectly. Option B is a rotated reflection.

6. **C**
The figure is rotated 180 degrees. Option A is a reflection. Options B and D are the wrong shape.

7. **B**
The figure is rotated 135 degrees anticlockwise. Option A is a rotated reflection. Option C has a different triangle. Option D has two circles.

8. **A**
The figure is rotated 45 degrees clockwise. In option B, the four-pointed star is the wrong colour. In option C, the four-pointed star is inside the wrong shape. In option D, the large star is six-pointed instead of five-pointed.

9. **D**
The figure is rotated 135 degrees clockwise. In options A and C, the black arrow is positioned incorrectly. Option B is a different shape.

10. **D**
The figure is rotated 135 degrees clockwise. Option A is a reflection. In option B, the two lines are not parallel. In option C, the black triangle has been rotated incorrectly.

Section 5 — Complete the Series

1. **B**
In each series square the figure reflects across and gets bigger.

2. **C**
The black shading moves from the centre out one row of shapes in each series square.

3. **E**
In each series square the triangles move round one position clockwise (the fifth series square shows that there are five possible positions for the triangles). In each series square a new white triangle is added in the next available position (going clockwise, starting from the grey triangle).

4. **D**
In this series, the number of pentagons changes in the sequence: two, three, four, three, two. The series square rotates 180 degrees each time.

5. **D**
In each series square the diagonal line and grey square rotate 90 degrees clockwise. The type of line changes in the sequence: solid, dashed, dotted, solid, dashed.

6. **A**
In each series square the arrow rotates 90 degrees clockwise around the central shape. The arrow leaves a dashed trail behind it where it has already been.

7. **C**
The shapes move round one place clockwise in each series square.

8. **D**
The entire figure rotates 90 degrees clockwise in each series square.

9. **E**
In each series square, the white circles move along one triangle to the right. Once the circles reach the furthest triangle in their row, they start again on the left of that row.

10. **B**
The whole figure rotates 90 degrees anticlockwise in each series square. The two hearts alternate between pointing up and down.

ASSESSMENT TEST 8

Section 1 — Find the Figure Like the First Three

1. **C**
All figures must have the same large white 6-sided shape. This shape must contain three black circles and at least one circle with horizontal hatching.

2. **B**
All figures must be identical apart from rotation.

3. **D**
All figures must have four shapes which are the same apart from size. The shapes must all be centred on the same point.

4. **C**
All figures must be half black and half white.

5. **C**
All figures must have two arrows inside the shape and one outside the shape. All arrows must point in the same direction.

6. **D**
All figures must have two overlapping white shapes which have the same number of sides. One shape in each figure must have a single curved side.

7. **D**
All figures must have one grey shield shape.

8. **A**
In all figures, the two small shapes must be the same shape, and one of them must be black.

9. **A**
In all figures, the star must be at the front of the set of shapes.

10. **B**
In all figures, there must be two squares and a hexagon (ignoring overlaps). The centre shape must be black and the outer shapes and the overlaps must be white.

Section 2 — Cubes and Nets

1. **D**

Option A is ruled out because the cube face with the spiral and the cube face with the black dot must be on opposite sides. Option B is ruled out because the cube face with the star and the black cube face must be on opposite sides. Option C is ruled out because the net doesn't have two identical faces.

2. **A**

Option B is ruled out because the cube face with the three thin lines and the cube face with the four-way arrow must be on opposite sides. Option C is ruled out because the white cube face and the cube face with the black zig-zag must be on opposite sides. Option D is ruled out because the cube face with the thin lines and the cube face with the star must be on opposite sides.

3. **A**

Option B is ruled out because the net doesn't have two identical faces. Option C is ruled out because the cube face with the letter N and the cube face with the grey bars must be on opposite sides. Option D is ruled out because the grey cube face and the cube face with the circle with a line through it must be on opposite sides.

4. **D**

Option A is ruled out because the face with the ellipse is never above the 'top' of the grey mushroom shape. Option B is ruled out because the black triangle should be opposite either the face with the letter E or the grey mushroom shape, so these three faces cannot be seen together. Option C is ruled out because the grey mushroom shape has the wrong rotation.

5. **B**

Option A is ruled out because the face with the heart and the face with the hexagon and circle should be on opposite sides. Option C is ruled out because the net doesn't have two identical faces. Option D is ruled out because the cube face with the three circles and the cube face with the loop must be on opposite sides.

6. **A**

Option B is ruled out because the dotted cube face and the cube face with the eye shape must be on opposite sides. Option C is ruled out because the cube face with the triangle and the cube face with the square in the middle must be on opposite sides. Option D is ruled out because the grey cube face and the cube face with the cross must be on opposite sides.

7. **B**

Options A and C are ruled out because the grey cube face and the cube face with the number 1 must be on opposite sides. Option D is ruled out because the 'handle' of the racquet shape must point towards the cube face with the overlapping circles.

8. **B**

Option A is ruled out because the net doesn't have two identical faces. Option C is ruled out because the face with the circle and the face with the two pentagons should be on opposite sides. Option D is ruled out because the white half of the circle must be closest to the cube face with three short lines.

Section 3 — Changing Bugs

1. **B**

The bug's eyes change from black to grey and its wings get bigger.

2. **D**

The bug's body reflects across and it gains an extra pair of legs.

3. **A**

The smaller bottom shape on the bug's left-hand side moves up to go inside the top shape. The same two shapes are then copied on the right-hand side of the bug's body and the colours are swapped.

4. **C**

The bug's body becomes shorter and wider and its hatching rotates by 90 degrees.

5. **C**

The spiral on the bug's shell reflects across. The shape of the bug's head gains a side.

6. **C**

All the shading on the bug's body moves down one segment.

7. **C**

The bug's wings turn grey and each of its legs gains an extra bend.

8. **B**

The shading on the bug's upper body swaps with the shading on the bug's lower body. The shapes at the end of the three tail lines each move one place to the right.

9. **D**

The bug's mouth gets bigger. The bottom triangle on the bug's body disappears.

10. **C**

The shape on the bug's back rotates 180 degrees. The end of the bug's body becomes spiked.

Section 4 — Complete the Pair

1. **A**

The whole figure rotates 180 degrees. The two small shapes swap shadings with the large shape.

2. **B**

The whole figure rotates 90 degrees clockwise and the number of points on the star goes down by one.

3. **B**

The outer shape reflects across. The inner shapes are cut in half along a central vertical line. The left half of each inner shape disappears.

4. **F**

The shape turns grey. All the separate long lines move closer to the centre of the figure.

5. **C**

The whole figure rotates 180 degrees. The two large shapes swap shadings.

6. **C**

The shadings of the bottom shapes move one place to the right.